James Gibbons Huneker

STEEPLEJACK

BY

JAMES GIBBONS HUNEKER

"I find no sweeter fat than sticks to my own bones."
—WALT WHITMAN

VOLUME I

NEW YORK
CHARLES SCRIBNER'S SONS
1920

UNIVERSITY CLUB
OF PHILADELPHIA

THIS BOOK

OF VANITY, DREAMS, AND AVOWALS

IS INSCRIBED TO MY DEAR FRIEND

ALDEN MARCH

EDITOR-IN-CHIEF OF THE "PHILADELPHIA PRESS"

(In whose columns the following pages appeared daily from June
9th to November 9th, 1918.)

And now when the Great Noon had come Steeplejack touched
the tip of the spire where instead of a cross he found a vane
which swung as the wind listeth. Thereat he marvelled and
rejoiced. "Behold!" he cried, "thou glowing symbol of the
New Man. A weathercock and a mighty twirling. This then
shall be the sign set in the sky for Immoralists: A cool brain
and a wicked heart. Nothing is true. All is permitted, for all
is necessary."   Thus Spake Steeplejack.

"I am not what I am."
                "Othello."

CONTENTS

CONTENTS

PART II

ILLUSTRATIONS

APOLOGY

The avowals of a Steeplejack! Why shouldn't a steeplejack make avowals? It is a dangerous occupation and, oddly enough, one in which the higher you mount the lower you fall, socially. Yet a steeplejack, humble as is his calling, may be a dreamer of daring dreams, a poet, even a hero. I, who write these words, am no poet, but I have been a steeplejack. I have climbed to the very top of many steeples the world over, and dreamed like the rest of my fellow beings the dreams that accompany the promenade of pure blood through young arteries, and now after a half century, I shall report these dreams and their awakenings; for the difference between the dream-world and what we are pleased to call reality is something which no poet, philosopher, or psychologist has yet explained. Whether we dream at night when our body vegetates, or our dreams overflow into our waking hours does not much matter. To dream is to exist. I dream therefore I am, might be the formula of a second Descartes. And who enjoys loftier dreams than a steeplejack? But alas! he must always return to earth, else perish aloft from the cold.

When a boy I was called a Johnny-look-in-the-air, because of my reckless habit of rambling into obstacles, from moving locomotives to immovable lamp-posts. I suppose I was dreaming; at least I was walking in that pleasing haze we call egotism. Now a large dosage of self-love is a necessary ingredient in the formation of

3

character, character called by the Greeks a man's destiny; that character which leads to success only when followed no matter the cost. Chamfort said this, but the fog-fed owls, to whose care our tenderest and most susceptible years are usually confided, cry anathema. Cynical! they say. Well, what if it be? A cynic like a pessimist, is only a man who tells unpleasant truths, while your optimist spins pleasing lies, therefore, is the more popular of the pair. Nothing succeeds like insincerity. A steeplejack never lies. His truth is the truth. At least I thought so years before I encountered this aphorism in the book of Max Stirner, an anarch. I tried to climb—always in the azure—but my muscles were undeveloped and wings I had none to speak of; the consequences may be well imagined. Many a tumble, broken bones, and what sentimentalists would describe as shattered illusions. Really, no illusions were dissipated. Fifty years have passed and I am still the incorrigible dreamer (with one eye on earthly banquets) and a steeplejack. So endure my childish egotism, doubled by the garrulity of an elderly person who ever carries his umbrella abroad even when the sun bathes in the blue bowl of the firmament.

An egotistical steeplejack, then, but not a spinner of yarns; that is, I hope, not incredible yarns; though lying is like a forest—the deeper in you go the more difficult it is to escape. The narration, on whose road I am starting out so gaily, may puzzle but it need not alarm you. It is the story of an unquiet soul who voyaged from city to city, country to country, in search of something, he knew not what. The golden grapes of desire were never plucked, the marvellous mirage of the Seven Arts never overtaken, the antique and beautiful porches

of philosophy, the solemn temples of religion never penetrated. Life has been the Barmecide's feast to me—you
remember the Arabian Nights—no sooner did I covet a
rare dish than fate whisked it out of my reach. I love
painting and sculpture. I may only look but never own
either pictures or marbles. I would fain be a pianist, a
composer of music. I am neither. Nor a poet. Nor a
novelist, actor, playwright. I have written of many
things from architecture to zoology, without grasping
their inner substance. I am Jack of the Seven Arts,
master of none. A steeplejack of the arts. An egotist
who is not ashamed to avow it. Everyone for himself
in this desert of egotism called life, cried Stendhal.

George Moore has said that "self-esteem is synono-
mous to genius," a delightful concept which suddenly
peoples our ark of mediocrity with wild genius. The
Russian proverb sounds a deeper note: Egotism is the
salt of life. Of pride we cannot have too much, wrote
poor Nietzsche, who has been unjustly abused for his pride,
he the humblest among men. This dictum of his was
but a counsel of self-perfection. Zola called attention
to the egotism of the English, because, as he naïvely remarked, their personal pronoun is capitalised while the
French write "je," unless beginning a sentence. This
is a slap at what Pascal described as the "hateful I."
I best like old Walt Whitman's declaration of personal
independence: "I find no sweeter fat than sticks to my
own bones." . . . Let us admit, strictly between ourselves, that we are all egotists, as we are all snobs, according to Thackeray. Some won't acknowledge this.
But it is true. A world without egotism would cease to
exist; every grain of sand is self-centred, every monad
has its day. Therefore, bear with me if I talk of my

petty personal affairs, bear with my "thunder and small beer," especially the chronicling thereof. A critic should confess his limitations, draw up at the beginning of a book a formal scenario of his temperament, prejudices, his likes and dislikes. A French critic, Hennequin did this, and has since served as an exemplar for the English writer, John M. Robertson. Then your readers would know what to expect, would discount radical utterances on hearing that your grandfather had been a Fenian or that your aunt was opposed to female suffrage. This is no Apologia, but an illuminating diagram. He who runs may see, may read. To be quite frank, I had rather echo the piteous prayer of Charles Baudelaire: "Oh! Lord! God! Give me the force and courage to contemplate my heart and body without disgust." To which we should, all of us, heartily reply: "Amen."

Taking it for granted that I am an egotist, a professional egotist, for I write to make my living (he who lives by the pen shall perish by the pen); that I am a newspaper man (not a "journalist," of whom the late Joseph Howard, Jr., said: "Newspaper men usually subscribe to pay the funerals of journalists"), why shouldn't I write my memoirs, relate my adventures among mediocrities? Benvenuto Cellini said that the writing of his autobiography was the duty of every eminent man— and also those not eminent, slyly adds Leslie Stephen, who was probably thinking of Pepys. It is my belief that every man on the threshold of life should write both his memoirs and his obituary so as to match them with the assembled mature patterns of his career. All is relative—even our poor relatives, as metaphysicians have observed—so it doesn't matter what you gossip about, whether it be the stars or clam-chowder. The important matter lies in the manner of gossiping. The style oft proclaims the man. (This is a medley of Buffon and Shakespeare.) In his charming essay on Autobiography, Leslie Stephen declared that "Nobody ever wrote a dull autobiography" and continuing said that "it is always curious to see how a man contrives to present a false testimonial to himself. It is pleasant to be admitted behind the scenes and trace the growth of that singular phantom, which, like the Spectre of the Brocken, is the man's own shadow cast upon the coloured and distorting mists of memory." Instead of ponderous philosophies what wouldn't we give for more personalia from the ancient world, another Petronius, another Suetonius, those wicked old gossips. Dame Quickly or Justice Shallow are as vital and important as Hamlet or Lear. Mediocrity, too, is the salt of existence. Didn't Mirabeau cry: "Mon Dieu, donnez-moi la médiocrité!"

No man or woman likes to be classed among mediocrities. I wonder why? We are middle-class—there is no "lower" or "upper" class in our country, that, William Jennings Bryan decided several years ago; our ancestors were for the most part proletarian—when they were not criminals dumped over here by England in the early eighteenth century—labourers, runaways, "patriots," the poor, the dissatisfied, and recently the very dregs of southeastern Europe; of whom should we be particularly proud? We should not assume either the airs of "fashionable folk" or of supermen. We are neither; though the Eternal Snob is always with us—like the politician. Max Beerbohm summed up the future of socialism in a memorable epigram: "If he would have his ideas realised the socialist must first kill the snob."

Why shouldn't we enjoy hearing ourselves called mediocre? It is our ingrained Bovarysme—the attempt to seem otherwise than we are. Thackeray when he wrote his Book of Snobs was not aware of the underlying philosophy in his subject. Since his day a young French philosopher, Jules Gaultier, has set forth with abundant testimony his doctrine that all life aspires to appear other than it is; the Eternal Camouflage, the Everlasting Masquerade. The snob is only a tiny manifestation of the cosmical lie that permeates all sentient beings. It is, in brief, an Evolution developed under the aspect of eternity; this clear thinking of Young France outweighs the subtle but sterile and scholastic philosophy of Henri Bergson. I have often wondered why, armed with such a viable theory as this of M. Gaultier some essayist has not made a plea for mediocrity. Supermen, superrogues, sentimental humbugs, are done to the death, yet not a word of praise is given the garden variety of the human plant. Like the "average sensual man" and "the man in the street" he is taken for granted. Mediocrity is the backbone of our country. The man in the street whose collective opinion, whose vote rules, whose fighting spirit protects us, isn't this chap, this "fellowe and his wife," worth studying? A majority of "exalted" souls would transform America into a howling wilderness. The word "mediocrity" has become debased in meaning. It formerly stood for the happy equilibrium of our mental and physical forces. The golden mediocrity of the Latin poet. To its possessor it spelled content, and, as long as the wolf was kept from the door, contentment reigned. That is the precise word—contentment not happiness, which is too ecstatic to last without burning up nerve-tissue or without insanity supervening. To be contented was once a gift of the gods; nowadays it means that you are commonplace, without social ambitions. And this is not well.

Notwithstanding that we are a nation of one hundred million humans (mostly busybodies and politicians, as Carlyle would say) we are each in his own fashion endeavouring to escape the imputation of mediocrity. In vain. Number is mediocrity. We think to order, vote as we are bidden, and wear the clothes we are ordered to wear by destroyers of taste. Why then this mad desire to be exceptional, whence this cowardice that shudders before genuine art, and espouses the mediocre because it is more soothing to fat nerves? Let us hear the truth. It is because, happily for us, mediocrity is the normal condition of mankind, and genius is not. We pretend that we are not mediocre—Ah! Bovarysme inescapable—yet we proudly point to our national prosperity. Says Emerson: "Is it not the chief disgrace in the world not to be a unit; to be reckoned one character, not to yield that peculiar fruit which each man was created to bear, but to be reckoned by the gross, in the hundreds of thousands, of the party, of the section to which we belong, and our opinion predicted geographically, or the north or the south?" I confess however I like to saunter from my own bailiwick and watch my neighbour. Anything human or inhuman interests. Not that I am a Paul Pry, but because curiosity assuaged is a prime condiment in the cuisine of life. We are all hypocrites, whether we call ourselves idealists or pragmatists. There is no such thing as altruism, only certain souls who, self-illuded, believe themselves to be disinterested. Be frank. Be egotists, like myself, and the rest of men and women and children—the supreme egotists. Confess in your narrow, timorous souls that there is nothing so interesting as yourself. You confess in prayer, to the most personal of gods. Yourself. The world is your dream. The world is my dream. I have only to die and it no longer exists. In telling you of my experiences I am not bound to consider your prejudices or compelled to apply a poultice to your vanity. If you don't care to take the excursion to the other side of the moon you need not. It strays away from my beloved Philadelphia, and as all roads lead to Rome, it returns to Philadelphia. A half century later. The loop is large, it includes many people, many customs, many lands. Come, let us be off! And I hope my bark of dreams headed in a trice for a remote and exquisite Cythera, does not bump into some paludian wharf at morose and melancholy Camden.

Pray accept me as a steeplejack of dreams, an egotist, a mediocrity, and these Avowals merely as the chemistry of saturation and precipitation. In an old book a character crys: "Five minutes more and I confess everything." Wise Mother Church was aware of one of our profoundest instincts when she instituted the sacrament of Confession. After this discursive prelude, I promise to tell you everything, even though it blisters the paper on which it is printed, which Edgar Allan Poe asserted would happen if a man wrote his inmost thoughts. Autobiography is but fiction disguised, from St. Augustine to Huysmans. If I bore you—which is sure to happen—I am not altogether to blame. Like the naïve old Frenchman who was living unknown during the most brilliant period of French literature, I desperately cry: "Even if nothing else, I am, at least, a contemporary."

PART I

IN OLD PHILADELPHIA

I

I AM BORN

Let us begin at the beginning. I am the second son of my parents, and was born under the sign of Aquarius, symbol of inconstancy, literally, before my time, for I am a seventh months' child; not, however, born with a caul like David Copperfield; yet an object of curiosity to the neighbours, and a cause of extreme solicitude to my parents. I was told by my old nurse, a devoted Irish servant, with us over a quarter of a century—where are such servants to be found in 1919?—that I reposed in a little box heavily wadded with wool, and on the mantelpiece, which in the houses of those days was broad and commodious. A queer way to begin life, the top of a hearth. No doubt I would have figured in an incubator if there had been such an institution. The fact of my premature birth is not of national importance, but it is a fact that has solved several puzzling questions for me. The health of my mother had been delicate for a year and the death of an infant sister brought much sorrow into her life. Naturally, such mental and physical conditions reacted unfavourably on my organism. I was what boys contemptuously call a cry-baby. That unfortunate cotton-wool pursued me for years. I was not only a cry-baby but a child that always kept close to its mother's skirts. I had, still have, the mother-cult. In early childhood it was an obsession. Mother's boys seldom fight back, and I was no exception. I am not an unqualified believer in heredity, because of the disconcerting slap in the face so often given the investigator by data. Weismann has asserted that acquired traits are not transmitted. This must be true as neither my father nor mother were tearful persons; if they were sentimental it was normal, and it belonged to their period, sometimes called the Mid-Victorian. Let us call it Before the War, that liberating war of 1861 which well-nigh disrupted the Union. My morbid sensibility may be set down to my unexpected appearance in the vale of sorrows, and I long suffered from shyness, absurd sentimentality and a horror of the actual. Need I add that I have bravely outlived this youthful bashfulness?

In everyone's memory there is at least one glittering peak around which cluster or swirl the mists of minor happenings peculiar to childhood. Naturally, I can't recall the outbreak of the war, but I remember as sharply as if it were yesterday a walk down Chestnut Street, clinging to my mother's hand, scared but curious. The entire world was out in holiday mood. Independence Hall was decorated with flags. People were cheering. Bands playing. The most vivid recollection, the high-light of the moment was the deafening sound of bells. There were the bells on the old-fashioned hose-carts, and they were rung by red-shirted firemen. Confused by the clangour, the crowds, I asked my mother what it all meant. She answered: "Richmond has fallen." I didn't understand. What could Richmond mean to a boy still in skirts? Although I was reading Dickens at the age of seven, it was years before I appreciated the significance of that phrase, the first one that I can recall from my mother's lips: "Richmond has fallen."

The next high-light was the excitement over the assas-

sination of President Lincoln. Philadelphia, no matter
her Tory leanings during the war of the Revolution, is
an intensely patriotic city, and that patriotism reached
my infantile sensorium despite the fact I had no com-
prehension of the tragic event. The way it was fixed in
my brain-cells came about in this fashion. An image is
more lasting than an idea, and the image was the result
of a picture, a living one, framed by either side of lower
Chestnut Street. Night-time. Torches illuminated a
vast and solemn procession which moved at a funereal
pace. It had seemed to me years, before this mournful
column passed the printing-office of my grandfather
Gibbons, at No. 333 Chestnut. From my mother's arms
I was permitted to peep from time to time through a
window on the third floor. The windows were crowded.
Our family must have been there. I fell asleep. I was
awakened by the words: "Here comes General Han-
cock." Another mystery. Dazzled by the moving lights
I made out a huge dark object, but didn't understand its
meaning. Nevertheless, I was unconsciously assisting
at the obsequies of the greatest man since George Washington to whom the United States has given birth—
Abraham Lincoln. His remains lay in state at Independence Hall, April 22, 1865, of that I remember
nothing. But the flare of the torches, the moving
catafalque, and the rumours of a people in mourning I
shall never forget.

The third high-light found me older and, for my age,
an omnivorous reader. Anything from Shakespeare to
the weather reports in the *Daily Ledger* were welcome.
Stendhal—Henry Beyle—boasted that his brain demanded a thousand cubic feet of ideas daily to stoke up
the cerebral system (a steamboat brain), but I needed

more; if not ideas, then words. The rather uncertain
science of meteorology in its infancy, enthralled my
imagination. The clouds were my constant preoccupation. A pillar of fire by night—the stars and moon—
the clouds in daylight. "J'aime les nuages. . . . là
bas. . . ." I could have cried with my adored poet,
Baudelaire. But the sad, bad, mad, and unhappy
Frenchman didn't bother me in 1870. I was too busy
on the roof of our house at 1434 North Seventh Street—
it still stands, this house, between Master and Jefferson,
although the trolley-car conductors have not begun to
point it out as my birthplace—watching for storms.
Well, one came, and for years I didn't wish to see another. It was on a certain Sunday afternoon, in May,
warm, sultry, threatening, stormy. From my observa-
tory—a barrel in the garret, my head popping out of
an aperture in the roof, I noted with joy and fear a tremendous disturbance in the western sky beyond the
Schuylkill River. Two clouds, of greenish-yellow hue
rushed towards each other, interlocked, and after a brief
struggle, melted into one ominous funnel-shaped apparition. The classic tornado shape, though evidently on a
miniature scale if contrasted with a Kansas "twister."
But size wasn't the quality that scared me, it was the
terrific speed and scream of the approaching monster.
I hurriedly closed the trapdoor and almost fell down-
stairs yelling: "Whirlwind, whirlwind!" Midnight
blackness had settled upon the city by the time our windows were tightly closed. The wind was terrifying, the
lightning and thunder made me hide under pillows.
That storm was accompanied by hail that broke more
windows and ruined more crops than any storm in or
around Philadelphia since then. The Camden tornado

of August 3, 1885, did much more harm to life and property. The exact year of this great hailstorm? I don't know. I've read Hazen's study, The Torando, but this storm is not mentioned. I fancy, it must have been in 1870 or 1871, about the epoch of the Franco-Prussian War. It was some years after the installation of the horse-car line on Seventh Street, which I remember, because as car sixty-six went by I was told that the year was 1866. The Franco-Prussian War I can recall as my mother, an ardent lover of France and all things French, argued the case with a neighbour, a German, and always lost her temper. From this dates my precocious interest in French art and literature, and I lay the blame on the Centennial Exposition of 1879 for my subsequent running away to Paris. I mention these three high-lights: war, assassination, and tornadoes, as proof that I was predestined, willy-nilly, to become a newspaper writer.

II

MY GRANDFATHERS

I come of an old-fashioned, middle-class family on both sides, notwithstanding the radical Celtic strain. My father, John Huneker, was the son of a John Huneker, organist of St. Mary's Roman Catholic Church on South Fourth Street. Somewhere in the old church-yard is my grandfather's tomb. I have not succeeded in finding it. The elder Huneker was organist in the year 1806, and the reason I know is a letter in my hand which is dated "Philada., December 22nd, 1806" and quaintly addressed "To the clergy and managers of St. Mary's Church." In this letter my grandfather, true to type, protests that since he is appointed organist of the said church he "proposed to be choir-director or else—!" The usual choir row.

A certain—the name looks like Mr. Ansan, but is hardly legible—had hitherto directed and instructed the choir. This didn't suit the plans of the old gentleman, hence the protest. It is characteristic of the Huneker tribe, as well as of the musical profession. All or nothing —Either—Or. No happy medium for them. Steeple-jacks. Dreamers. Only hard knocks from experience made them come to earth. How the dispute was set-tled deponent saith not, but as my grandfather was or-ganist of St. Mary's many years, I fancy he had his way. At this juncture I have a painful duty to perform. Far be from me to betray a lack of piety in the matter of such a forebear (I never saw him). His daguerreotype shows him to have been a well-set-up man with regular features, and evidently of a florid complexion. He composed a sacred anthem for voice and organ in 1826. Worse remains. He actually published the composition. It is entitled, "The Vale of the Cross," words by Roscoe. It is distinctly bad, not mediocre, but stupid, indifferently written—there are false progressions, banal harmonies—and I regret that after so many years my conscience forces me to criticise adversely the work of an ancestor. I shan't speak of the open-fifths and parallel octaves; to-day the new men in music violate every rule of the old masters; need I refer to Richard Strauss, Schoenberg, Stravinsky? But my grandfather did not possess the brilliant gifts of these modern composers. If his blood didn't flow in my veins, I should be constrained to add that his creative gifts were not much in evidence in this composition, no matter his executive ability in the handling of organ manuals and treading the pedals; otherwise he is said to have been a kindly gentleman. With you, I also breathe a sigh of relief at accomplishing my duty. Later I fear I shall be compelled by the same motive to criticise my maternal grandfather for his manipulation of the anapestic measure, also for writing sonnets of thirteen lines, though Sydney Dobell did the same afterwards.

In New York you ask a man what will he take; in Boston, who is his favourite composer; in Chicago, how many he has killed that day; but in my dear old town the question always resolves itself into—were you born above or below Market Street? Anyhow, this street was the social Rubicon when I was a boy. On this side of the Pyrenees—Truth; on the other side—Error. I was born in No Man's Land, a barbarian in the outer wilderness. But while the Hunekers were not of an

aristocratic strain we were not newcomers in the land.
I wonder how many fashionable folk in New York,
Boston, and Philadelphia can trace their family back to
the year 1700?   It doesn't matter much, but the blare
of social trumpets still deafen me when I visit my "home
town," so that I feel like querying: "Did your family
come over before or after the centennial?   I used to ask
my father who were his ancestors.   His whimsical reply
was: "Pudding-weavers down at the Neck," which made
me laugh, but left me wondering.   What's a pudding-
weaver?   I know where the Neck is, or was.   Hog
Island has an affinity with such puddings.   Produce
farmers, perhaps—Oh! Chopin, Oh! Verlaine—perhaps
my grandfather's father made blood-sausages.   I refuse
to believe it, only—that subtle allusion to the weaving
of black pudding!   Martin I. J. Griffin, an authority on
historical research, a genealogist, particularly interested
in old American Catholic families, wrote my brother,
John Huneker, that "Mark Honyker, in 1782, gave
twenty-five pounds to enlarge St. Mary's Church. He
was an uncle of John Huneker.   Your family in Philadelphia goes back to 1700, and were among the earliest
Catholic settlers."   A tradition is that the family originally stemmed from Hungary, then an autonomous
state.   An old Viennese Bible, dated 1750, spells the
name Hunykyr, though we can't claim alliance with the
noblest among Hungarian families, Janos Hunyadi. Well
I recollect the fear this bible aroused with its pictures
of the damned in hell; indeed, I conceived my first prejudice against the theological hell because of those cruel
illustrations.

There are various strains in our blood in the paternal
line: Hungarian, English, and, no doubt, sturdy Pennsyl-

vania Dutch; the Irish blood we derive from the distaff side; Gibbons and Duffy. But my father's mother was a Bowman and related to the Coopers. From data furnished by our second cousin, George E. Walton, I learn that Charles Bowman, while a theological student fled to America because of political opinions, and on June 13, 1777, took the oath of allegiance to the State of Pennsylvania. He was prominent in business as in civil and religious affairs later, and with Messrs. Oellers, Drexel, Reufner, and others, Charles Bowman became responsible for the building of the Roman Catholic Church of the Holy Trinity, at Sixth and Spruce Streets, of which he was a trustee. His associates withdrew their names and support, and unfortunately left Bowman to complete the church, which resulted in his mental and financial breakdown. He died, broken-hearted, about 1820, and was buried in Holy Trinity Churchyard. There is a book of the Bowman genealogy published at Harrisburg, 1886, but it seems that the Philadelphia branch is separate from others of the same name. Charles Bowman married first Miss Faunce, by whom he had three daughters: Mary Bowman, who married Harry Voigt; Elizabeth Bowman, who married my grandfather, John Huneker; Frances Bowman, who married Francis Cooper, Jr., the maternal grandfather of George E. Walton. After the death of his first wife, Charles Bowman married a widow, Mrs. Fox, who had a son, John Fox, the father of the late Hon. Daniel M. Fox, formerly a Mayor of Philadelphia. With Daniel M. Fox I studied law and conveyancing at No. 508 Walnut Street, in 1876 —or went through the motions of studying. His sons are Henry Korn Fox, well known in that city, and William Henry Fox, at present Director of Art at the museum on

the Eastern Parkway, Brooklyn. The Coopers and
Bowmans were patriotic, and participated in the Revolutionary War, as well as the War of 1812. Even if
we were not F. F. V.'s, we could belong to the sons and
daughters of the Revolution. Some of us do. Since
the recent happy recrudescence of patriotic sentiment
in this country it is consoling to know that your family
stock is so deeply rooted in the native soil. But the
Gibbons side is another story. That once told we shall
quickly get afloat on the stream of memories.

The acute sensitiveness, the instability of temperament, the alternations of timidity and rashness, the morbid exaltation and depression which were, and still are,
the stigmata of my personal "case"—as the psychiatrists
put it—come from the Irish side of my house. To be
sure, the two months' shortage in normal gestation
played the rôle of a dissolvent in my character. Every
human is a colony of cells. His personality is not a
unit, but an aggregation of units. Duple, triple, sex-
tuple personalities have been noted by psychologists in
abnormal cases. Yet I firmly believe this dissociation
is commoner than psychologists would have us believe.
When President Woodrow Wilson spoke of his "single-
track mind," he merely proved that by powerful concentration he was able to canalise one idea, to focus it, and
thus dispose of it. This inhibitory power is not possessed
by everyone. I, for example, have a polyphonic mind.
I enjoy the simultaneous flight of a half-dozen trains of
ideas, which run on parallel tracks for a certain distance,
then disappear, arriving nowhere. This accounts for
my half-mad worship of the Seven Arts which have always
seemed one single art; when I first read Walter Pater's
suggestion that all the other arts aspire to the condition

JOHN HUNEKER
My Grandfather
(1804)

ELIZABETH BOWMAN HUNEKER
My Grandmother
(1804)

of music, I said: "That's it," and at once proceeded to write of painting in terms of tone, of literature as if it were only form and color, and of life as if it is a promenade of flavours. Now, I admit that this method apart from its being confusing to the reader, is also æsthetically false. It didn't require Professor Babbitt to tell us that in his New Laocoon. The respective substance of each art is different, and not even the extraordinary genius of Richard Wagner could fuse disparate dissimilarities. The musician in him dominated the poet, dramatist, and scene-painter. And in this paragraph I am precisely demonstrating what I spoke of—my polyphonic habit of thinking, if thinking it may be thus called. I often suffer from a "split" or dissociated personalities, hence my discursiveness—to call such a fugitive ideation by so mild a name. But I started to tell you of my maternal grandfather and I am winding up on Wagner. Talk about "free fantasy" in a modern tone-poem, or a five-voiced fugue, or a juggler spinning six plates at once!

James Gibbons was born in 1801 in Donegal, the "far down," the "black north" as they say in Ireland. Not finding the politics of his land to his taste he did what millions of his countrymen have done, he emigrated to America. This was in 1820. He married Sarah Duffy and settled in Philadelphia. I knew him slightly but never had very strong affection for him. When he died in 1873, I was just in my teens. The man was reserved, haughty, and to my younger brother, Paul, and me he seemed needlessly harsh. My first dislike was born of his admonishment that if we misbehaved or worried our mother he would cut off our fingers. There was something peculiarly Celtic in this cruel threat, not that the Irish are bloody-minded or treat their children roughly, but the race is imaginative. It deals in the hyperbolical. Its temperament keeps it oscillating 'twixt hell and heaven. Above all, the gift or curse of expressiveness has never been denied the Irish. They love highly coloured phrases. They are born rhetoricians, from a Dublin jaunting-car driver to Edmund Burke. My grandfather was an orator. He dealt in superlatives. To hear him declaim his own patriotic verse—it was patriotic or nothing—to proclaim the wrongs of Emerald Isle, to denounce the enemy, the Sassenach—Ah! where would George Moore have been with his Erse and his aristocratic condescension to the men of County Mayo! My relative was seldom so exuberant. His hatred for England and the English is historical among his sympathisers. Probably the gravest defect in my character is my inability to hate anyone, or anything for more than five minutes, except hypocrisy and noise. They say a man who can't hate can't love! I don't subscribe to that. Probably I come by my indifferent temperament from my father, who would curse like a sea-pilot and in a change of breath caress the cat. "Here, Pussy!" he would say, after consigning to the demnition bow-wows one of his workmen. But I can love, intensely love an idea or an art. I am a Yes-Sayer.

The fulminations of my granddaddy never got under my skin. Occasionally he would take me on his knees —bony they were, and hurt me—and thus adjure me: "James, you are my grandson, and named after me. Never forget the accursed enemies of your country." Meaning the English. I promised him, naturally, and ever since have bravely battled with the English language, the charmed tongue of Chaucer, Shakespeare, and

Swinburne, and I am always defeated in the verbal fray.
A martyr to English literature and Irish patriotism.

I recall certain long summer afternoons the babble
of men's voices, the cigar smoke, and the clinking of
glasses when a Fenian pow-wow was held in our dining-
room. I also remember the cynical smile of my father,
who detested Fenianism with its blow, brag, and bluster.
He knew. I have since discovered that the sincerity of
my grandfather couldn't be challenged. But my father
distrusted some of the "patriots" who surrounded James
Gibbons. And justly so. Joseph Conrad has said that
in every revolution the bad characters come first to the
surface. This is particularly true of the Fenian movement of the sixties. As to the validity of the cause I
may say nothing. But the patriotic motives of such
men as James Gibbons, Patrick J. Meehan (editor of *The
Irish-American*), James Stephens, the Head-Centre of the
European Fenian Brotherhood (he died about 1901), of
General Sweeney, Charles Roberts, John O'Neill, and
many others, no one could impugn. James Gibbons was
the vice-president of the American branch of the Brotherhood, and while he was not a rich man, he had an abundant income from his printing-press on Chestnut Street.
That thriving business was swallowed up by the "patriots," who did not then disdain, as they do not disdain to-
day, the humble savings of the servant-girl. I speak by
the card, for I have often heard my grandfather savagely
attack these blood-suckers who, with the flag of the Emerald Isle—how often I have been dazzled by that golden
sunburst—in one hand, outstretched the other greedily
grasping the pennies of the deluded Irish lads and lassies
whose hearts were bigger than their brainpans.

James Gibbons sacrificed his money, his family, him-

self in the vain pursuit of patriotism. He was called the
Irish Poet, Patriot and Printer, and while his powers as
a poet are not considerable he put such vehement passion
into his utterances that one must overlook his limping
and monotonous verse. I hold in my hand a small,
unbound book, bearing the title: Miscellaneous and Patriotic Poems by James Gibbons. Printed for private
circulation, 1870. A harp decorates the green cover.
Also a quatrain beginning: "Oh! harp of my country,
the pride of her sages." and the last line, "Thy music
still lives in each Irishman's soul." On the fly-leaf is the
following, written in an abominable scrawl—I know from
whom I inherited my handwriting: "To my dear grandson, Master James Huneker, with the affectionate re-
gards of his grandfather." Rather touching, isn't it,
from a man who never considered his family, friends, or
self-interest when confronted by his duty to the cause,
who dreamed, Ireland Free, ate, drank, and lived with
the idea. Only Erin—the devil take the hindmost!
His was a fanaticism that would have ennobled a baser
cause, and the Lord only knows the Ould Sod has its
grievances. But to capture the British Empire via
Canada has also seemed to me, as it did to my father, the
maddest of dreams. The Irish and the Polish are of
spiritual kin patriotically. Individualists, they are never
happy under any form of government.

However, James Gibbons and his associates did not
think this, nor were they discouraged after the first dis-
astrous battle in Canada. England was not the only
object of my grandfather's abhorrence. He was a violent, nay, a virulent prohibitionist; they called themselves Temperance Advocates in those days, but they
nowise differed as to intemperate speech from the pro-

hibitionists of 1919. All fanatics are alike. The truth is
seldom their aim. They become propagandists no matter
the silliness, inutility, or the positive evil of their cause.
Consider the anti-vivisectionists, the opponents to vac-
cination, or any such baleful cults. James Gibbons, as
his obituaries tell me, and as I know by word of mouth
from my mother, was largely instrumental in bringing
Father Matthew to this country about the middle of the
last century. Our family has, or had, many letters from
that great apostle of temperance, Father Matthew, also
from Archbishop McHale to James Gibbons, who was a
member of St. Augustine's Church a half century, and
an active and zealous worker in St. Vincent de
Paul's Society, for an equal period. He was devoted
to the succour of poor orphans, and I often heard his
poem, "The Lament of the Orphan Boy," recited or
sung. The rind of the man was sometimes forbidding;
he had suffered from many disillusionments; but his
heart was as sentimental as an Irishman's only can be.
I have seen his eyes fill at the mention of a child's sorrow,
or of Ireland. At his funeral the organist of St. Augustine's, Henry Thunder—the father of the present conductor and organist, Henry Gordon Thunder—played
"The Exile of Erin." He was an exile his life long, and
if he had remained in Ireland he would have died either
from disgust or on the gallows. There was short shrift
for "traitors" in 1820.

But to these poems: they are dedicated to his daughter, Mary Gibbons Huneker. The author calls them
"fugitive pieces," and they are. Most of them are dog-
gerel, though the best are marked by unfeigned pathos
and burning sincerity. Those are musical to the ear,
written in the simpler forms, and strongly influenced

by Tom Moore, Campbell, and Byron. "'Tis sad to say farewell, love, Thy absence gives me pain," was once upon a time a popular song. It has a tuneful jingle that is pleasing, if not too original. I like the image, "When the stars hung out their silver lamps above the dark blue sea," even if it is since faded to fatuity. There is a poem dedicated to ex-President Tyler—we were intimate with the Tyler family—but the "gem" of the collection is "A Dream," which appeared in the Philadelphia *Evening Journal*, April 22, 1863. I wonder why they didn't hang the poet from a lamp-post. It was during the Civil War, and a year of red-hot partisanship. The Copperhead was an outcast. Abraham Lincoln had not been canonised by martyrdom. Nor had he been idealised. He was plain Old Abe, and half-mockingly, half-affectionately called "The Rail-Splitter." He was caricatured, abused in print, and fathered with many a doubtful joke. But he was also the "Old Abe" who penned the Emancipation Proclamation, the "Old Abe" who delivered the Gettysburg speech—the English of which has not been bettered by any one of his successors in the White House; an English which came from the Bible and Bunyan, and hot from the heart of the great man who wrote it. Therefore, my astonishment is all the greater that punishment, swift, condign, did not follow the publication of the vitriolic verses signed by James Gibbons, and doubtless inspired by that other James S. Gibbons, a Quaker, who composed the once famous lines beginning: "We are coming, Father Abram." My grandfather's amended version began: "We are coming, Abram Lincoln, with the ghosts of murdered men." I repeat, I wonder how he escaped death or imprisonment. Both were summarily dealt to men for a less offence. That was the time when Secretary of War Stanton is reported to have made his speech: "When I tap this little bell, I can send a man to a place where he will never hear the dogs bark." I quote from an exceptionally treacherous memory. But if a nonconformist, James Gibbons was a loyal citizen and not against our government.

I fancy the fact that he was a poet saved Mr. Gibbons from punishment. The other verse in his little book is harmless enough. "A National Temperance Song," dedicated to Francis Cooper, Esq., a relative, the music by B. Cross, the father of the late Michall Hurley Cross, fills my cup to overflowing. A Gibbons a poet, even a poetaster, is credible enough, but a Gibbons a prohibitionist is flying in the very face of probability. Yet it was so. Before the Fenian movement netted him he was often on the temperance platform, sometimes in company with Father Matthew. It is the only blot in our 'scutcheon—a reformer among the Gibbons and Hunekers. And a temperance reformer. The pity of it! I much prefer the admirable attitude of James, Cardinal Gibbons, of Baltimore, a connection of my grandfather's, who has pointed out that true temperance is to be found in moderation, not in total prohibition. So fierce were the sentiments of James Gibbons on his darling themes of temperance and patriotism, that at a meeting of Irish-Americans in Buffalo, while he was addressing his audience the floor fell in, carrying with it the concourse of patriots. But the orator, undismayed, hung on to a window-sill and continued his passionate address on the wrongs of Ireland. This anecdote may be apocryphal. I never heard how many were wounded in the affair. It was said afterwards that to kill a Gibbons, the only sure way was to heave a brick at his head when one of the tribe was caught praying. This is an old Donegal superstition. But though the family can boast several ecclesiastics, not one has been overtaken in prayer by an enemy. Nor by the same token have any of the Hunekers.

Among my grandfather's papers I found a copy of a letter, dated November 8, 1867, and addressed to "His Excellency, Andrew Johnson, President of the United States." The handwriting is that of my mother, who wrote many a "State paper" for her father. In this letter the writer airs his usual grievance: "Prominent Republicans have left nothing undone to seduce by flattery and fair promises the Fenian or Irish vote from its allegiance to the constitutional party of the country; how far they have been successful the late elections will answer." Gibbons then makes an appeal to crush the enemies of Ireland in the country and stop the "insidious tyranny of England." . . . "I need not remind your Excellency that England has never acknowledged citizenship in an Irishman, when her interest or her hate stood in the way." Toujours England. Whether President "Andy," as he was endearingly called by an ungrateful constituency, ever took action in the matter I can't say. I play Bach fugues every morning after breakfast, but my technique in American history still leaves much to be desired.

Another letter which throws light on the man and contemporary events came to me from Richard McCloud, attorney-at-law, Durango, Colorado. It is dated May 7, 1909, and runs thus: "In reading the *Bookman* for ‘May, 1909, I came across your portrait and learned that

you were born in Philadelphia, and that one of your
grandfathers was an Irishman, a poet, and also vice-
president of the Fenian Brotherhood some time in the
early seventies. That grandfather and I were great
friends. I was one of the Senators of the Fenian Brotherhood, and one Sunday in 1870, a short time before the
last raid on Canada the Senators had a meeting in
Philadelphia at the house of your grandfather. He was
a good speaker on many subjects. I lived in New York
and had a desk in the Custom House, and was a student
in the Columbia College Law School. James Gibbons
and I made a trip from New York to Chicago in 1870
to attend a Fenian convention called by the Senators to
stop the second raid on Canada proposed by President
John O'Neill of the Brotherhood. I got passes for Mr.
Gibbons and myself from New York to Chicago on the
New York Central Road through Canada to Detroit,
etc. I had two small tin boxes containing all the Fenian
papers for the convention, brought from headquarters
in New York. Mr. Gibbons and I sat together in the
train. After we crossed Suspension Bridge at Niagara
Falls, the Custom House officers were coming through
the cars and Mr. Gibbons became uneasy and said to me
that we would be arrested because of the Fenian papers.
I quieted him by showing him that my passes were
granted because of the New York Custom House, and
that the boxes would not be examined. And so it happened, when the Canadian officers reached our seat.
However, on our return, we did not pass through Canada
as we were watched by Pinkerton detectives from Chicago, as we learned from private sources. James Gibbons was a true Irish patriot, and sacrificed his printing
business for the cause of Ireland. I was married in 1870,

after the second raid on Canada, and my best man was
Joseph I. C. Clarke, of New York city, who has since
made a reputation as a literary man. My father-in-law
is still living, and he was a great friend of James Gibbons,
who was frequently entertained at his residence in
Norwich, Conn. His name is Michael McQuirk. Excuse
this screed. Yours, Richard McCloud."

A brave old friend. I hope he still lives. The Clarke
alluded to is no less a personage than J. I. C. Clarke,
formerly editor of the New York *Journal*, poet, orator,
and patriot. James Gibbons was of medium height, as
lithe and swift as an Indian, swarthy of skin, his eyes
grey-blue, his hair white and primly parted, his expression stern, yet his glance was the glance of a visionary.
He was a visionary. Another steeplejack. A dreamer
of that wildest of dreams, the political separation of
Ireland from England. He spoke with eloquence. He
was logical. His familiar pose was that of a statesman,
his right hand thrust in his frock coat. I think about his
only weakness was his belief that he resembled his political idol, Henry Clay. There was sufficient resemblance
to justify this belief. He was a man of character and
intellect. No Celtic instability there. He was as stub-
born and unyielding in his faiths, religious and patriotic,
as the rock of Gibraltar. With his brains and iron will
he should have risen to eminence in any profession,
whether the law, politics, or the church. I think that
he would have made a model bishop. But he preferred
to follow his dream, a beautiful unselfish dream, all the
more beautiful because it was unrealised. He was ex-
ploited by a conscienceless crew. With his imagination
he was doomed to be a leader of forlorn hopes. Ah! the
Wild Goose, which George Moore calls the symbol of

the restless Irish temperament. Despite his occasional chilliness I revere the memory of the man, though I shall never forget the cruel image evoked by him. My hands were my petty vanity. I was called a "fingersmith"— good old Northern Liberty word—and to chop off those fingers seemed the acme of the horrible. He didn't mean it. It was his heightened and Celtic way of saying things. James Gibbons was a fighter born; till the day of his death he fought windmills, and like the noble Spanish Don, of Cervantes, he never knew they were windmills. He thought it was for humanity's sake. And it was for suffering humanity that he fought without a thought of self, or ultimate success. Of such rare and heroic stuff was he fashioned.

III

FAMILY LIFE

These retrospective hallucinations would be incomplete without an account of my parents; not of overwhelming interest to you, but it is to me, hence its inclusion in these pages. Stendhal has said that a man's first enemies are his parents, and there is just enough truth in the paradox to lend it wings. We are the product of inherited tendencies, to give to an unknown quantity a word; we are usually brought up to believe what our fathers and mothers believed. They are our pacemakers in life. Their religious faith is thrust upon us without our asking. Their prejudices, social, political, are ours. It is a man or woman of character who breaks away early from the yoke, supposing that it is a yoke and that our beliefs are sincere. But the profound impressions of childhood are seldom erased. You may fight your life long against them, and uselessly. I, who am not of what is euphemistically called the religious temperament, cannot pass a church without saluting, and often entering. Two rituals fascinate me. The Hebrew and the Roman Catholic. In Paris I went to the Greek church, and occasionally in New York. The liturgical chants first sung when mankind was in its infancy, before Egypt was, and perhaps during the Atlantean golden age, are echoed in the Kol-Nidrei of the Day of Atonement and in the Dies Iræ of Passion Week. The call of the Muezzin from the minaret of the Mahometan mosque is a cry that has sounded down the corridor of time from immemorial days and lands that vanished in the last glacial epoch. The soul of man is older than his handiwork, and his soul has always aspired after the vision. Totem and fetish, tabu, magic, animism, and idols are incorporated in the solemn church services of to-day. Religious emotion is as old as humanity. Baudelaire would not permit his friends to mock his grotesque wooden idol, because, as he whispered, a god might be concealed in it. The idea of divinity lurking everywhere was one of the charms of the pagan world. Man was accomplice in the eternal mysteries. Religion, that most ancient and jealous thing, was a forest peopled by gods, pluralistic deities. Some men outlive this feeling. I cannot. And the æsthetic symbolism of the Mass is alluring. But suppose that it would have been possible to have consulted me at the age of understanding. Would I have subscribed to the tenets of the Roman Catholic Church? Or, to take a commoner example, was I asked whether I preferred being a Democrat or Republican? Stendhal is not so far wrong in his assumption, though in his personal case he was the victim of a cruel, illiberal father, and a nasty-tempered, nagging aunt. This was his Aunt Seraphina, made famous in his journals. For his mother he entertained a feeling that edged the idolatrous. I was luckier than Henry Beyle of Grenoble. My parents were not my enemies. To them I owe everything.

My love of pictorial art was fostered at home, my passion for music stimulated in a musical atmosphere. My father was an easy-going man with a waggish disposition and a large fund of dry humour, which found expression in pithy, if not always parliamentary expres-

sions. He called a cat a cat, as they say in Paris, and
sometimes the names of his cats evoked a shudder, but
the shudder always resolved itself into laughter. Those
shrewd, crisp vocables born somewhere in old Kensington hurt our ear when they impinged too sharply on the
tympani. Yet they usually disposed of a variety of
upstart pretension, of false sentiment. This John Huneker hated humbug. His hatred was not of the bilious,
corroding kind, but gay, sometimes too broad in speech,
and ever salutary. He had a barytone voice, rich, vi-
brant, and, like little Galli-Curci, he occasionally sang
off the pitch. It wasn't as much, I fear, lack of method
as some aural defect. Nevertheless, he was in great
demand at social gatherings where he won applause by
his imitations of Italian opera singers. My memory cells
can still recall his singing of buffo arias, side-splitting in
their innocent fun-making. Also many old-fashioned
English ballads. "The White Squall," "My Boyhood's
Home," "The Ivy Green." His "Down Among the
Dead Men" was justly esteemed. It would have won
favour from Colonel Newcome in any Cave of Harmony. And those caves were prevalent in the early
forties of the past century. Philadelphia boasted a
dozen, a combination of chop-house, tavern, and concert-
room. There was a chairman, usually some well-known
"booze-fighter" and all-round "genial" with a resonant
voice, or else some actor. Billy Burton, among the greatest of Falstaffs, like the elder Hackett, and Edgar Poe's
employer on *Burton's Magazine*, was an admirable host.
The convivial gentlemen damned the King and drank
toasts to the memory of Washington. "Black-Eyed
Susan" was their favourite theatrical entertainment,
though, when it came to "heavy" tragedy, then the

phalanx turned out to welcome Edmund as well as the
younger Kean or the elder Booth.

Many a time I have listened to my father's stirring
stories of the Macready-Forrest row. He espoused the
cause of the English actor, principally because of his love
of fair play. Macready was badly treated. All that
Dickens wrote of our intolerance and rough manners was
exemplified in the Macready affair. Feeling never ran
so high in Philadelphia as it did in New York—witness
the Astor Place riots; but it was pretty bad. In reality,
my father considered Edwin Forrest the more powerful
actor of the pair. Macready, he said, was cold, his art
cerebral. If Forrest had not the polish, he possessed
dramatic temperament. How he could thunder in the
index, whether in Othello, Lear, or Metamora. He tore
passions to shreds, but he communicated thrills to his
audience. He was before my time as an actor, but I saw
him once at his home in North Broad Street. With a lot of
boys I sat on his brownstone steps of a warm Sunday afternoon. No doubt Mr. Forrest was long-suffering in the
matter, for suddenly, to our dismay, the door opened
and a terrible-appearing old ogre with disordered hair
shouted in a voice that might have been heard on Girard
Avenue: "Get out of here, you blankety, blank, blank,
blank!" We "got out of there," and swiftly. Richelieu
was never more wrathful, Lear more tragic.

Of the elder Booth my father related that one Sunday
morning on Walnut Street, opposite the now historical
theatre, his attention was arrested by the clattering of
hoofs and the sound of many footsteps. A crowd swept
around Ninth Street following a horse upon which sat,
or rather crouched, old Booth, who faced backward,
holding on literally for dear life to the tail of the animal.

It was one of the accustomed outbursts of the great actor, a "uric-acid storm," the specialists now call it. The following Monday evening he played a Shakesperian character, none the worse for his experience. There were giants in those days.

Music, while never a profession of my father's, as it was of my grandfather, played a pleasant rôle in his life. His voice and amiable personality brought him into the best company of the town. He belonged to the Poe circle: Judge Conrad, William Burton, John Sartain, the engraver who has written of the men at these gatherings—Poe himself, Booth, and Pierce Butler. Judge Conrad would recite the Lord's Prayer in a way that moved Booth to tears. My father would sing "As I View Now Those Scenes so Charming," from "Sonnambula"—the battle-horse of the barytone Badiali. And if Poe was not too sullen or melancholy he would recite "The Raven," and freeze the spines of the company. As I have told elsewhere, my father confessed that he never saw Poe the worse for liquor except once, and then it was a thimbleful of brandy that disturbed his equilibrium. A handsome, dapper little man, reported my father of Poe's person, and a sad reticent man, with the fixed glance of one immersed in doleful memories, and an eye that was beautiful in colour and the saddest that he ever saw. When Edwin Booth played Hamlet, he looked like Poe, I was informed; not a physical but a spiritual resemblance, my father probably meant.

My father entertained all the visiting musical celebrities. He knew Thalberg, Louis Moreau Gottschalk, Vieuxtemps, and a host of others. Ole Bull went around our dining-table on his thumbs, his feet free from the floor. He was an athlete, this grand old Norwegian

violinist, who looked like Liszt or the enchanted Merlin—
as pictured by Burne-Jones. He was a bit of a charlatan in his old age, and played all sorts of tricks on his
magic fiddle. But he touched the hearts of his audiences
with "Home Sweet Home," "Way Down Upon the
Suwanee River," "Old Dan Tucker," with his reels, jigs,
and once in a while a Paganini caprice. He never, to
use a homely expression, played over the heads of the
people. There was his secret. Art could go hang. My
father heartily approved of this attitude. Naturally I
did not. Art for me was cryptic, else it was not art.
Many the battle we had on this not very subtle question
in æsthetics. Thalberg, in company with Madame
Lagrange, played with unqualified success. He knew
his public and tickled the ears of the groundlings with
his fantasias and variations on popular operatic airs.
The prayer from Rossini's "Moses in Egypt" was a
favourite, and as played by the greatest singer on the
keyboard—Thalberg had the mellowest touch among
his contemporaries—and with his lyric thumbs he intoned the melody. He had studied with the harpist,
Parrish Alvars, who, like Bochsa, also a harpist, was a
visitor to America. Arpeggios, coupled with a lovely
touch in cantilena and an impeccable technique made
this virtuoso the sensation of his time. A natural son of
Prince Dietrichstein, an Austrian magnate, by a celebrated Italian opera singer, Sigismund Thalberg was not
only rich but an aristocrat born. When he appeared
my mother sat in the audience an interested spectator
for the reason that her husband was on the stage and
figured in the programme. "Why, there's John!" she
exclaimed as the pianist emerged. The resemblance is
striking. I have the old photographs of both men.

Mutton - chop whiskers were in vogue with high neck-
cloths, and watch chains that wound serpentine fashion
about the wearer's waistcoat. And like Thalberg, my
father was slightly bald, ox-eyed, and aquiline of visage.
At one concert Gottschalk, fresh from Paris, a pupil of
Camille Stamaty (he never studied with Chopin, as bi-
ographers say, but he played for Chopin and heard that
marvellous Pole play; the reason I speak by the card is
because I asked a pupil of Chopin's, Georges Mathias,
in Paris, and he assured me that Gottschalk, then considered a brilliant talent, was never under the tuition
of Chopin), with Thalberg played the elder pianist's
fantasia on themes from "Norma" arranged for two
pianos, and my father remembered the difference of the
scale-passages; Thalberg's scales were a string of pearls,
the scales of the New Orleans virtuoso were glittering
star-dust. Louis Gottschalk, with whose family I was
intimate, had a more dramatic temperament than Thalberg, who was impassive, and a believer in Baudelaire's
line: "Je hais le mouvement, qui déplace les lignes."
Linear his art, rather than colourful, yet his touch was
golden. In Gottschalk's playing there was something
Lisztian and diabolic.

I was taken to many concerts and operas by my
father, and when he didn't take me I sneaked away and
paid a quarter of a dollar to hear singers and pianists
and violinists who, by any reasonable standard of comparison, would be worth ten dollars to listen to in 1919.
There is no Carlotta Patti; there may be equals of
Vieuxtemps, but not in grace or finesse, and I defy you
to find me a second Anton Rubinstein. In 1869, I think,
Carlotta Patti sang the "Queen of the Night" in Mozart's
"Magic Flute" at the Academy. In the cast were

Formes, Hablemann, and the formidable basso Herr-
man. The opera was sung in Italian. Never shall I
forget the prima donna who limped down a "practicable"
staircase to the footlights and then showered on our
delighted ears a cascade of dazzling roulades. There
was no doubt about her F in altissimo, clear, round, and
frosty. She was a cold singer, the very timbre of her
voice was icy when compared with the warmer, richer organ of her more celebrated sister, Adelina. But Carlotta
was the more brilliant of the two, an incomparable
coloratura singer, whose memory has not been disturbed even by Ilma di Murska, Sembrich, or Melba.
Carlotta visited us later with Theodore Ritter, a polished
pianist, and for the last time in company with her husband, a violoncellist, De Munck, by name. This was
during the decade of the eighties. The third sister,
Amalia Patti-Strakosch was a contralto. I never heard
her sing. The only son by Caterina Barili's marriage
with Salvatore Patti was Carlo Patti, a violinist, who
married in 1859 the actress, Effie Germon. My father
praised Caterina Barili as a dramatic soprano. By her
first marriage she had the two Barilis, Antonio and
Ettore, both operatic singers, the last named a famous
Rigoletto. He became choir-master of St. John's Church,
and taught many singers. His son, Alfredo Barili, went
to Cologne, where he studied under Ferdinand Hiller, the
composer-pianist (oh! Hiller's F sharp minor Concerto,
how I loathe your smug Mendelssohnian melodies, your
prim passage-work); and in Paris with Theodore Ritter,
then a friend of his Aunt Carlotta's (once at a Turkish
bath the frolicsome Alfredo turned a hose on his preceptor with consequences too awful to relate. I think
his aunt stopped his spending-money for a month). He

is now in Atlanta. A younger brother, Henry, is a singing teacher. Alfredo Barili was patient and friendly enough to give me piano lessons, and made a prediction that came true when he assured me that I would never become a pianist worth hearing.

The Academy of Music has not changed much since the days of Carlotta Patti, Brignoli, Annie Louise Cary —now Mrs. Raymond, and with few exceptions the greatest contralto of them all—Minnie Hauk—my first Carmen—Clara Louise Kellogg, Nilsson, Adelina Patti, and Campanini. Colonel Bonnafon was kind enough to show me the green room where hang portraits of Carlotta Patti, Brignoli, Christine Nilsson, Campanini, Salvini, Charlotte Cushman, and others. The old chandelier still hangs in the auditorium, though the frescoes are new. Only the ventilation-plant and the tablets in the lobby, to the memory of Michael Cross, Charles Jarvis, and Fritz Scheel, made me conscious of the passing years. A half century before I had declaimed with schoolboy fervour from the historical stage, some piece or other at the commencement exercises of my school, Roth's Military Academy. I then and there made a blighting failure as an incipient elocutionist and a budding actor. But when I came out in Locust Street last year and saw Sautter's where as a lad I doted on the ice cream and cake, the illusion of the stability of youth was renewed. In New York a week suffices to destroy a landmark; in Philadelphia the tone of time longer endures.

BLACK AND WHITE

When in 1894 my father's collection of black and white was sold at New York the catalogue enumerated several thousand pieces: mezzotints, line-engravings, etchings, and lithographs. It was not a large, but an important gathering. All schools were represented. Quality ruled. Knowing that with his means he could not indulge in the luxury of a gallery of paintings, he wisely "went in for" engravings. That collection not only educated my eye, educated me in the various schools, but it gave me the first æsthetic thrill of my life. The walls of our house were hung with choice specimens of the gravers' art. I ate my meals facing an old mezzotint of John Martin, "The Fall of Nineveh," a huge plate, coarse as to technique, disorderly in composition, yet revealing an imagination monstrous, perhaps, though none the less stirring. Both Charles Lamb and Macaulay have commented upon the grandiose visions of the eccentric English mezzotinter. Melodramatic, violent, morbid, these same visions gripped all England for a brief period during the early Victorian days. Not a colourist, the designs of John Martin show him to have been a Turner, à rebours. His predilection for biblical and Miltonic subjects was the outcome of a mind deeply saturated by religion. His vast temples, his multitudes in sackcloth and ashes, the horrific happenings must have endeared him to Poe as they did to Wordsworth. However, he was not a first-class mezzotinter. In none of his work is to be found the velvety tone of Richard Earlom, or the rich colour suggestions of Valentine Green. Bituminous blacks and glaring whites, his mezzotints are not unlike his paintings. But their glory is their vivid dream-architecture as is the same in Piranesi's plates.

In our living-room, then called the sitting-room, there was a cabinet devoted to the collection, a small chamber filled with numerous portfolios, and carefully arranged as to schools. It was my father's principal pleasure to look through his plates, rearranging them, weeding out mediocre specimens, while vaunting to me the beauties of a Goltzius, an Edelinck, or Drevet, a J. R. Smith copperplate, a Sharpe, or a Woollett. Stately examples of the French and English schools were framed, and were literally "lived with." No especial school was favoured. Lucas Van Leyden and Albrecht Dürer were to be found, as was the grey-haired Man, or the large Bervic plate of Louis XVI. Landscapes after Claude, fruit and flower pieces by Huysums were there. Better training for the student's eye I don't know than a collection of black and white. The emotional glamour of colour is absent, though its symbols are suggested; the very skeleton of composition is bared, and the art of design, abstract and concrete, may be learned. What long happy summer afternoons we spent, my father and I, as remote from the actual as if we had been in the moon. At least once a week old man Bonfield, as he was familiarly called, would drop in and salute us in his bluff English manner. Bonfield was a marine painter of excellent talent and training. He patterned after the Dutch marine painters, Vandervelde, in particular. He loved Constable and Turner. He could render with a broad, flowing brush the rhythms of water and clouds. He helped to form my father's taste in engraving. Keppel was another. He carried prints from New York to his various clients in Philadelphia. About 1850 mezzotints and steel plates were easier to buy than now; also etchings, for then there was no craze over signed examples. That phase evolved later. The consequence was that at what would be ridiculous prices to-day, my father acquired all sorts of plates, brilliant, bad, and indifferent. As his knowledge increased he became wary, and would accept only proofs, before-all-letters. His etchings were his pride. Rembrandt largely figured, but not Whistler, for the good reason that he was not then an etcher. I doubt if he ever appreciated the subtle needle of James the Butterfly, although he had acquired some splendid plates of Whistler's brother-in-law, then known as Dr. Seymour Haden. When this accomplished craftsman visited Philadelphia and lectured in the small hall of the Academy of the Fine Arts, I attended the affair and remember the florid complexion of the artist rather than his words of wisdom.

This was about the time that Fortuny's "Gamblers" was shown at the Union League Club, and its price, seventeen thousand dollars, was mentioned with awe. Henry C. Gibson was buying Cabanel and Bouguereau then, and I don't suppose he had eyes for the superior art of the great Spaniard. Luckily the Academy owns one sterling picture, "View in a Spanish City, Sevilla." A few years afterwards I saw the Fortunys of the Stewart collection at Paris, especially the almost miraculous "Choice of a Model"—which in this decadent epoch of muddy colour, lumpy modelling, and freakish design would be patronised by myopic youth. I have paid a tiny tribute to his genius in "Promenades of an Impressionist." "The Gamblers," to be truthful, didn't make as much of an impression on me at that time as Benjamin West's apocalyptic "Death on the Pale Horse," still hung in the Academy. I realise now the overwhelming superiority of John Martin in the matter of invention when compared with the more successful Quaker mediocrity.

Those summer afternoons spent with our collection set my mind wandering on a dozen different roads. It was the hub of the wheel, of which the spokes were archæology, architecture, history, foreign languages, music, and what-not, all growing out of the numerous subjects dealt with by the artists. I verily believe my first longing for foreign lands and travel was born among these etched and engraved plates. The Centennial Exposition of 1876 completed the victory over my inborn timidity and aversion from strangers. The wheel came full circle in 1878, when I ran away—with my parents' connivance—to Paris.

But I mustn't forget that other collection of prints around the corner on Logan Square, the truly imposing gallery of James L. Claghorn. Sunday afternoon was the chosen time for the gathering of the clans. Then Mr. Claghorn was in his glory. An enormous man with abundant white hair, a smooth-shaven face, ecclesiastical in its mixture of benignity and shrewdness, large blue eyes and a cordial manner, made the personality of this connoisseur an agreeable one. To me, a slender half-scared boy, he was very cordial. I helped to shift portfolios, lift out prints for his inspection, and doing this for some years, I gained more than a glimpse of this magnificent collection, which, when compared to our modest portfolios was as the sun is to a star of the tenth magnitude. All the world worth knowing in Philadelphia passed through the Claghorn galleries, and also many foreign celebrities. James Claghorn was that rare and rapidly vanishing specimen of humanity, a merchant-prince. The collection was sold after his death to Mr. Garrett, of Baltimore, and is now housed at Princeton College. Our plates when sold did not fetch a big price owing to various reasons. My father's ventures in oil pictures were confined entirely to the American school, Philadelphians preferred. Peter F. Rothermel's "Trial of Fabiola"— after Cardinal Newman's novel—portraits by William Hewitt, and Isaac Williams, marines by George Bonfield, snow-pieces by his son, Van Bonfield, a fruit-piece by George Ord, then a well-known still-life painter, a head by Thomas Sully, a supposed Gilbert Stuart, a contested Teniers—which I own—and a dozen other paintings by men of minor talent all testified to my parent's faith in native talent. Some of the artists were constant visitors: Peter F. Rothermel, well known for his "Battle of Gettysburg," the elder Waugh, W. T. Richards, Hamilton, the marine painter, William Hewitt, Bonfield, and Isaac Williams, Peter Moran, John Sartain, Dr. W. P. Baker, these with William Dougherty, of Girard Avenue, a collector of prints and a man of taste, usually figured at our Sunday-night gatherings. Thomas Sully, the portrait-painter, was a rarer caller. Hewitt was a born mimic, and I can still hear him with my father sing an old song, "Paul and Silas Went to Jail." It sounded like a travesty of a darky camp-meeting "spiritual." Rothermel, tall and drily sarcastic, seldom opened his thin lips; Isaac Williams was, like Hokusai, an old man mad-about-painting. He was the theoriser of the group. He had a technical treatment ready for every pictorial subject, but it wasn't original. Reynolds for children, Gainsborough for young women, for male heads, Rembrandt, for sacred subjects, Raphael or Correggio — don't smile. Those were the days of Raphael worship, of Correggio idolatry. Velasquez was unknown, as was Vermeer, but

Murillo and Ostade—Ah! What marvellous artists. The pre-Raphaelitic group was not known, and the school of 1830, the Barbizon men, had not come into its own. Realism was abhorred, Sully, Peale, and Gilbert Stuart most admired. The growing vogue of Bouguereau, Cabanel, Lefebvre was deplored; too much nudity for the prudish public; but Gérôme was applauded to the skies, Gérôme and Meissonier. "The Duel in the Snow," lithographed by Gérôme, after his own design, was popular. And there was a rumour from Parisian ateliers that two portraitists, Carolus Duran and Leon Bonnat, were considered promising. It all sounds before the deluge, doesn't it? Yet I have heard fierce discussions over chiaroscuro, as it was called then; over the disposition of the model—usually a studio mannikin—over complementary colours, over the arrangement of a palette, yes, the very problems that were agitating a certain small circle in Paris; the Impressionists, Manet—who was not, strictly speaking, one of the group, though in the revolt against the Institute—Monet, Pissaro, Sisley, and the rest. In 1867 the Salon of the Refused was opened through the influence of the Emperor Napoleon III. That was about the period when the new and heretical theories had been wafted across to the United States. Not one of the artists I mention had a good word for the innovators, but they discussed them, not by name, but their theories, and you don't discuss a corpse. Impressionism is no new thing. Nevertheless, the Philadelphia artists based their theories on a sound foundation; what they didn't see was that tradition often proves a traitor, when you don't play off your own bat. For them the fact that Rembrandt handled lights and shadows in a masterful way meant complete surrender to his personal methods. Any deviation spelled anarchy.

I was allowed to "stay up" a little later than custom-ary on Sunday nights. As vividly as this morning I remember sitting on William Hewitt's knee, and after he had crooned some quaint tune, the conversation touched on lighthouses; of all subjects in the world. Finally the Eddystone light was reached. What was the secret of its resistance to the sea and storms after several failures in building, no one knew. Full of the subject, for I had been reading the history of Plymouth, I boldly spoke up: "I know." My father looked at me as if at a crazy person. "You know? How do you know?" he asked. "Let the boy alone," said Bill Hewitt. "How do you come to know, Jim, about the Eddystone lighthouse?" I needed no further encour-agement: "I know, because John Smeaton dovetailed the stones when he rebuilt it." A roar of approbation greeted this tour-de-force of memory—I wasn't more than seven—and my father's eyes twinkled. He was evidently proud and pleased. Polonius-like he remarked: "Dovetailed is good." The word enchanted me. I repeated it for days: dovetailed, dovetailed. I was as bad as Flaubert with his infernal "Taprabona," or as the old woman with her blessed word, "Mesopotamia." I can't hear "dovetailed" pronounced to-day without seeing the smoke-filled room, its walls plastered with engravings, the cheery voices of old friends, my father's kindly, bearded ruddy face. Dovetailed; dovetailed. Even at that early age I was spouting words of whose meanings I was often ignorant. And how many did I not mispronounce! I loved Æsop's Fables and once I quoted to my sister: "The mountains that were in labour"; but I pronounced the last word with the accent on the last syllable, and was rewarded with shrieks of laughter. I had fancied that "labour," like Labrador, was a land somewhere in the Arctic Zone. That the phrase indicated the birth of a mouse did not seem so interesting nor exotic.

IV

MY MOTHER

Tell me of your mother and I'll tell you of yourself.
As a man speaks of his mother so you may estimate his
character. Arthur Schopenhauer was right when he
said that from his father a man derived his will, but from
his mother he inherited his intellect. The exception
proves the case; and while we have traversed many
psychological leagues since Schopenhauer, in the main
we adhere to his theory. He only wrote of genius, but
his idea holds good for the average man and woman.
The few wits I possess came to me from my mother, who
was a woman of brains, above all, of character. Before
twenty she was the principal of a high school somewhere
in Kensington. She saw men shot in the streets during
the Know-Nothing riots of 1844, and also the burning
of St. Augustine's Church on Fourth Street. She always
had the faith, but these outrages on the Irish and on her
religion crystallised this faith. She was not a theologian
in petticoats—a more detestable thing than a female
politician—nor was she a propagandist, like her father,
James Gibbons. But she was consistently pious and a
practical churchwoman. Her erudition was notable.
In matters of theology I never met her superior among
her sex. I was inducted into the noble literature of
Bossuet and Père Lacordaire, early in my teens. The
Paroles d'un Croyant of the unhappy Abbé Lamennais I
was not permitted to read at such a tender age, though

51

my mother spoke of him in pitying terms. Revolt against Rome meant to her revolt against life. Yet she was not a bigot. She did not condemn to the everlasting bonfire dissenters from her faith.

My Aunt Susan Gibbons, a character who would have intrigued Dickens, made up for my mother's tolerance. "He will roast in hell after death, and the devil will baste his ribs," she would exclaim, to the intense delight of the children. She not only put the enemies of Mother Church into the darkest and deepest circles of the fiery pit, but also the objects of her personal animosity. Like her father she loved politics. A Democrat had a chance for heaven, no matter his habits; a Republican, however, was doomed. No appeal. Irrevocable. And then the dear, irritable spinster would go into the kitchen—where she was fervently hated by our two Irish girls as an interloper and a spoil-sport—and fry oysters as appetising as Finelli's, fabricate a chicken-salad which reached our very youthful souls, and Oh! she baked biscuits which melted on the tongue. What matters a woman's theology if she cooks like an angel? Aunt Sue did thus cook, but she paddled us like a devil. She made herself our mother, ex-officio. She was not without a touch of spinster acidity, and her occasional cruelties were Celtic. She had native humour. Celtic also the voicing of her sentiments concerning Republicans, Protestants, and people who didn't subscribe to the tenets of Fenianism. She was a family institution, this aunt of ours, and when a nurse was demanded, who could nurse the sick with such tenderness? But when you were safely launched on the route of convalescence she put off all such weaknesses as affection or solicitude for your well-being, and became her old self: witty, sharp of tongue, and the implacable antagonist of anyone who dared to combat her prejudices. Forty years she sparred at the table with her brother-in-law, my father, and as her tongue was more nimble, her wit more agile, her vocabulary larger, she generally got the best of him. It was all in a vein of good temper, yet the sparks flew, especially if the old man ventured on any allusion to the clergy's love of even cheer. Then Aunt Sue would bristle. According to her, all priests were ascetic. "Like Father McBlank," would interrupt my father, alluding to a concrete case, a fat, jolly priest, with a healthy appetite and thirst, God bless his memory! What fulminations ensued. "John Huneker, the Old One will surely get your carcass." My father would hum "Lillibulero," and the incident was closed. But as a teacher of the young she had few rivals. Like my mother, she began as a public-school teacher, and while her intelligence was as acute as her sister's she had not the emotional depth nor the stability of character; nevertheless, she had the art of imparting knowledge, and many girls, now matrons in this city, will recall her school on Spruce Street, where she leased a floor in the house of the late Dr. Brinton.

A mother's influence should be like gentle rain on the sandy soil of youthful egotism; a boy at twelve has portioned out the globe in his fancy. Life is before him and it is created for his pleasure alone. Anyone who comes between him and his nascent desires is a rash intruder. Why can't we accept the wisdom of our elders' judgment, when we are cautioned not to fly from the nest before our wings are full-fledged? The answer is to be seen in the actions of any girl or boy with a particle of self-assertion, and, as a rule, young America has more than its share. Because each soul must traverse

the dolorous path of experience for itself. There is life
knocking at the doors of our senses bidding us come out
and enjoy its multifarious pleasures. Always pleasure,
never pain, it matters little if our mother bids us beware.
She knows the bitterness of the dregs. She recognises
the illusions. And yet we fly in the face of her admoni-
tions. If we didn't we shouldn't live. My mother who
had sounded the heights and depths, knew that children
provisionally accept advice. She had mastered the art
of holding on and letting go, which is the secret of wisdom.
So I had a pretty long rope to hang on. I can't recall
a single instance of a blow from my father. He would
fume, mildly speak harsh things when I played truant,
but in five minutes the sea would be serenely smooth;
besides I took advantage of his weakness. Boys are
almost as cunning as girls in this respect. My sister
Mary had only to play the theme of the A flat Sonata
of Beethoven (opus 26) and she could wheedle anything
from my male parent. I took a lesson from her book.
I discoursed of Raphael Morghen and his engraved Madonna, or of the joyous landscapes of Claude Lorraine.
All was forgiven.

But my mother was never trapped by such obvious
subterfuges. Her perception of right and wrong had the
incisive clarity of an etching by Meryon. Her conscience,
safest of monitors in her case, would not allow her to
juggle with the moralities. She earnestly wished that
I should enter the clerical life. Early she realised the
hopelessness of her wish. I hadn't the vocation. Nor
did the well-meant promptings of some of the sisters at
Broad and Columbia Avenue, deter her from seeing the
cold truth. This old convent was my delight on Sunday
afternoons. There I was petted by Mother Frances de

MARY GIBBONS HUNEKER
My Mother

JOHN HUNEKER
My Father

Sales, and Mother Augustine, and I always promised,
like the meek little humbug I was, to become a priest
when I grew up. This valiant declaration was rewarded
with candy. I liked candy then. I also liked to play
in the nuns' garden. The Sisters of Mercy is an order
whose rule appealed to me, as did the Jesuit's. I have
a weakness for the Jesuit order, not because it is worldly
—that venerable delusion—but because its members are
masters of the gentle arts, and, whatever else they may
be, they are liberal in spirit. The Sisters of Mercy are,
among other things, a teaching order. They know the
souls of their pupils. Now I am what an old and very
dear priest calls "a hickory Catholic," yet I love the
odour of incense, the mystic bells, the music, the atmosphere of the altar, above all the intellectual life of the
church. There is a world of thought suspended like
Mahomet's coffin above the quotidian existence of religion. It is not free to everyone, nor is it an arcanum
forbidden all but the few. Its literature had penetrated
my very bones when boys of my age were playing marbles. No wonder some of our ecclesiastical friends saw
in me the making of a fervidly pious young priest. But
some did not. Father Boudreaux, a French priest and
author, did not; nor did the Reverend Dr. Kent Stone,
a convert, noted for his unction and oratory. He saw a
row of books on my table and shook his head. He had
his misgivings when he noted the four volumes of Charles
Baudelaire—the critic Baudelaire, and there are few to
surpass him in clairvoyance, interested me as much as
the poet—the essays of Walter Pater, Matthew Arnold,
the poems of Swinburne, Rossetti, of Poe and Gautier.
Rabelais, Montaigne, Goethe, Aquinas, and Emerson had
their place, and Schopenhauer, and there were sermons

by Lacordaire, whose harmonious French I savoured, and Bourdaloue; Madame de Swetchine and Eugénie de Guérin were there. I read the sister before I saw the pantheistic prose-poem of her brother Maurice, "The Centaur." This poet whose sensibility was as exquisite as Chopin's, I still love. But he didn't die a moment too soon for his artistic reputation. My chief offence, however, was Walt Whitman, the 1867 edition of his "Poems." Professor George Saintsbury had introduced me to the genius of Baudelaire—who waxes in greatness with the waning of the years—and Professor Edward Dowden of Dublin, sent me in eager haste to modern French literature—that is, modern in 1875 or thereabouts. I had introduced myself to Whitman by securing his volumes and later (1877) by visiting the Bard of Camden in his lair on Mickle Street. But I had seen him for years on Market or Chestnut Streets, a Homeric man, good to gaze upon, with his magnificent head and bare chest. I never saw him without a forlorn pup at his heels. But I have told you all this in Ivory Apes and Peacocks. He is one of the peacocks.

Dr. Stone knew that a youth who poisoned himself with such powerful and pernicious toxics as Baudelaire and Whitman had no inner call to religion, though its ritual appealed to his æsthetic sense. I read all day when I had a chance, read everything from editorials in the *Public Ledger,* which seemed to me masterpieces of common-sense, to Dante and Shakespeare. The Divine Comedy had just appeared with the fantastic illustrations of Gustave Doré. The poem and pictures gripped us, and I see myself playing Lucifer to my brother Paul's Minotaur in our back yard. Every circle in the Inferno we tried to imitate. Many rows with my old nurse, Maish Finn, ensued. To-day the "terza rima" of that sombre and magnificent poet is as alluring as ever. Possibly Doré and his vivid fancy first attracted us. Don Quixote was another magnet. And Bunyan, with his glorious apotheosis of the soul, which we accepted as sheer facts, thanks to his sober, convincing prose, became a masque of boyhood. But the dream of a sacerdotal dedication was further away than ever. My mother once remarked: "What can you expect in the future if you turn your mind into a sewer for all these vile poets and infidels?" She didn't know that Baudelaire is the Catholic poet par excellence, one whose morose delectation would have been congenial to John of the Cross, Ruysbroeck, or any early mystic. Contempt for life is in his words, hatred of self, fiercer hatred for woman, a hatred so cuttingly expressed by the monk, St. Odo of Cluny, "quomodo ipsum steroris saccum amplecti desideramus!" truly a judgment on feminine beauty in the manner of the early Church Fathers. (I quote this from Affirmations, by that philosophic and erudite critic, Havelock Ellis, a writer after my own heart.) Or, Arthur Schopenhauer, with his convincing pronouncements of the nothingness of life! Isn't he in consonance with the wisdom of the church? Not the pellucid style and charm of Cardinal Newman could offset the deadly lessons in pessimism of the poet and philosopher; Walt Whitman and his Bowery Boy Emersonism, his anarchic defiance of the ordinary decencies of life completed the disruption of my character. Hereafter these were the dissonances in my little harmonic scale. The spiritual dichotomy was complete. My mother was right—and yet, and yet, life is to be faced, not feared. Prove all things, said the

Apostle. I might have made a short cut to salvation if I had listened to my mother. But I didn't. I was wrong. And if I had to go through it all again I should proceed approximately the same. Cowardice is a more fatal spiritual lesion than vainglorious rashness. For each man must weave the web of his own destiny. There is a time to be static and there is a time to be dynamic. The trouble was that I too often played the dynamic at the wrong time. What I most wonder at, and also admire, is the tolerant spirit exhibited by my mother. She protested, but she allowed me my intellectual freedom. Once I saw her genuinely indignant. She caught me on the roof reading Strathmore, by Ouida, a novelist she detested. Like Max Beerbohm, I had conceived a passion for this extravagantly romantic writer. Not even "Guy Livingstone," from whom Ouida derived, cured me of her sentimental sensuality. Dickens did, and when I reached, in due course of time, Thackeray, the Ouida measles had quite disappeared.

But the school was looming up, school and its odious tasks, its discipline, its convict-like confinement. It was a foregone conclusion that I should be sent to a sectarian establishment, though not to the parish school. I had been taught my catechism by the good nuns, and also at our parish church, St. Malachi's, on Eleventh Street near Jefferson. Gaunt Father Kelly had scared us with his harsh manner, and I soon feared him. It was an adventure, too, the trip from Seventh Street. Gangs of rival boys laid in wait for us and many times I ran homeward, dodging stones and brickbats. The old lawlessness of the fire companies had been abolished, but not altogether. The South Penn Hose Company fought the Cohocksink Hose at every fire. I saw a building burn down on Marshal Street one bitter cold morning while red-shirted heroes in the old style fireman's hat beat each other with spanners, hose-pipes, and fists. It was magnificent, but it wasn't fair to the householders. Like their elders, the young "toughs" who played in the Ninth Street lots descended, a horde of savages, on the more civilised purlieus of Franklin or Seventh Streets. "Baste the dudes," "bang the squirts" were passwords. Any boy who wore a clean collar was considered effeminate; nor did the girls escape. The cotton-dollies wearing sunbonnets from up Kensington way would assault any girl with pretty ribbons or hair carefully combed. On election nights the guerilla warfare was terrifying. Bands of young ruffians—some of them I know to-day as distinguished lights on the Bench, at the Bar, also in the Eastern Penitentiary—swept down on our bonfires, ruthlessly stamping them out; worse, actually stealing the flaming barrels (so sedulously stolen by our gang earlier in the week) and then dumping them in a cage, which they dragged over the cobble-stones, with yells of triumph. One November evening my father tried conclusions with them. They escaped his slipper, his only weapon of offence, and he limped back, quite forgetful of one foot in a stocking. These affairs deeply impressed me. I was a physical coward, and dodged a fight whenever I could. But one afternoon I was cornered. Then the scared boy became desperate. For weeks that conflict was the subject of gossip and curious comment. I put a bully down and out, but there was much critical asperity over my methods. I was said to have fought unfairly. Why? Simply because I transformed my left arm into a revolving flail—if such a thing could be—and knocked the other chap senseless. I won't say that admiration was withheld, but it was qualified. "You hadn't ought to done it," was the final judgment of a veteran pugilist of ten. And I shouldn't, but I won. Later, on Chancellor Street, down-town, in my famous fight to a finish with bare knuckles, with Jimmy Kelly, my old tactics availed me naught. I had both eyes blackened, swollen lips, one tooth loosened, and an ear magnified to the size and colour of a ripe tomato. After that downfall I abandoned all hopes of the prize-ring.

Another time I was rescued by my elder brother at the corner of Eighth and Jefferson Streets. Vacant lots. A covey of vicious lads. The gas-house gang. I only played the witness, incidentally dodging flying missiles. But the enemy didn't count opposed to the skill, strength and courage of my brother. He sailed into them like an armoured cruiser, battered down their defence, and finally chased them from the field. That night a parlour window was broken by a half brick. They never forgave us. I quit the dangerous route, except on Sundays, when protected by my parents. I had been confirmed at St. Malachi's by Bishop Wood, afterwards Archbishop, as I had been dedicated at St. Michael's by Bishop Gibbons, later Cardinal James Gibbons. I was taken by my mother into the Sacristy of St. Michael's and kissed the hand of that distinguished churchman. Furthermore, I had been given in confirmation the name of St. Aloysius of Gonzaga, the patron saint of purity. That was handing over a hostage to fortune. The devil must have smiled when the news reached his apartment in the infernal tropics. He was at my elbow in twenty-four hours, and has never left it since. At three score and ten I hope to rid myself of this particular pest, but

not till then.   (Ah! the braggart, I hear him whisper.)
After my first communion at the convent this diabolic
familiar came in conflict with my guardian angel.   I
fought with my junior brother over a silver watch, and
we punched and cursed till separated.   No denying the
existence of demons.   Again my mother shook her head.
My worldly vocation was undeniable.

V

I GO TO SCHOOL

The school selected for me was Roth's Military Academy at No. 337 South Broad Street. The building still stands, the façade unchanged. From Seventh and Jefferson Streets to it was a long distance. It seemed unending. I took the walk every day in fair weather, usually in company with my brother and sister. We were intimate with several Jewish families; the Aubs, the Eisners, the Bacharachs—be still, my heart, one beautiful maid, Bertha by name, with Oriental eyes and tresses won my admiration!—and the chattering crowd would go down Franklin Street to our various schools. I don't know whether customs have changed, but many of my sister's school companions were of Jewish origin. Roman Catholics and Jews got along very well as any Catholic convent list then proved. One morning we were alone, my sister and I, and at the corner of Eighth and Poplar Streets were suddenly attacked by a lot of boys who cried: "Jew, Jew, where's your pork?" It was the first time I had been called a Jew, but not the last. Being liberal in our notions we did not feel insulted, until the fighting blood of the Gibbons was aroused in my sister. I was too puny to be of assistance. She needed none. Firmly grasping the straps of her leather school-bag, she whirled it about as if it were a Zulu club; the same circular tactics that won my first battle. The rout was unquestionable. She banged those boys so badly that thereafter we were never molested. In my eyes she became

Boadicea. What made me a peculiar victim was the
cadet uniform I was compelled to wear. A torture! On
our caps were the letters B. S. C.: Broad Street Cadets,
which was jeeringly transposed to Broad Street Cleaners
by the hoodlums. "Envy," said my mother. But I
didn't think so. It was the hatred of any boy for another who is differently dressed. That uniform—what
unhappy hours it gave me! How I loathed its grey and
black, its buttons, its cap! Professor Roth, our principal, ranked the soldier only one step below the priest
in the social hierarchy. A good soldier makes a good
citizen, he declared. A good citizen makes a good husband, a pious churchman. Obedience was his watch-
word, and then the health-giving drill, the physical development in the gymnasium! This military discipline
and the Latin language were the two obsessions of the
worthy man, for obsessions they were.

It was the alphabet and Latin, arithmetic and Latin,
grammar and Latin, geography and Latin, history and
Latin, mathematics and Latin, the arts and sciences and
Latin, and of course, religion and Latin. Before I could
parse an English sentence I had Cæsar pumped into me.
At twelve I had bolted the Latin literature, and to-day
I can't read Cicero without mental nausea, though
Horace is always at my elbow. Greek literature was then
a sealed book, not because Mr. Roth disliked it, he was
too much a humanist for that, but that he loved Latin
the more. The consequence is that I know little Latin
and less Greek. But the solid foundations were laid
and aided me in modern literature and in the study of
the law. We read Greek in translation from Xenophon's
Anabasis to the decadent writers. I had not then any
taste for Huysman's favourite fourth and fifth centuries

A. D. Latin authors. St. Augustine, however, seemed as romantic as Rousseau or Amiel. But English! Ah! That was the weak joint in the Roth educational armour, the three R's I mean. The curriculum was the ordinary one. We ploughed through it in a matter-of-fact way. I'm weak on grammar and algebra to-day. But a page of Livy or a quotation from Plutarch would fire the enthusiasm of our chief, and farewell to Prescott or differential calculus. French came next in the favour of this remarkable Irishman, and Jules Verne, then fresh on the horizon, he translated for our benefit. It was like a rummage-bag, this system. You put in your hand and at hazard drew forth anything from Aristotle to Plain-Chant. Choral singing was a rule enforced. Leopold Engelke our preceptor. He was an excellent violoncellist, and like so many musicians of the time he taught singing and played the organ. We sang everything, more or less, in tune; we sang the Gloria from Mozart's reputed "Twelfth Mass," and we sang with infinite glee a rollicking air to the words of "Johnny Schmoker." Negro minstrelsy was in its golden prime, and Carncross and Dixey's on Eleventh Street furnished us with a repertory of "nigger" melodies. Happy days? Not a bit of it. I hated them then, and I look back to them with a sense of relief that they are over and done with. It is a common error among grown-ups to fancy that childhood is the happiest period of our lives. It is usually the most miserable. Often I wished that my childhood could be abolished. I envied my elders; envied their freedom from constructive criticism, from bullying, from flogging, and a hundred other cruel impediments between my wishes and their fulfilment. There were plenty of boys who thought as I did. Tom Sawyer and Huckleberry

Finn are delightful fairy books for the old, who wish
their school-days had been so recklessly vagrant and filled
with impossible adventures. I was like boys of my age
and enjoyed myself out of school, but study killed the
joy of living.

Goethe, supposed to be the happiest man in history,
confessed at four score that he could remember only four
weeks of positive happiness in a long life, and those weeks
were scattered, resolving themselves into days, hours,
or mere fractions of a minute. Perhaps if the truth be
told, few lucky men could boast even four weeks. I can
recall one brief blazing second of absolute happiness,when
I actually said to myself, "I am happy." It was like the
moments of ecstasy that are said to presage an epileptic
seizure, when the arterial tension is dangerously high and
approaches a cerebral crisis. I was about ten or twelve.
It was at the corner of Seventh and Oxford Streets, where
the old hay-market stood. Hay in those days was not
baled and sent to market as it is now; the hay-wagon
was in its glory—the hay-wagon with its driver concealed
in front, and a string of urchins tagging behind. You
may see this hay-wagon in the paintings of John Constable engraved by Lucas. The day was an early spring
one; saturated with sunshine, the air eager and nipping.
A feeling of contentment flooded my consciousness. A
hay-wagon went by. I was as if transfigured. I mur-
mured: "I am happy." I fancy it was the sensation
superinduced by a perfect balance of body and spirit;
that and youth. The Greeks named it ataraxia. I have
never experienced the feeling since, not even in the trans-
ports of calf-love. Only a few years ago, as I looked at
the Walnut Street Theatre, a hay-wagon, old-fashioned
as ever, moved up Walnut Street and turned into Ninth

Street. In a vivid flash a bolt from the blue of my
locked memory-chambers came the incident I relate. I
saw the old hay-market on Oxford Street and the hay-
wagons, felt the cutting sunshine, but I didn't repeat:
"I am happy." That seldom comes more than once in
a lifetime, and, to be quite philosophical over the matter,
it is just as well, for then the reactions are fewer. You
may not attain paradise, nor do you tumble into hell.
I can conceive of no more awful suffering than the prolonged rapture we call happiness. Human nature can
endure misery, but not without peril to its immortal soul
can it wallow in happiness. Some cynic has observed
that life would be tolerable were it not for its pleasures,
and Lord Brassey, traveller and yachtsman, after a long
life of enjoyment, has told us that he positively loathed
his existence because of its happiness.

My school companion and deskmate was Lewis Baker,
afterwards on the stage, and John Drew's brother-in-law.
His father was Lewis Baker, an excellent comedian,
first at the Arch Street Theatre, later with Daly in New
York. All I remember of Lewis is that he invariably ate
my luncheon, and knowing there was no escaping this
expropriation I begged our cook to give me double ra-
tions, which she did (she always spoiled me). But the
appetite of Lewis at once became more ferocious. I, who
had been dubbed "hollow-legs" by my satirical father,
because of my capacity for a miscellaneous cargo of food,
was silenced by Lewis Baker's prowess. So we came to
daily blows, and finally Professor Roth conducted us to
the death-cell where he slapped our hands with a heavy
ferule. Why I should have been punished I couldn't
discover. It was my first collision with the inherent
injustice of all things mundane. And I revolted. On

general principles, I became the worst behaved boy in my class. I stopped studying. I played "hookey." I defied my legal guardians. I was "agin" all forms of government. It was only one of those little temperamental outbreaks which any teacher recognises as inevitable. Mr. Roth was not a tactful man. We were students by compulsion. He took little account of individual variations in character. It was the same old mould-theory of education. Dress alike, walk alike, think alike. Nietzsche has defined the Prussian as "long legs and obedience," and Roth's idea of a boy was as a receptacle for the Latin language, and a capacity for repeating "Amo, Amas, Amat" ad nauseam. Automatons, well-drilled but incapable, any one of us, of forming a personal opinion—beyond hating our masters. I respectfully submit that this is the wrong way. Our receptive brains are so stuffed with indigestible facts that only lifelong experience frees us from the abominable clogging. I don't know how it was in the upper classes of this school, which I never reached, thanks to my inveterate laziness, but it must have been the same.

VI

THE PLAYERS

John Drew and my brother, John, were classmates, and their friendship continued after their school-days had ended. They joined the Malta Boat Club and often rowed double-sculls on the Schuylkill course. Young Drew was already on the boards, a promising beginner. I saw him make his début in "Cool as a Cucumber," at the old Arch Street Theatre, then under the management of his mother, that sterling actress and admirable woman, Mrs. John Drew. Later his sister, Georgia Drew, not yet married to brilliant, irresponsible Maurice Barrymore, also made her first bow before the footlights in this theatre. My father decorated the establishment from time to time, and was a friend of Mrs. Drew. After some friendly dispute over the colours I heard him call her "Mother Drew." I was aghast. It seemed as sacrilegious as calling Sarah Siddons "Mother." But Mrs. Drew only laughed and shook her forefinger at my father. "Now, John Huneker," she cried, "if this theatre isn't decorated on time, then I'll open it with your scaffolding in it just the same." She could play Lady Gay Spanker, Mrs. Malaprop, the adventuress in "Home," and also remain a shrewd woman of business. She was my first Lady Teazle, Mrs. Malaprop, and Queen Gertrude in "Hamlet," and I worshipped her. When I saw her for the last time on the stage, in "The Rivals" with Joseph Jefferson, she was venerable in years, but her vivacity made the audience oblivious to her age. She was a fine comedienne, and her gifted grandchildren, Ethel, Lionel, and John Barrymore, owe her much, and with her son, John, have much to be proud of their lineage. My chief dissipation was this same Arch Street Theatre. The stock company has always seemed to me to rank in completeness with any other, and the visiting "guests" were distinguished.

Another of my passions was E. A. Sothern, the father of E. H. Sothern, Lytton, and Sam Sothern. Lytton is dead. I thought him more talented as an actor than his brother, Edward. But who knows? I was very young and impressionable, and perhaps my intimacy later on with Lytton may have influenced my judgment. He was a handsome, winning chap. But one thing is certain: none of the three sons rivalled their father in art or personality. Pathos was his weak point, and he knew it; nevertheless, his David Garrick mellowed with the years. I believe his Fitzaltamont in that screaming burlesque, "The Crushed Tragedian," recorded in reverse fashion his aspirations. He had wished to enact tragedy, but nature forbade him. There was a twinkle in his eye, an intonation in his voice that won his audience from the moment he set foot on the boards; but the tragic temperament he had not. Yet there was one speech, a soliloquy in "The Crushed Tragedian," that he delivered with genuine feeling; it sets forth his ambition to become the greatest tragedian that ever lived. It always gave the audience pause when spoken by Mr. Sothern, a respite from his laughter-breeding antics. The piece was wretched stuff; nor was Lord Dundreary much better. Laura Keene gave it up in despair. So did John Sleeper Clarke, whose Asa Trenchard was capital. "Our American Cousin," as it was then known, was all

Sothern. Aut Sothern aut nihil. His English "swell" of the day—the Ouida and "Guy Livingstone" period—was a finely wrought piece of art. Remember, too, that the elder Sothern's Dundreary was far from being an imbecile, caricature as he was of the heavy guardsman type. He had a keen eye for his personal interests, witness his stuttering speech: "I require all my influence for my own family." Not Richard Mansfield as Beau Brummel exhibited such polished art as Sothern in this poor play, although it was no worse in quality than Clyde Fitch's travesty. When Sothern played Dundreary at the Walnut Street Theatre, it was with a different cast. Linda Dietz from the Haymarket, London, was the Georgina. Mrs. Walcott, Bailey, Atkins Lawrence—who would have been a "movie" idol now—with Charles Walcott as Trenchard and Hemple as the valet, not so competent, if I remember aright, as the inimitable Binney of W. H. Chapman. This was years after the original performance of the piece.

Amusing as he was in "Brother Sam," with a blond make-up and not appearing over twenty-five years of age, Mr. Sothern was more in his element as David Garrick. Only Salvini—in "Sullivan," the foreign title—effaced our impression of his drunken scene. As Sydney Spoonbill in "A Hornet's Nest," by Byron, this English comedian was vastly entertaining. His native elegance, his personal charm, his handsome features, his lightness of touch, recall what we read of the palmy days of Charles Mathews. He was the best English-speaking comedian I ever saw except Charles Coghlan, and Coghlan was not so lovable as Sothern, who was a gentleman on and off the boards. His son, E. H. Sothern, inherited more than a modicum of his father's deft art, and, while I applaud his ambitious efforts as a Shakespeare tragedian, I think the American theatre lost one of its best light comedians because of this vaulting ambition. We remember his early impersonations at the old Lyceum on Fourth Avenue, New York, when he was supported by Virginia Harned, and in "The Highest Bidder." Possibly his high-water mark was in "If I Were King." His Claude, Hamlet, and Macbeth were not convincing, but his Malvolio had good points. However, it is ungrateful to bear down too heavily on the temperamental shortcomings of an earnest, studious actor, the son of a distinguished sire, who, despite his physical limitations—he lacked the necessary inches for tragedy—did so much for Shakespeare in this country in conjunction with fascinating Julia Marlowe. Arthur Symons praised the pure diction of this artistic pair, when they played in London. The crisp, too-staccato speech of Sothern was counterbalanced by the rich, organ-like music of Miss Marlowe's voice. Such a voice I have not heard since Adelaide Neilson's.

Sothern was not the only attraction at the Arch Street Theatre. I forgot to add that once I saw him play "opposite" to Mrs. Drew in "L'Aventurière." Edwin Booth, then in his prime, was a visitor there. I hardly lived on earth after his Hamlet and Iago. I had seen Charles Fechter's impersonation, blond wig, Soho accent and all; but I was not old enough to mark the differences in the two readings. Fechter had seemed to me—superb actor that he was—to be a robustious, periwigged fellow, who, all fat and fury, ranted too much. And as it was toward the close of an exceptionally brilliant career, he was too flabby to be an ideal Prince of Denmark. He was then married to Lizzie Price, of the Arch Street Company, and lived at Doylestown. We shuddered at the expression of malignity of his Obenreizer in the dramatised version of "No Thoroughfare." His Bertuccio in "The Fool's Revenge" must have been played in the same sinister key. I never saw it, but I saw Edwin Booth as the Jester and was more than satisfied. Only Victor Maurel in "Rigoletto," the operatic version, paralleled Booth in the part; as he did later as Iago in Verdi's "Otello." The Arch Street "stock" was excellent. Watching it for years from the family circle (twenty-five cents) I became familiar with a wide repertory of plays; restoration comedy, the classics of the eighteenth century and the entire range of mid-Victorian pieces. Tom Robertson and H. J. Byron were favourites, and "Caste" was considered a test for any theatrical company, as indeed it was, and as indeed it would be nowadays. Just put some of the belauded actors who are drawing full houses in such amusing rubbish as "Oh, Boy," "Oh, Girl," "Hello Bill," "Oh, Rot," into the parts of Old Eccles or Sam Gerridge or Polly Eckles and you would see the muddle they would make of these contrasted characters. I've often attended performances of the "little theatres" with their bandbox art, and wondered over the rawness of the acting. Want of stock training is the cause. Any fly-by-night company in my youth could, at a few hours' notice, give better interpretations of not only Shakespeare, but also modern comedy, than these young men and women, who make a dab at Nora Helmer, agonise over Oswald Alving, wriggle through Hedda Gabler, but can't speak clearly or convincingly, or, for that matter, walk across the stage without sex consciousness. I won't pretend to deny that Ibsen isn't a thousand times superior to Robertson or Byron, Pinero,

EDWIN BOOTH

Arthur Henry Jones, or Shaw, but their now conventionalised drama was once fresh and full of "fat" for the actor. Studying a variety of rôles is the best exercise for young people. It is the problem, ethical or otherwise, of the play that now captures their interest when it should be the problem of acting. Think of Barton Hill, Lizzie Price, W. Davidge, Bob Craig, John Drew, Mrs. Drew, the two Walcotts, Sam Hemple, Ed. Marble, and others whose names may be found in the annals of the day, and all in "stock" company. Charles Walcott in particular was a versatile actor. And H. E. Meredith. Craig was always comical. Why, any one of these men and women would be stars in comparison with the half-baked professionals of to-day. Nor is this belief the jaundiced expression of a bored old man. It is history. When these stock companies went out, whether in Philadelphia, Boston, or New York, the art of acting deteriorated. The average plays of yester-year were no better than those of the new century. Mediocrity never varies; but the actors have disappeared. And the "movies" have given them the final push over the precipice into oblivion.

P. S.—My father made the same complaint circa 1875.

VII

THE OLD TOWN

The Philadelphia of my school-days was a prettier, a more provincial, withal a pleasanter place to live in than the Philadelphia of this year of grace. I was younger, and when one is young the world is seen through enchanted spectacles; nevertheless, there are well-defined criteria by the aid of which I can verify my childish judgments. The city was greener, trees abounded, and flowers, lawns, and gardens; not only in yards, but facing the houses. Fountains were more plentiful. The rural appearance was more pronounced, a grave defect in the eyes of tasteless persons who prefer the ugliness of tall factory-like buildings; the uncouth mobs, and hideous noise of New York. Philadelphia, to be sure, was not cosmopolitan, yet it was more attractive, and at the risk of being paradoxical, more European. Certain sections of The Hague, Haarlem, Amsterdam, and Utrecht in Holland, recall to me the city of my early youth; the rather prim two and three story brick residences, the white marble steps, gardens behind, and the immaculately kept brick pavements, these and a dozen other resemblances came to my mind when I lived in the Dutch cities—of whose placid, well-ordered life I am exceedingly fond. Best of all to a musician with sensitive ears was the absence of unnecessary noise, for there is unnecessary as well as unavoidable noise. When the horse cars first jogged through Seventh Street, we all exclaimed at their clangour. The market carts which came in from Montgomery County at dawn on Wednesday and Saturday, rumbled over the cobble-stones, but they were quiet in comparison with the cars. And now the overhead trolley is deafening. It fills every alley with its buzzing, and the metallic clanking of the cars put Philadelphia on the map as one of the noisiest cities in the Union.

No fear any longer of the cruel aspersion of rusticity. The grass does not grow in the streets. The city is become a metropolis, if it is only the metropolis of Pennsylvania. Remember, I am not finding fault. I am merely telling you that fifty years ago Philadelphia was a sweeter-smelling, more picturesque, and a less noisy spot than now. The population that of an important town, but not too populous. There were many Germans, few French or Italians, some English, and a rapidly growing influx of Hebrews. But we all mixed well. After the Native American outburst in the early forties the city settled down and until the Civil War its peace and prosperity were practically undisturbed. A comfortable city, with plenty of elbow-room, good cheap markets, superior cookery, service of a sort long since vanished, and a social life, which, while it had its exclusiveness, its snobbish reactions, did not impeach the mass of the people from sanely enjoying life. Yes, I fully admit the provinciality. They are still narrow - minded concerning innovation, particularly in the Seven Arts. Philadelphia has always been prudish, and not without a taint of hypocrisy. As to the snobbery, that is the extension of the old Tory spirit. Philadelphia boasted an aristocracy in the early eighteenth century, still boasts one. Families with a pedigree that go back to the glacial epoch continue to live on side-streets, poor but solemnly proud. It is a flattering illusion, this ancient family tree, and

only cruel iconoclasts care to destroy it.   In the broader
aspects of life, in First and Last Things, Philadelphia has
always been pre-eminent: religion, patriotism, the family.
For "new-fangled heretical inventions" she has ever
shown a distaste.   She has been called a village—a village, when she boasted a million inhabitants—and she is
voted "slow" by visitors from the Bronx or Flatbush.
But this is another delusion, like the "noiseless" legend.
If the truth be told, and it may wound the moral sensi-
bilities of some, Philadelphia is an extremely "lively"
resort, from which strangers hurry to recuperate at ease
in Manhattan.   The hospitality is occasionally excessive,
the civic thirst abundant.   I speak nowise in an apolo-
getic fashion.   A great city should live freely, largely,
though not loosely.   (Ha!)

The settlement by the Quakers lent to William Penn's
Town a spirit of sobriety.   The Quaker bonnets, dove-
coloured gowns, shad-bellied coats, and broad-brimmed
hats were to be seen everywhere when I was young.
The women, old or youthful, were pleasing to gaze
upon; demure glances did not detract from the charm
of the girls.   The graveyard on Race Street, the Meeting
House on Fifteenth Street, the silent services, where grace
descended without the assistance of brass bands, baboon
antics, or newspaper notoriety—this Quaker cult was
very attractive in its simplicity and sincerity.   Down-town
the males of the flock drove shrewd bargains.   Not even
a Rothschild could beat a Quaker in the real-estate game.
They said "thee" instead of "thou," but the quaint
friendliness of the address excused its incorrectness.
Despite the more vivid, garish display of colours and
exotic costumes of our streets, the absence of the Quaker
garb is a distinct loss.   It was a peculiarly personal note

in the civic symphony. The Salvation Army costume
by no means replaces it.

The town was far from being built in 1870. The suburbs had a disconcerting way of bobbing up after you
went further north than Columbia Avenue. We seldom
dared West Philadelphia, or the more tremendous neighbourhood of the Neck. Young rowdies made life unsafe
when out of our own bailiwick. I invariably took one
route to school. I would leave the house at eight, traverse Seventh Street to Spring Garden, never forgetting
to look at the house where lived Edgar Allan Poe. We
then would traverse Spring Garden, a street of delightful
shade, till we reached Broad. Down that wide avenue
of noise and bustle we went to Pine Street, and there the
doors of the school yawned for us. It took exactly one
hour for the trip, not a slow record considering the slim-
ness of our legs. We hated Seventh Street because of
that inordinately long block or square between Girard
Avenue and Poplar Street. But before the Baldwin
Locomotive Works we stood transported. My passion
for machinery became inflamed by the spectacle of a
monster locomotive, suspended, its wheels whirling at
the rate of sixty or seventy miles an hour. It was the
final try-out. With full steam the machine stood on a
vast truck and ran on imaginary rails, officials and engineers in the cab. No conjurer's show or transformation
scene in pantomime so enthralled me. I had no premoni-
tion that later I should be a humble member of the great
army enrolled under the flag of Mathias Baldwin, Matthew Baird, Charles Parry, and others of the extraordinary organisation, with its three thousand employes
(now five times the number), and its capacity for turning
out daily a locomotive completed. Yes, the shops were

a magnet, going and coming from school. Above Callowhill Street, we met a dangerous obstacle, the unprotected tracks of the Reading Railroad. We had already passed our first on crossing the tracks of the Chestnut Hill and Germantown Railroad, and, as a rule, we avoided these by going west via Spring Garden. The Reading Railroad was another fascination, the shifting of the trains often made us late at school, with the usual penalty of a pensum of a hundred lines after hours—a singularly idiotic and gratuitous form of punishment.

Another dangerous diversion and temptation, was Penn Square, then in four public parks, railed in, as was years before Union Square in New York. Henry James remembers the latter, but I don't think our greatest master of fiction ever saw Penn Square, upon which now stands the ugliest municipal building in the United States, bar none. Even Camden, Trenton, Brooklyn make more appeal to the æsthetic eye than this clumsy congeries of jumbled architecture surmounted by a statue that borders on the blasphemous and burlesque. But at the period of which I am talking the parks with their green, gravelled walks proved a soothing interval in a morning's walk. Perhaps Mr. James would have found these breathing spaces evocative of old London. The dignified residences, the shade trees, the leisurely traffic, the splendid sweep of Broad Street, which one could survey north and south, these were more agreeable than the present encumbrance, which might have been so modified as to leave our show street unimpeded from end to end. Were these public buildings erected as an ineluctable barrier to balk the hungry social aspirations of the outcasts north of Market Street? Or, were the beautiful parks butchered to make a politicians' holiday? Who

shall say, I don't know; but I do know that I was repri-
manded more than once a week for tarrying in this delectable region.

Below Market, Broad Street was lined with homes,
although the La Pierre House, then a leading hotel, stood
near Chestnut Street. The Academy of Natural Sciences
was, if I remember rightly, at the corner of Sansom Street,
on the west side of Broad Street. A certain slender,
agile, bright-eyed young man was always ready to help
us when we sought paleontological mysteries. We craved
for the buried bones of what not impossible saurian.
If there had been a giant crustacean we should not have
been surprised. Everything happens in childhood, even
flying-machines and pterodactyls. With a patience that
was touching, Dr. Edward J. Nolan took us from case
to case, from room to room. Although he may have
forgotten this, it is so, and the now distinguished librarian
and scientist still occupies, I am happy to say, the same
position at the new academy on Logan Square, although
he doesn't have the time to pilot around his little friends,
for the most part grey-beards. Otherwise, I don't find
Broad Street considerably altered as to façades. The
old Natatorium is abolished, but the building stands
across the street from the Art Club—that jewel of architecture, hidden in the shadow of the Bellevue-Stratford.
In the Natatorium the two Payne brothers taught the
young idea how to swim. They were German, one
smooth-spoken the other brusque. I can't recall which
was Jules, but he taught me my first strokes; as in a
dream I hear his guttural: "Ein, zwei, three!" for he
mixed languages. We went there daily in the summer-
time. A season ticket was not costly. You could hire
trunks or bring your own. My chief memory of the

place, apart from many pleasant hours in the water, was the split skull I got from diving in shallow water. It served me right. I was showing off, and the consequences might have been fatal. I still carry a part— alas! a widening one with the years—in my hair caused by the scar I received. For that trick I was scolded by Mr. Payne and banished eight days.

Years before the advent of the Rathskeller above Chestnut Street—high buildings are comparatively recent—there was a small but well-known resort on the west side of Broad between Chestnut and Penn Square. It was called "The Keg," and kept by the Gasslein brothers, Joseph and Charles, the sons of old man Gasslein, who had a place fifty years ago further up town on Callowhill or Noble Street. "The Keg," so called because of its symbolic barrel over the entrance, entertained many distinguished visitors. There was a little garden at the rear with rustic tables. The cheer was simple, but pure—I wish I could say the same of contemporary brews—the company varied and usually interesting. Joe Gasslein, since dead, was an amiable host. I once saw Edwin Booth there in company with his manager, and to his amusement, as well as sorrow, he heard spouted Hamlet's speech to the players by an old fellow-actor, ruined by drink. A capital fellow and an excellent mime. His first name was Joseph, and when he whispered into the sympathetic ear of Mr. Booth, it was done with the sinister air of Iago poisoning Othello's mind. Poor old Joe! He had supported Booth, Barrett, John McCullough, had been in the company of Adelaide Neilson. A man of ability, educated in the best stock companies, of good presence, he let himself slip down-stream, and because of a love-affair. But usually when a man with an alcoholic breath tells me that a broken heart drove him to rum I suspect him. He would have drunk even if he had married the girl. Women may be blamed for a lot of things, but they are too often a convenient excuse for a thirsty throat. Joe had that in excelsis. He was playing at Wood's Museum, at Ninth and Arch Streets at this time—I am years ahead in my narrative—and played villains with terrific force. A shocking villain. How we shivered at his curses deep in "Jack Harkaway," when, as Barboni the brigand, he swore to be avenged on jesting Jack. And in "Ruth, or the Curse of Rum," how awful was his remorse, his delirium tremens and his death. "Father, dear father, come home with me now, the clock in the steeple strikes one"—or was it nine? But that touching verse, which wets my eyes and dries my throat—probably association of ideas—was spoken in "Ten Nights in a Barroom," not in "Ruth." After either piece Joe would appear at the "Keg" thirstier than ever. No wonder! How few recall the old actor. Perhaps John Gasslein, perhaps Albert J. Hetherington—with his miraculous Pepys-like memory—and myself. The Keg has gone the way of all liquid.

If the weather was rainy we rode, generally in the Tenth Street cars, then crossed over Pine to Broad. A favourite return from school was up Ninth Street. There stood above Green Street, near the old depot—there were depots in those days, not stations—a restaurant where the fish-cakes were ideal. The price, too, was ideal, ten cents, with oyster soup obligingly thrown in by the oysterman. Did they taste? But ten-cent pieces were rare. In this establishment I first heard recited, "We don't give bread with one fish-ball," and by a school companion, Philip Dollard. The appositeness of the recitation lay in the fact that they would not give us bread with our fish-cake. "Ain't potatoes as fillin' as bread fer ye?" demanded the guardian. This was about 1871 or 1872; for in the same place we heard the news of Jim Fisk's shooting, and the name of Josie Mansfield. Our curiosity was further piqued on learning that Ed Stokes, the slayer, hailed from our town, and was of Quaker stock. What gossip ensued on upper Franklin Street and the vicinage!

Another vanished landmark was the old Bellevue, at the corner of Broad and Walnut Streets, where now stands the Manufacturers' Club. The late George Boldt directed this hotel, whose cuisine was noted for its quality. It boasted many distinguished guests, not to mention the Clover Club dinners, famous for their witty sessions. Colonel William M. Bunn, one time Governor of Idaho, often presided. I recollect his lithe figure and characteristic head, steel-grey eyes, and imperturbable bearing. He looked then not unlike Robert Mantell. He still lives. Fred Fotterall, Dick Townsend, Ned Rogers—known as Montezuma, and the nephew of Fairman Rogers, the noted driver—frequented the Bellevue, which had an atmosphere its stately successor has not duplicated. (Ah! the pathos of distance.) The younger Rogers was a great swell, and his abundant side-whiskers, called "Piccadilly Weepers" after Lord Dundreary's advent, were the envy of the younger crowd. (This nickname is quite venerable in England, where as a challenge the costers used to plaster a curl of hair on either side of their temples, and call the ornaments "Newgate Knockers"—in French the "bullies" of the Fau-

bourgs call them "Accroche-Cœurs," *i. e.*, heart-hookers.)
The blond magnificence of Montezuma Rogers made my
heart beat. He seemed to step from a page of Ouida,
illustrated by George du Maurier. Incidentally I may
remark that I owed him a debt of gratitude for he saved
me from a nasty fall down an open trap in front of Lippincott's book-shop where I had been staring at titles.
He saw me backing towards the trap and rapped over
my heedless shoulders his dandy's stick, saying to Dick
Townsend: "There's a Johnny Look-in-the-Air for you!"
Dazzled by his "weepers," I didn't have presence of
mind enough to blurt out my thanks. A handsome trio,
Rogers, Fotterall, and Townsend; all have since crossed
the great divide. Another good-looking set was composed of Stephen Whitman, Emile Perdriaux, and Prince
Iturbide, the latter a gay young Mexican, who seemed as
if he had just deserted the Paris boulevards. All these
men went to the Bellevue. So did Brooke Dolan, Frank
McLaughlin, Frank Ash, Paul Huneker, Burt Lee, and
other kindred souls. I never discovered who threw the
big and costly crystal punch-bowl of the Bellevue into
the middle of Broad Street, and then danced some sort
of a savage ritual over the fragments. Whenever I questioned Mr. Boldt at the Waldorf-Astoria his memory
would become hazy. But he did tell me who footed the
by no means insignificant bill. There were ructions and
the rumour of ructions for a long time.

Here are a few additional names in the old Arch Street
stock: Ada Rehan (season 1875–6), F. F. Mackay,
Thayer, Adam Everly, the elder Davidge, Charles Thorne,
Louis James and Fanny Davenport. Some of these became famous at Daly's and. Palmer's. Bob Craig was
the Dick Swiveller to Lotta's Little Nell. His Toodles

and Bob Acres only fell short of Clarke's and Jefferson's.
Think of Dombey and Son with John Brougham, as
Captain Cuttle, supporting Mrs. Drew. Barton Hill was
versatile, as his "Rosedale, or The Rifle Ball" and Shake-
spearean rôles demonstrated. Edwin Adams played at
the Arch in "Dead Heart," Charles Mathews, too, in
"A Dress Rehearsal," though I confess I didn't see him.
Lewis Baker and his wife were in the company. The
Walnut Street Theatre had a capital stock, the Walcots,
Effie Germon—sister-in-law of Adelina Patti—Roland
Reed, Griffith, Annie Ward Tiffany; Roland Reed was
"the young man by the name of Guppy," and Mrs.
Walcot was the Jo in "Bleak House." Edwin Forrest
played his farewell performances at the Walnut, in Cori-
olanus and Jack Cade. John Sleeper Clarke as Toodles
and Dr. Pangloss was irresistible. At the Chestnut
Street Theatre, where I made my début as a dramatic
critic at ten, I saw my first play, or pantomime. What
was "The Three Red Men"? Blue fire and heroics
probably. Later the stock was composed of such names
as Wilbur Lennox, Frank Mordaunt, Josie Orton, in
"The Octoroon," put on for a run; then the Gemmill
régime; W. E. Sheridan, Lily Glover, Frank Norris,
George Hoey, and others I've forgotten. I do remember,
however, the Louis XI of Sheridan, also his Sir Giles
Overreach in "A New Way to Pay Old Debts," though
he never excelled E. L. Davenport in the rôle. Charlotte
Cushman I saw once, as Meg Merrilees, but she was too
old for my young eyes, a hag spouting fire and fury, a
terrible creature, who caused me more than one nightmare. "Our Boys" at the same theatre in 1876 ran six
months, for those times a long run. George Holland was
in the cast. E. L. Davenport is one of my choice mem-

ories. Next to Salvini's and Booth's I never enjoyed such acting. The summit of intellect and emotion was never quite compassed, but to tell the truth, I liked him better than I did Henry Irving. Davenport, it has always seemed to me, never received his critical due. For most theatre-goers in the nineties he was only the father of Fanny Davenport—not a remarkable artiste, though she was handsome and intelligent.

Davenport had not the "divine spark," but he gave his audiences a very fair imitation of it. He was scholarly. He was also poetic and passionate as Hamlet, while his Richelieu was only topped by Booth's. To see him play William in "Black-Eyed Susan" and Sir Giles at one performance was a treat. His Brutus, too, his Othello, and his Bill Sykes could they be matched in artistry and verisimilitude to-day? His Bill Sykes was simply nerve-shattering. Frank Mordaunt's assumption paled by comparison. F. F. Mackay was a finished actor. Do you remember his Eccles? I recall the Western Sisters, Lucille and Helen. Lucille played East Lynne; Mrs. D. P. Bowers was striking in "Lady Audley's Secret." Helen Western was a celebrated Mazeppa—Adah Isaacs Menken, of course, the greatest —at the old Continental, Walnut and Eighth Streets. Those were the exciting days of "The French Spy," "The Wild Horse of Tartary," and Count Johannes, a veritable "Crushed Tragedian," who played behind a net, because of the enthusiastic generosity of his audiences in the matter of bilious eggs, onions, and hard sand. And Hughey Dougherty sang "Sweet Evelina" at Carncross and Dixies. Ah me! I suppose some of these plays would be hooted off the boards to-day, but they were good fun forty years ago.

VIII

I AM A PENMAN

To recapture the first careless rapture, as Browning sings, is not easy, if indeed, possible. What the critics call the innocence of the eye is seldom renewed. Some artists possessed the virtue their life long; Titian and Frans Hals, for example. Any one who has visited Haarlem will remember that veracious group of old Dutch ladies painted when the artist was past eighty— and the town drunkard! Well, those were exceptions. Lesser mortals must be contented with only one optical virginity, and if that is sufficiently vivid to accompany him on his progress to the Hollow Vale he should not complain. With me memories of inanimate objects, houses, streets, trees, sounds and scents are in the nature of hallucinations. They appear in puissant relief. But to pin down to paper these waking dreams, that's the rub. For instance, there are bosky avenues on the west drive of Fairmount Park through which I could find my way blindfolded on a dark, stormy night. And a certain bench, just below Strawberry Mansion on which I sat of moonlit summer nights—how many years ago?—and held hands with a girl who had the golden tresses of the Venetian school; Giorgione, Paris Bordone, Tiziano. (Elaine! Elaine!) That bench I see in all its enchanting angularities whenever I close my eyes and ring up my cerebral Central, Fairmount Park, 1880.

After I had attained the age of unreason, which sets in with a man at his fifteenth year, or thereabouts, I was discovered as a penman whose handwriting bid fair to outshine in illegibility the classic scrawl of Horace Greeley (you have read Mark Twain?). Since then every newspaper office that I worked in has made a rediscovery of this disconcerting fact: *The Evening Bulletin, The Recorder, The Morning Advertiser, The Sun, The Times,* and *The Press* chapels recognise my penmanship a block away. There was a standard joke in one composing-room; the compositor who set up my copy, and the proofreader who corrected it—poor, dear chaps—were always pensioned by the proprietor when they went to the blind asylum. Gallows-humour, this, but it threw some light on my case. My mother realised that my script was impossible—I had recovered from the locomotive craze—and after discussion I was sent to the writing academy of Samuel Dickson on Dock near Walnut Street. He was an old acquaintance of my father, and one morning after commending me to his good graces my father left me in anything but a cheerful mood, confronted by paper and pens, the sight of which then produced nausea, as they even now do, only I call it eye-strain; it sounds more important, more pathological, when it is really old-fashioned laziness. To reach Dr. Dickson's Academy—a pretentious title for shabby chambers—I daily walked down Seventh Street, and turned eastward at Girard Avenue. The old market houses, low, shambling, one-story structures, ran for blocks as far as Eighth Street or Ninth Street—the Chestnut Hill Railroad tracks; perhaps they extended further, even as far as Twelfth Street, but I'm not sure. They were jolly, bustling resorts for all the housewives in the ward. Walking down the avenue, I would stop at St. Peter's German Church, go in sometimes, not to pray,

but to hear old Pop Hertel play the organ, an instrument
of which I am fond. There was a candy shop at the
corner of Fifth Street, where gingerbread was to be had
at fabulously low prices. The beldame who kept the
shop was a creature who alternately bullied and wheedled
her childish clientèle. Her usual expression reminded me
of the sour-sweet taste of cream thunder-turned. She
was of German origin and the school children said she was
a witch, a gingerbread witch. Fiercely she would lean
and ask: "Vot ye vant?" to which the inevitable answer was: "Vot ye got?" "Vot ye want?" she would
repeat in menacing tones. "Vot ye got?" was the Irish
echo. This silly litany would go on sometimes for five
minutes. Her features never changed, her eyes never
twinkled, yet I believe she enjoyed the game of question
and answer, though once I saw her take off her wooden
shoe and chase an irreverent boy who dared to upset
her scheme by asking first "Vot ye vant?" This annoyed her; like Sarah Battle at whist, she must have the
"rigour of the game," as well as a clean hearth.

Slowly sauntering down Fifth Street, I would proceed
as if on a visit to the dentist. When I arrived at Fairmount Avenue, I would gaze across the street at the
residence of the Hon. Daniel M. Fox, once Mayor of the
city, and would note the window in his bedroom, from
which on election night he made a speech to his con-
stituents. Old York Road achieved I footed down its
inviting width. There was at the junction of Fifth
Street and the Road the Betz Brewery. Only a year
ago I retraced my early footsteps, but my souvenirs were
pleasanter than the realities of 1918. Old York Road
had well kept residences in my youth; now the entire
thoroughfare is sadly down at the heels. Shabby is,

perhaps, too complimentary a word for it. I noticed
that our East Side is rapidly keeping company with New
York's. After a visit to Essex and Grand Streets in
1908, Henry James in his American Scene called the
East Side, "Jerusalem Disinfected." He exaggerated
slightly, though not as to racial roots. In certain quarters of our town you feel as if in some foreign ghetto;
Vienna, Budapest, Cracow, Warsaw. I was depressed
by my walk; the poverty, the absence of foliage, the
crowds, all reminded me of the Yiddish belt in New
York. I looked in vain for the Italian colony which is
elsewhere. Franklin Square had nicely kept residences,
but no longer, though the old Fox mansion on Fifth
Street is precisely as it was. York Road alone has
changed. On Sixth Street my eyes were astonished by
the name of Martin Wisler over a furniture wareroom.
Impossible! I went to the door on the sill of which
stood a young man with blond curly hair. Again impossible! In the seventies I often passed this establishment and always saluted by his name, young
Wisler, cheerful, blond, curly-haired. There he stood,
the same lad with the jolly smile, and yet he was different; years bring their changes. I inquired of him his
name. He told me. He was a Wisler. "My father's
inside at his desk. Go in, he will be glad to see an old
friend; you won't find him much changed." I peeped in.
Yes, there sat Martin Wisler, and he did look many years
younger than he should have, considering that he was
my contemporary. But I hadn't the courage to enter.
I feared I was the one who had changed, feared that he
wouldn't remember me unless I told my name. So I
whispered to his son: "Another time, your father is
busy. Never mind my name. I'll surprise him again,"

and I saved myself by flight. I was a moral coward that afternoon. Or was it vanity?

I would pass St. Augustine's, with its dramatic history —how often has my mother told of the wild night when it burned down to the drunken howls of frenzied "native" Americans. Finally, at Walnut where it debouches into Dock, I could see my goal, my "jail" I called it. Dock Street and its surroundings have changed surprisingly little. The house where lived my writing-master still stands, and still needs a coat of paint. When I would enter on the second floor there sat a portly, middle-aged gentleman of negro strain. His broad face, flat nose, eyes showing plenty of white, were unmistakably negroid, which his shining, coffee-coloured skin did not deny. He always wore his hat, indoors and out, as Walt Whitman would say. I was told the reason. His hair was kinky; hence the hat. It was a tall stovepipe of ancient lineage, and was almost covered by a deep mourning-band. He was probably a native of an English-speaking West Indian Island. His speech was excellent English, yet softly streaked by something exotic. He used big words. He wrote formidable phrases. His handwriting was, in my eyes, extraordinary. A master of all styles from the conventional Spencerian to the ornamental letters used in addresses, testimonials, and the like; he was a first-class craftsman. "A clear round hand, my boy," he would say to me, though his kindly expression would be replaced by a vexed one after he watched my futile attempts. He would then sigh, remove his owlish horn spectacles, wipe his vast forehead without removing that eternal hat, and then, without modulation whatsoever, would exclaim: "Ah! James, the Magorians, James. If it wasn't for those Magorians, life would be all skittles and beer." And I, thinking this a quotation, would encourage him with a wan smile. The Magorians! What the deuce were Magorians? I often puzzled over this enigma of the Dock Street sphinx. The Magorians! Were they the Babylonish scarlet-women from the Seven Hills? I never encountered painted Jezebels on Dock Street, unless the limber-hipped, unkempt fishwives who paraded after dark in quest of fresh air, not human bait. What did old man Dickson mean by the Magorians? I did not dare ask him because he was a Turveydrop in deportment, a Turveydrop of the ink-well that Dickens would have appreciated. I asked my elders but they all leaned heavily on the scarlet-woman theory, especially William Hewitt, the portraitist. "He means the girls," he would mutter. If so, why then the British symbol of skittles and beer? Even at that ingenuous age girls, and skittles, and beer formed an indissoluble trinity. And why precisely Magorians—a lurid, suggestive word, a planetary word. I remembered having read a tale by Douglas Jerrold, its title forgotten, which described a fashionable soirée in London. At the height of the festivities, as the society reporter would say, a little fusty old fellow attired as a cobbler appeared in the drawing-room. He made his way to the hostess, blazing in her diamonds, arrayed like a queen. Squatting before her in true shoemaker pose, he shook his forefinger at her: "Now Sue," he said, "now Sue, this will never do. Put on your clothes and come home." (Or words to that effect.) The dénouement? There was none. She quickly left the room, returning in a few minutes enveloped in a shawl (1850), and white-faced and with staring eyes went away with the mysterious stranger. Her husband? Or did she owe him a hopeless bill for cobbling? Jerrold doesn't explain. The story left a queer taste in my memory. So did the Magorians. In the meantime my handwriting steadily became worse. It's as bad now as it was four decades ago, and as I can't use a clanking typewriter, and won't dictate, I have been forced to write millions of words. And yet I call myself lazy. Basta!

Despite the talk about living in the open air and active sports, I think the boys of my day were hardier and less spoiled. Of the girls I can't speak with authority. No doubt they were more coddled, more protected then, and the voice of the chaperone was heard in the land. For a young woman to go alone with her young man to a theatre or a ball would have hopelessly riddled her reputation. The young ladies of various fashionable boarding-schools were given their morning and afternoon walk up and down Walnut Street, or around Rittenhouse Square, which like Logan, was railed in. These processions with the girls paired-off were events for the young chaps. What pretty girls they were! (Dostoievsky has written: there are no old women; an old woman is younger than an old man.) Anyhow, the girls were pretty then. The Chegaray Institute in particular piqued our juvenile gallants. This choir of lambs were fleecier, softer-eyed, plumper and comelier than other flocks. They had the innocence of the serpent, the wisdom of the dove. They never flirted. They only looked at you. And then your aggressive masculinity crumpled before the idol. Occasionally, in the spring of the year, when the moon was full, they betrayed a disposition to throw their little bonnets over the windmill, which was natural; but Madame Chegaray, who was an experienced tactician, knew how to handle the situation. She grimly told any mother that when the crisis became acute she dosed her refractory patients with a good, old-fashioned remedy, brimstone and molasses. The rest is silence.

IX

THE GOSSIP OF THE DAY

The startling sensations of the day such as the Fisk-Stokes shooting, the James Gordon Bennett-Fred-May duel, the cataclysmic earthquake and tidal wave in Peru (1868) when an American battleship was safely landed in the hills among the trees far from the water, Colonel Bob Ingersoll's lectures, temperance revivals, the Keeley motor, the "new" dietary of Dio Lewis, bustles, chignons, and the divorce of Adelina Patti from her rake, Marquis de Caux, the Beecher-Tilton case, Lydia Thompson's Blondes, these and a thousand others fluttered our excitable young brains. I regret now not having kept a commonplace-book. It would prove a guide for a rapidly failing memory. I do, however, remember that after Fred May cowhided Bennett on the sidewalk of the Union Club, there was a challenge, and the duel came off somewhere in Maryland. This was denied the other day when Bennett died. He had been engaged to Miss Caroline May, the sister of the aggressor, who only did what any other brother should have done. James Gordon Bennett, as a young man, was heroic in his cups; that is, his capacity was that of a hero. Byron or Landor said that brandy was fit for heroes. It was really old Sam Johnson who said it first. He didn't know the proprietor of the *Herald* who was heroic with champagne as well as brandy. Bennett often repeated, and according to the newspapers of the period—I read the Philadelphia *Times*' account—he told Fred May he was sorry,

that he wasn't worthy of his sister; but later said "that
he would give any man one hundred thousand dollars to
take her off his hands" (*Times*). He was cowhided for
this, and the duel followed—a French duel, I suppose, as
the participants lived many years. This was one episode
in the extraordinary career of that extraordinary man,
"Commodore" Bennett, who was surely made to figure
in fiction or drama.

The Peruvian earthquake at Arica caused as much
excitement as the one in San Francisco. As for "Bob"
Ingersoll and his warmed-over Voltaire and Huxley, I
can only speak by repute. He raised an awful rumpus,
more of a rumpus than even Darwin, Tyndall, and Huxley combined. Those were the days of Star-course
lectures. T. B. Pugh, or Major Pond managed them.
We had Gough, the temperance agitator, Proctor, the
English astronomer, the beautiful Mrs. Scott-Siddons,
lustrous-eyed, but lacking dramatic temperament, the
South American pianiste, Teresita Carreño, another
beauty, Seraphael, the boy-wonder (really Henry Waller,
the English pianist, said to be a scion of royalty; the
"son of the P-e of W-s," as the society journals subtly
put it), Leopold Lichtenberg, the biggest violin talent
of the country, the elder Bellew in Shakespearean readings—and scholarly readings they proved—and how
many others? I remember at one of these affairs—not
quite so ghastly as Chautauqua lyceum courses—a prohibition humbug drank water all evening, and at the close
of his speech he was so "het up" by enthusiasm for the
cause that he stumbled and fell as he left the stage.
The curtain was quickly rung down. Gin, like water,
is colourless. Father "Tom" Burke filled us with joy
by his attacks on the "Sassenach." Ireland is always

about to be, but never is free. We went to the circus, then Adam Forepaugh's, on North Broad Street, and Smith's Island, in the Delaware, was a haven of happiness. A Coney Island in miniature, without its disagreeable drawbacks, we swam and were at peace with the world. But the island was a menace to navigation, and it, too, disappeared, like so many other pleasant things. Nor should I forget the excursions on the little Schuylkill River steamboats.

Fairmount Park, after Independence Hall, the crowning glory of Philadelphia, was then as now a wonderful playground. The approaches to it were not imposing, as they will be when the new boulevard is completed. The entrance at Callowhill Street was distinctly depressing; dark, damp, dirty; but the old waterworks, the mysterious wheels, above all, the smell of brackish water, stirred our childish imaginations. What a pretty walk was that along the river till the last boat-clubhouse was passed. Trotting horses attached to modish traps, buggies, and the selfish sulky, with its solitary driver, flew by, harness shining, the metal on the spokes glittering in the sunshine, which seemed more suave than now. Philadelphia summers are trying because of their persistent sultriness. There is no salty sea-breeze at sundown to relieve the heated atmosphere, as in luckier Gotham. Yet we never suffered. Children seldom do. We jumped and romped, rolled hoops, shot our marbles, kept our nurses shivering with fright when we fell overboard in the park fountains, and at the end of "a perfect day," we would run home all the way from Lemon Hill, eat till our tiny waists would bloat, go to bed and sleep the untroubled sleep of little devils.

The park seemed more umbrageous then; I say

"seemed" for it is precisely the same, probably plus more trees, and if I seem to make unfavourable comparison it is only "seeming." Sans teeth, sans hair, sans strength and spirits, his youth to an old man is overflowing with honey and sap. The wild locusts and the seamy side of disillusionment come later. We picnicked on Lemon Hill, we trooped to Strawberry Mansion when Levy played his golden-toned cornet. We ate catfish and waffles on the picturesque banks of Wissahickon Creek, and gorged planked shad at Gloucester. To fish in the Wissahickon was a joy, with Manayunk across the ocean. The annual regattas on the Schuylkill were religiously followed. Didn't I have a brother a referee on the judges' boat or in the singles; two brothers in fact? With what nervous anticipation we would stand at the end of the course and watch for the winner! When the Malta boys won, our throats automatically released a yell, a rebel yell, at that. The Centennial regatta especially appealed to us, for a home crew—I've forgotten the club—beat the British visitors. From Schuylkill Falls to Rockland Bridge, the course was black with people. But the London Rowing Club beat Yale by a second, and there was gloom in the camp. For baseball I never entertained the same admiration. It was too violent, but I was mildly interested in the Red Sox and similar organisations.

As the population of the city was so much less than to-day's you could go for miles in the park and meet but few folk. Picnics were quite the thing. There were no trolleys; as the park was near, and we usually walked. I notice now that a regrettable puritanical spirit has turned this leafy paradise into a thirsty desert. That's the way to do it. Make people uncomfortable. Tell

them if they are thirsty to drink lemonade or gassy
soda water. Muzzle them with good advice, but forbid them burgundy and terrapin, or pretzels and beer.
As for beer, poor, vulgar, despised beverage, that is
being chased off the globe. Yet Philadelphia was famous
throughout the world for its brews. Old Brewerytown
may go but not its memories. There was a certain
little garden attached to Conrad's brewery on West
Poplar Street, long since disappeared, where of Sunday
afternoons you fancied yourself in Europe. I maintain
that simple pleasures of this sort react more favourably
on civic life than despotic measures. You can't sup-
press legitimate thirst, but you can follow the example
of continental nations and canalise it; make it sociable
and enjoyable. Catfish and waffles without light wine
or beer is like Wissahickon without its historical creek.
Oh! America! Happy hunting-ground for humbug, hys-
teria, and hypocrisy. Vacations were sometimes spent
at Chestnut Hill, at Squan River, or Atlantic City—
preferably the latter. We usually victimised our Aunt
Eliza, who lived on Atlantic Avenue—Pacific Avenue was
a mere sketch. You could see the ocean from your
back porch on Atlantic Avenue. When, a few years ago,
I flew over the Island in Beryl Kendrick's hydroplane,
I noted the changes in the coast-line. The Thoroughfare
is hardly the same; Brigantine Beach is slowly being
brought closer by sand bars. But the boardwalk is
unique. It was a poor affair fifty years ago—for it is a
half-century since I climbed the tower of the lighthouse.
Cape May, on the other hand, has changed, but not for
the better. It was "Queen of the watering-places" on
this New Jersey coast when Atlantic City was a modest
fishing resort. However, our favourite playground was

Fairmount Park, "annihilating all that's made, to a green thought in a green shade," as old Andrew Marvell sang. (Young Kendrick fell last June and was killed.)

In a word, life in Philadelphia ran on oiled wheels. Even to-day, after the huge clatter of New York, and despite its own contribution to the Moloch of Noise, there is something mellow and human about the drowsy hum of Chestnut, the genteel reaches of Walnut, the neat frontage of Spruce Streets. The stranger is at the first bored, then lulled, at last amused by our intimate life. London or The Hague recalls Philadelphia to some of us. The fine disdainful air of Locust Street, the curiously constrained attitude of the brick houses on side streets—as if deferentially listening to the snobbish backyard remarks of their statelier neighbours, the brownstone façades—these things demand the descriptive genius of a Dickens to make them real; Dickens who discerned human expression in door-knockers, and on the faces of lean, lonely, twilight-haunted houses. The water-fronts fascinated me. Port Richmond on a misty day would recall London, which city I had never seen, but secretly worshipped. I have since wondered at this curious mental transposition of cities and the sensations aroused by them; particularly the slightly perverse wish to be at home when in Europe. Philadelphia never seemed so desirable as when I lived in Paris. Nostalgia? Perhaps. But an absurd one. I longed for Paris when I returned to Philadelphia, and I perpetually saw "European" in the most ordinary and domestic things. That way lies cosmopolitanism, and cosmopolitanism has played the devil with my life—making me a wanderer when I was happier at home, making me think Brussels beer was

better than the brew I drank at old Pop Kemper's place
on Sansom Street, forcing me to deny, I blush to say,
that Fairmount Park was superior to the Prater, the Bois
de Boulogne, or the Thiergarten.   It is.   But an inverted
snobbery made me say the opposite.   In matters
spiritual and artistic it is the same.   To be sure I never
denied that Mark Twain wasn't our most American of
writers, one who would outlive the pallid philosophy of
Emerson, the swaggering humbuggery of Walt Whitman, or the sonorous platitudes of Longfellow; that sort
of snobbery I never cultivated.   I adored Poe, and sadly
wonder over the certain condescension among our native
critics when speaking of him.   He drank.   So did General Grant.   He drugged.   So did Coleridge, De Quincey,
and Charles Baudelaire.   He was inconstant.   So were
Byron, Shelley, Swinburne—oh! billions of humans; what
man some time or other hasn't carried a harem under
his hat?   Or dreamed of houris never seen on sea or land!
But European poets could live recklessly while this unhappy American was hunted to his grave for his temperamental variations; and once buried was quickly exhumed
by the moral buzzards.   As Baudelaire, who gave Poe
European fame by translating him, wrote: "Since when
are the jackals permitted to defile the graves of genius
in the United States?"   Why don't critics and public
alike pose the important question: Is the work good?   Is
the work bad?   Do this and the moral will take care of itself—that misery-breeding moral, varying like a weather-
vane according to clime, time, and circumstance.

But restless bones, and the fear that home-keeping
youths have homely wits, drove me across seas and back
again.   Even as a lad when I stood at Market Street
ferry, I wished to be in Camden.   I would stay on a car

long after the point was passed where I should have alighted. These were only growing pains, I know, yet showed, like straws, which way the breeze would blow later on. Girls, when maturing sometimes nibble at slate pencils or sip vinegar; this doesn't impeach them from becoming the happy mothers of twins, or joining the suffragette brigade. I remember a terrible story of abnormal passion manifested by an up-State Judge, from Reading, or Lancaster, or Harrisburg? Once a year he would disappear, and visit the Quaker city. Then at the Girard House in the secrecy of a locked room he would let loose his worst instinct, and for a week wallow in debauchery. But here is the odd part of the story, one vouched for by the best authority, the man himself. His degrading obsession was oatmeal and cream. Fearing the accusation of gluttony in his native town, he would come here and stuff himself till miserably ill with oatmeal, then, pale, his soul at peace, he would return home meekly accepting the suspicious glances of his wife and the broad jests of his friends. But his morbid craving had been satisfied, and without peril to his immortal soul; besides he was considered a slily wicked chap, a "deevil amang the wimmen." What man, vain or otherwise, could resist such flattering implications?

X

MAGIC

A new mania invaded my consciousness about this time, and captured me in the very citadel of my being. Magic, black and white. As was so often the case the spark that set me afire came from a book, the Memoirs of Robert Houdin, most amiable of Frenchmen, most ingenious of conjurers. He was the first to utilise electricity as an aid to his magical mechanisms; he literally invented so-called Second Sight; and while his magic is quite out of date, he may be fairly called the Columbus of his profession, the modern Columbus, because magic is as old as the Atlanteans, and every religious mythology has its legends of the art. Before I read Houdin, old Signor Blitz had made our young eyes stare with his tricks and his ventriloquism. And Heller, magician and piano-virtuoso, had linked in my imagination the two arts. Heller, whose real name was Palmer, and an Englishman, was an excellent pianist. A grand piano always stood on the stage surrounded by his infernal apparatus; cones and cabinets, glittering brass, and the complete paraphernalia of the successful prestidigitator. Heller played the operatic fantasias of Thalberg—then considered extremely difficult—with technical finish and musical taste. He had evidently studied in a good school and his touch sang on the keyboard. What he accomplished in the other craft I have forgotten. But he was a degree higher than Signor Blitz. Hermann was defter at card tricks; I mean the original of that name, not his

nephew. Houdin I missed in Paris though I attended
a seance at the Houdin Theatre, somewhere down the
grand boulevard and conducted by his son. Maskelyne
and Cook at Egyptian Hall, London, were, in my opinion,
the most remarkable of all the illusionists I had seen,
and I saw all I could from Blitz and Perry to Keller and
Harry Houdini. Exposing the spiritualistic humbuggery was another sensation of the day, for after the toe-
cracking exploits of the Fox Sisters of Rochester, came
messages red-hot from spirit-land with cabinets and tam-
bourines, banjos, and apparitions. Need I add that the
recent death of Eusapia Palladino, the Italian medium,
with the newspaper accounts of her curious career, only
prove that victims still abound. Think of such a great
scientist as Professor Crookes being fooled by the Katie
King materialisation! Poor old Professor Zoellner went
mad over the fourth-dimension, and it was because of
this charlatanry that Pepper invented his famous ghost.
We saw it at the Academy—how many years ago?—and
after that only imbeciles could be convinced that me-
diums had supernatural communication with alleged
"spirits." Supernormal these women are, and their
catalepsies have proved of value to psychiatrists. But it
is all of the earth earthy.

Then there was the plump nymph who slumbered in
mid-air, her elbow resting on an iron upright. She, too,
has gone the way of things inutile. No one believes in
her nowadays. The crystal clock-dial suspended by a
wire, one of Houdin's inventions, was a novelty in the
seventies. But these elaborate mechanisms did not
tease my fancy as did the personal address displayed in
pure sleight-of-hand. To make vanish a solid ball, to
throw a pack of cards in the air and with a magic dagger

transfix the card chosen in the audience—by a confederate, or else "forced"—to stand before a table and with
mystic gabble make eggs open and become bouquets, or
pull rabbits, and water-filled glass globets from a silk
hat—ah! how my heart beat in the presence of those
marvels. I had read of the mango-tree, of the disappearing rope-ladders, of East Indian Yogis, yet none
appealed so much to my fancy as nimble finger-tricks.
I became an adept—and a nuisance to the family. I
would dazzle the servants by juggling with apples, potatoes, plates. From my unhappy aunt I would pluck
oranges, and finally I became so mad over the thing that
I gave exhibitions in our nursery to gaping boys and
girls collected from the neighbourhood (admission five
pins per person). These affairs always broke up in a
fight, free to all comers; either my brother Paul would
become a recalcitrant confederate, and forget to return
to its owner the real handkerchief, or else some inquisi-
tive urchin in the audience would force his way behind
the curtain just as I was cooking up some dark enchantment. I was really suffering from virtuoso fever—the
inclination that drives deluded people on a concert platform there to sing or play and make a show of themselves.
Deeper rooted still was the desire to illude. The escape
from the actual. The yearning for the miracle. It
found its account with me—later in music, at once the
most sensuous and spiritual of the Seven Arts; the one
art which extends partially over the line into the unex-
plored fourth dimension of mystical mathematics. Music,
mathematics, mysticism. The oldest of triune sub-
stances. Mysticism didn't bother me as a boy. It was
the Will-to-Deceive, as the psychologists would say, that
made its appeal. The Great Adventure then was to

bamboozle my little public, and to this very day I retain a certain finger ability in palming coins or handkerchiefs. Alas! the vanishing globe full of gold-fish is beyond my present capacity, but I can play in a respectable style Handel's fire fugue and keep its complex web of four voices distinct. Music, executive music, is also prestidigitation but allied to beautiful sounding patterns. And music is an order of mystic sensuous mathematics, as I wrote in my study of Chopin.

To complete the ruin of my regular habits my principal, Professor Roth, fetched from London an illustrated catalogue of Bland, whose magic shop somewhere in Soho was a resort of the profession. I longed for apparatus. I went to great lengths to secure the coveted articles, and at the shop of Yost on Ninth near Arch Street, I met my Waterloo. The proprietor was a little, dark-skinned man, whose large black eyes would hypnotise you as he performed inexplicable passes, removing out of time and space a weighty object. I literally sat at the feet of this Yost the Yogi. I must have had the shining brow of the neophyte. Perry, the magician, was a visitor at the shop and could handle a pack of cards with skill. I neglected my books. I was become a weekly truant. The grand débâcle was at hand. Formerly it had been Wood's Museum that deranged my studies; the Lauris, Harry Hawk, the leading lady, Lily Hinton, and the stock company, not to speak of old Joe Nagle, these had all contributed in turn to divert me from the straight and narrow path of scholarly rectitude. Magic finished me, and there was irony in the gift of Professor Roth, for that Bland catalogue lost him a pupil. After a brief but very intense interview with my father, my magical toys were returned to the original owner. I was removed from school—an expensive one, by the way—why waste time there when I wouldn't study? I became an old man overnight, a senile dotard of twelve. Another dream smashed! What my future?

XI

A YOUTHFUL MACHINIST

My parents were surprised when I boldly suggested that I study to become a mechanical engineer. What I thought of in the recesses of my idiotic skull was the realisation of an old dream: to become a locomotive engineer, and make daily runs between the depot at Ninth and Green Streets and Chestnut Hill. Had I not been found by an agonised nurse beneath a locomotive at Chestnut Hill picking the cylinder? Had I not pushed the controlling lever of a machine and set it spinning down the steel grooves through the narrow cut below the Hill, and if it had not been for a fireman—the engineer had gone away—in the coal tender I should have come to grief as I couldn't stop the locomotive? My bias towards machinery was unquestionable. At last my vocation. Finally, yielding, it was decided that I should learn the trade from cellar to garret, and to that end I was apprenticed to the Baldwin Locomotive Works, before the steam-hammer shop of which I had so many times been ravished by the spectacle of sooty giants, flying sparks, the clash of metal, and the fierce blaze of the furnaces. I was suddenly lifted from the ditch of depression. I forgot my magic, and only had a vision of that locomotive test, its wheels a few feet off the ground, revolving at a superhuman speed amid the hissing of steam and the anxiety of the judges above in the cab. My ultimate goal was the job as engineer on the railroad. Other boys longed to be policemen or soldiers or engineers, and I recall one queer little chap who confessed that he wished he had been born a girl (how we hooted him one afternoon for this admission, the brevet in our eyes of a coward). But a locomotive and fifty miles an hour for me. To-day I hate motor-cars, speed, dusty roads, and the honk of the horns. Why?

The great day came and early one sultry September morning (I have kept the date, September 17, 1872), I went in company with my patient father to the works, to the machine-shop at the corner of Seventeenth and a little street I have forgotten (isn't it Hamilton?). There we met William Parry, a member of the firm, and whose family had intermarried with a cousin of ours, a Baird. Mr. Parry had been a workman and was the most active and practical of the great Baldwin-Baird corporation. He was amiable to me and seemed to think it natural that I should yearn to become an engineer. We entered a vast, gloomy shop. The noise deafened me. Men, half-naked, hammered on anvils; machinery spun around; the place was damp and smelled of smoke. A thin, stooped man in middle years, and wearing spectacles, saluted my father: "Hello, John," and my father answered: "Hello, Pete." I was told that he was Peter Farnum, an old Northern Liberty friend of his. He was a kind man but, oh, my! his face and bare arms were greasy. The idea of physical impurity had always revolted me. I was soon to shed such girl-like nonsense. After Mr. Parry had said a few words to Mr. Farnum, he shook our hands, saying: "We'll make a man of your boy, John," and left us. His departure was as if the sun had hid behind a cloud. With my father he was one of the last links with the outside world. Already, I was repenting of my determination to become an engineer, already I suffered from homesickness. The practical Farnum told me to come next morning ten minutes before seven, and bring a pair of jumpers, overalls, he called them; then he would set me to work. I arose at five A. M. the following day and ate breakfast with my father, who, as an old workman, had never cured himself of his early-rising neurosis. I ate a rare beefsteak, so as "to put hair on my chest" as my father realistically phrased it. Then a bundle under my arm, a full dinner-pail in the other hand, cap on head, and my heart a cinder in my bosom, I walked down the street in a hazy dawn and reached the shop a half-hour too soon. But the men began to straggle in, coughing, grunting, some smoking pipes, all wearing the resigned yet resentful expression of humans about to begin another day of hateful slavery. Talk about the "dignity of labour" to working men and watch their incredulous sneers. Dignity be hanged! they used to say to me at the dinner-hour, it's the grinding misery of long hours—ten hours in those times—the poor pay and the risks of the job, and after my short experience I heartily agree with their views, and I'm neither a socialist nor an anarchist, much less a sentimental agitator, parlour rebel, nor amateur busybody fomenting trouble among the proletariat—to whom the world will presently belong, the bourgeois having had his fling since Napoleon I. But I have lived with these men, seen their futile attempts to make both ends meet, to avoid the temptations of drink, good-fellowship, and the natural desire for a little relaxation after so many hours of blinding toil. To-day steel-workers occasionally end as multi-millionaires. Wages are higher. The workman is better housed, and hygienic conditions improved. Nevertheless, labour is not always ennobling.

Since my experience at the Baldwin shops, I have seen
the coal-miners of Belgium in the "black lands," and
look back at Baldwin's as an earthly paradise in comparison. Whenever anyone tells me that we should all
remain in the position God placed us, I wonder what
this particular moralist would say if he found himself
in the cold dawn of a drizzling autumn morning ham-
mering screws amidst a hell of fire, fury, and noise; or
in a boiler-shop chipping with a chisel? It's no fun,
hard work, and as I was born constitutionally lazy, I
loathe it. To be driven like stupid sheep or angry goats,
into an enclosure, and there work or starve—ha! just
try it once yourself Mr. Universal Panacea! I know
that the labour party makes mistakes, that it is as
tyrannical in its essence as trust combinations, mo-
nopolies, and other oppressive institutions; yet I can't
help sympathising with the workman, and that much
I learned from hard experience, something my kind father
never allowed me to see at home. No wonder. Later
I read Proudhon, Marx, Lassalle, Stirner, and Mackay
to find the same arguments.

But I had only set foot on the first rung of the ladder of torture. Pete Farnum showed where I could
stow my kit, a locker with a key which he bade me use
if I expected to keep intact my copious luncheon of cold
meat and buttered bread. Workmen are as honest as
any other class, but borrowed food doesn't come under
any rubric of the decalogue. I put on my new and coarse
overalls, too large by half for me. I stood waiting for
further orders, a picture of scared sickly youth. How
I wished myself out of it all! Then there surged into
my view another face. It belonged to Woody Mendenhall, the superintendent, a small, wiry, terribly active

man, with blond hair and an imperious way with him
that sent my heart into my boots. The boss! But he
proved a pleasant boss, only he was in such a hurry,
and his oaths were so crisply blurted out that I feared
him. He told Mr. Farnum to send me out into the yard
to get the pedestals that support the piston-box of the
locomotive. Each shop in this enormous hive has its
particular part of the machine to produce and perfect.
In our shop it was the cylinders. My initial task was to
knock off with a hammer and a chisel the roughness of
the casting on the pedestals; rust and bubbles were thus
removed. But first I had to get my pedestals. They
lay in the yard, and after a snow it wasn't pleasant to
dig them up. Then lugging the ugly casting into the
shop I would put it in a vise at my work-bench and proceed to maul my thumb with a twelve-pound steel hammer. How heavy it was! I discovered that technique
is demanded in such a prosaic occupation as hitting a
chisel squarely on the head. A light, elastic wrist, economy of movement, a shrewd eye, and—bang! Again
on the first knuckle of my right-hand thumb. However, practice improved my stroke, its speed and precision, and after a week I began to touch the chisel. But
my colleagues, otherwise the gang, wouldn't let me alone.
I was called "the dude" because there was a rumour
that Mr. Parry, a boss among bosses, had me under his
wing; then, too, Pete Farnum was nice to me; worst of
all, my white hands and slender fingers damned me in
the eyes of my new acquaintances. I think I might
have been forgiven my "pull," but that my hands were
against me; "skinny fingers," as one fellow derisively
said, fingers that never did, never would, do a day's
hard work. He wasn't a bad prophet, this same Harry,

whose family name I shall never know. The work was hard, the workmen not sympathetic. But at the end of the first week came pay-day, that magical word which sesame-like opens all doors. I had rather swaggered at home, patronising my younger brother, and forcing the proletarian note, especially rejoicing in my grimy personal condition. I believed it the real thing to appear as dirty as I could. I even went so far as to smear myself with soot and grease. It seemed quite in the key of the toiler with his hands. But that pay envelope! That settled my social status. It was my first attack on capitalistic reserves. I was earning my living by the sweat of my brow, and the sum was precisely five dollars and twenty-five cents—piece-work. I wasn't apprenticed as I had expected. The system of apprenticeship was no longer in vogue at Baldwin's. My wages looked large in my eyes, for they were all mine. However, I didn't buy a private yacht at once, though I cast eyes on a small sailboat for sale, second-hand.

As soon as I manifested a friendly disposition my mates returned it with interest. They were decent chaps, few dissipated, and admirers of men like William Parry, Peter Farnum, and Woody Mendenhall, who had once worked with their hands. When they learned that my father, too, had used his hands to earn his daily bread, their respect for me was not decreased. I told them that my grandfather worked with his hands, but pressing down organ keys didn't impress them as genuine labour. It was playing. Their fetish was the human hand, the true tool of humanity. And they were right. Carlyle couldn't have put the case more clearly than Andy, a Scotchman with whom I chummed: "Ye see, lad, it's this way. If ye don't use your hands to earn your bread, you're a softy. No good. You're living off the working man. You're an aristocrat. That's my belief." Otherwise Andy was not very radical. He read Hugh Miller's Old Red Sandstone after luncheon and hummed hymn-tunes. From him I learned to respect the hand as the mightiest lever of civilisation. My own hands were the dirtiest in the shop, and I gloried in them. Besides Andy, who was tall, thin, dark, there was another chum, Tommy, and as we became inseparable, we were usually saluted in mock Scotch dialect: "Wha's cooming the noo? Tommy, Jemmy, Andy!!" Tommy was a reddish blond Englishman with a broad Northumberland brogue. I knew it was Northumberland accent because he told me so. He was a steady worker, his leisure hours he spent with his books. On clear Sundays he took fatiguingly long walks with Andy. I accompanied them only once; that sufficed. He held that the American workman would be fresher if he walked more; he hated saloons and was a teetotaller, but not rabid when it came to another man's drinking. Live and let live was his motto, though I did hear him giving Andy a blowing up on Blue Mondays. Andy liked his little drink, and on Sundays it was always a large one. But he never missed a day at his job.

My dinner-pail was an object of much curiosity. When my mates saw it the first day they gasped. Our cook, who spoiled me from my birth, would fill it with several pounds of cold meat and other items in proportion. There was enough to satisfy the stomachs of two hungry men. I look back with envy on my assumed capacity, for I never finished the portions. My friends helped me, and would then stare at me as if I were prize-cattle. The appellation of "hollow-legs" pursued me from my father's dining-table to my humble work-bench. I was positively embarrassed by the rough, good-humoured remarks passed on my appetite. I appreciated David Copperfield's feelings after his encounter with the ferocious waiter at the inn, and the land-lady's obvious worriment when she whispered to the coachmen: "Take care of that boy, George, he is wisibly swelling" (I quote from memory). As cold food didn't agree with me, I ate a hot dinner in company with Tommy and Andy, at a boarding-house somewhere on Hamilton Street. The change, and the fresh air were tonics. I consumed more than ever. In the meantime my pay-envelope did not grow. I have since consoled myself with the knowledge that I earned more as a mechanic than I did at any time later when engaged in the practice of the law or conveyancing.

But my hour was at hand. I was about to come to grips with a superior force. Our shop was full of whirling monsters that from time to time would seize a man and tear him to pieces. There was an organised hospital service in the establishment, not to speak of accident-insurance for the employes. I had been warned from the beginning to avoid the drills, lathes, and other scoopers of lives. My jumper was too full in the sleeves. Tommy begged me to have them altered. I promised this. The holidays were at hand. Night work gave me a chance to earn some extra money. I was running a drill-press by this time; that is, I bored screw holes in an iron beam for the pedestals aforesaid. It was a job that needed no particular skill or judgment. The spot for the hole was indicated by a chalk mark. I enjoyed the play of the machine and was fairly industrious until

one unlucky December night I turned to answer a neighbour when—bang! I felt my sleeve caught in the
rapidly revolving drill and the room, machines, and men
turned around me as in a dream. I cried out, but couldn't
hear my voice, and then my head was knocked against
the iron table. I heard music singing in my ears and
went to sleep without pain. It was a pleasant death.
When I came to myself the voice of the sardonic Harry
fell on my ears, and it smarted more than the balsam
apple which they poured over my skinned arms and
chest. "He swung around the circle like General Grant."
It must have been the time of General Grant's world-
tour as the expression "swinging around the circle"
was in everyone's mouth. But it did seem cruelly in-
appropriate. Andy had proved my saviour; with the
quickly operating wits of a practical workman he didn't
seek to drag me from the dangerous drill, but simply
pushed the belting off the lower wheel, the machine came
to a standstill, and I fell to the floor. All the same it
was a narrow squeak.

There was a compensation; Emerson insists that
always there is one. In this instance it proved to be
the official ambulance, with a driver, a surgeon, red lights,
and a gong. My mother's feelings may be imagined
when this terrifying apparatus halted at our house, and
good-hearted Peter Farnum went in to break the news.
I can see my mother, white-faced but cool, helping me
up-stairs. I wasn't much damaged. Skinned alive was
the sensation, yet no bones were broken, and my case
was considered a mere accident compared with the
swift, horrid entanglements of unhappy men in a belt,
there to be dragged to the ceiling and mangled. However, I had become a hero without heroism. I hadn't

cried, though there were tears of agony in my eyes when
that infernal juice of the balsam apple was sprinkled
over my raw flesh. Even the nervous shock failed to
register. I was of tougher material than anyone suspected, for I had always played on the belief of my mother
that I was delicate because of premature birth. My
nurse had predicted that seventh-month children never
came to maturity. Therefore, my speedy return to
normal health surprised. My mother kept the handful of rags that had been torn and twisted by the drill.
I signified my intention of returning to the shop. I
suspect it was more from a spirit of bragging than
any love of the job. Of machinery I had my bellyful.
But I wanted to go back and back to Baldwin's I went.
There were Tommy and Andy to see, and there was
Boss Farnum to thank for his kindness. I was called
General Grant by Harry, who didn't like me, and received with mild wonder by my two chums who said
they had given me up; they praised my pluck, but advised me to get a lighter job. "You will never make a
workman, Jemmy," added Tommy. Thenceforth I transferred my friendship to an engineer in the big boiler-room
on the Eighteenth Street side. With him I shared my
copious dinners, and was rewarded by a chain of scalp-
freezing stories. He told me that one day when he had
run out for a wet of ale he had forgotten the water-cock
and the boilers ran low. On his return he was aghast.
"The boilers were foaming, my boy. Foaming. All
was lost. I expected a blow-up every second. I had
turned on the water, but it was too late." Breathlessly
I exclaimed: "Did she blow up?" (Every machinist
knows a boiler is female?) "No, she didn't, but it was
a close call," he grumblingly acquiesced. "I ran out

and shouted to the shop that she was foaming." That "foaming" caught my fancy as much as Mrs. Joe Gargery and her rampages.

Despite my good intentions with which to pave Hades, nature intervened. A bone-breaking cold kept me in bed for a week, and the New Year found me tired of the glittering mirage of locomotive engineer. This time my father had something to say. He had observed my reading and scribbling, also my too glib tongue and a marked capacity for idling, and, naturally enough, he jumped to the conclusion that I would make a lawyer. I have read elsewhere that early in life I had my conscience extracted by a psychical surgeon; perhaps my father thought of this, too; anyhow, I said farewell to Baldwin's, which had done me some good; early hours, hard work, and the association with what Walt Whitman calls: "Powerful uneducated persons." I found in them, as I still find, more strength of character, less insipidity, and sincerer traits among workmen than I do in other strata of social life. And also a solid education, the education of life, not books. Having little time, a serious workman only reads the best. Without effusion my old comrades wished me well. Harry I didn't see, but Tommy and Andy I hated to leave. I promised to visit them every Sunday, and never did. I was become an idler with clean hands, a dude, living on other men's labour. I knew that Tommy and Andy had disowned me, so I promptly forgot them.

XII

LAW MY NEW MISTRESS

My superficial education soon betrayed itself. No arithmetic, little writing, less grammar, and a plentiful lack of history, would these deficiencies bar me from the study of the law? My Latin and French, said my father, "might be of use." My mother was sceptical. So was I. However, on a cold, cloudy Monday, January 13, 1873, I was again a sullen lamb led to the slaughter. Dr. Ellwood Wilson, who had brought most of the family into the world, had a son, a promising young lawyer, Ellwood Wilson, Jr. His offices and residence were at No. 1112 Walnut Street. The house, a double one, is intact to-day. Across the street was the home of old Dr. Gross, and many a time I saw young Haller Gross come down the steps in gorgeous raiment, for he was as great a dandy then as Fred Fotterall, Dick Townsend, Ned Rogers, Louis Beylard, John King, or any of the Philadelphia Club and City Troop men. Mr. Wilson consented to take me as a law student, although I said nothing that would indicate even a fairly reasonable desire to study. I simply did as I was told. My adventure as an engineer in quest of a locomotive had left me rather shame-faced. The daily life of a law student was apparently a lazy one. There was no salary attached, hence I didn't kill myself. Mr. Wilson was amiability personified. We began with Blackstone, Justice Sharswood's Commentaries. Dry reading? I didn't find the work dry, as its English was an antidote for the inevi-

table barrenness of the theme. The intricacies of common law were disclosed and explained. What racy old
English wrote the worthy Blackstone. In my father's
engraving cabinet there was an engraved portrait of the
great man, robes and all. Yet, I invariably deserted
him for Wharton and Stille's Medical Jurisprudence.
There was metal more attractive. The horrors of crim-
inology had never been set down so attractively since
I had devoured Eugene Sue's Mysteries of Paris. Naturally, I didn't make perceptible progress in the law. I
absorbed the curriculum as a sponge absorbs liquid.
My preceptor examined me at intervals, and it was then
I first noted what I call my mechanical memory. I
memorised as would a parrot. I repeated pages without
knowing their meaning. The big technical phrases I
gobetted as a dog does a bone. Terminology of any sort
always appealed to me. I became proficient in phrases.
With medical, or scientific terminology, it is the same,
whether anatomy, geology, astronomy, or cookery, the
technical verbalisms were easy to remember. My judgment centres were not much exercised, so that when I
underwent regulation examinations at the Law School,
or during the law course at the University I had no
trouble in reeling off page after page, because I simply
let my memory prompt and turn over in my mind each
page as it was finished. But put me to writing out opinions on a possible case, and my vaunted memory col-
lapsed. Not taking the slightest interest necessarily I
had nothing to say. Later in life I met pianists who
could play hundreds of pieces. I have questioned them
and in nine instances out of ten I found the same mechanical memory as mine. They saw the note-groups
and the pages, but the musical idea, or its emotional ex-

pression, did not much concern them. Ideas were then not my shibboleth. I soon hated the law as only representing conventional usage, and musty precedent filled me with disgust. I had no need of reading the dictionary, the writer's keyboard, for the reason urged by Théophile Gautier, to increase one's vocabulary; I rather studied it for Walter Pater's reason: to know what words to avoid. So is it in music. The supreme virtuoso conquers because he understands and feels. His memory is filled by the larger designs, the greater emotional curves of a composition, and not merely by a succession of notes. But this obvious truth I was to discover years afterwards.

I loafed and invited my soul to reading and staring from the large window on the north side of the house. I became acquainted with the green bags of legal luminaries. I knew them all by name and fame. I saw Richard McMurtrie go quietly by in earnest converse, or Daniel Dougherty, a household name and friend of my parents—with his characteristic stride and flowing locks. Richard Dale, then a student at the Law School, would wave his hand and swing on as if the universe depended on his getting to Washington Square before 10 o'clock. Lewis C. Cassidy or George Tucker Bispham would pass, or old Judge Sharswood would move along, preoccupied with his eternal legal problems. (Is there anything under the stars more sterile than the law? Rabelais doesn't exaggerate.) But my chief delight was to watch G. Heide Norris march by in all the splendour of very, very baggy trousers, and very, very high collars, accompanied by a friendly male echo likewise attired. From Mr. Norris I imbibed a passion for expensive collars. As with Victor Maurel, the collar became a cult.

At 11 o'clock, rain or shine, the British consul, Mr. Kortright, would heave into view; portly, choleric, pink-skinned, eyes of porcelain-china blue, and dressed as if for Pall Mall, this pleasant old gentleman was tremendously admired by me. If I saw Dickens' types everywhere, in Mr. Kortright I found the ideal Thackeray clubman. It was what Henry James calls "the emotion of recognition," and the exercise of this emotion became an overmastering one. It was that memory of mine beginning to seek analogies. I hadn't then read Hegel, but, when I did, his identification of opposites was an easy metaphysical morsel to swallow. I was always matching patterns—men, women, ideas, sounds, sights, and smells.

Mr. Wilson possessed an excellent library, and while I neglected Somebody or other on Contracts, Kent's Commentaries, or Coke on Littleton, I read De Foe, Smollett, Richardson, Fielding. Ah! what bliss. Clarissa Harlowe I mixed up with Tom Jones, and mistook Mrs. Booth for Roxana. Launcelot Greaves and the Knight of the Burning Pestle were the same, and I enjoyed Moll Singleton more than I did Robinson Crusoe. I had outlived my dime-novel and Jack Harkaway days, though I confess when the author of that famous series for boys, Bracebridge Hemynge, visited America, I went to see him with more pleasure than I experienced when I squeezed the chilly hand of Matthew Arnold in Association Hall some years later. My reading was not confined to English. French had been a master passion; all things French, painting, sculpture, and literature. Horizons widened. The world was not contained in Philadelphia. With the Centennial Exposition I suffered my first severe attack of cosmopolitanism. That tropical summer of 1876, shall I ever forget it? The heat was so sustained and exhausting that I did not visit the exhibition grounds till the autumn. The city was gay. Jacques Offenbach conducted at his garden, Broad and Cherry Streets; Theodore Thomas gave open-air concerts in the old Forrest mansion. The streets were tinted by a hundred exotic costumes, and Finelli fried his oysters in oil. Our town was put on the map of Cosmopolis overnight. General Grant had started the machinery on the opening day—he was feeble on that occasion, and had to be supported—and half the world closed it. I heard Richard Wagner's five thousand dollar Centennial March played by the Thomas Orchestra, and wondered how so much money could have been wasted on such commonplace music. But the Baireuth Music Festival was in progress and I eagerly read the account in the *Times*. Wagner was still a dark horse, his theories those of a madman, his music unmelodious. Think of it! And "Tristran and Isolde" one prolonged melody from the prelude to the death-song.

My interest in the law languished. I was otherwise occupied. The 4th of July, 1876, was not only the most memorable day in the century, but also the hottest. In a temperature of 105 degrees in my bedroom under the roof I wrote a short story, The Comet, and I don't doubt that the temperature stimulated me to lurid description. It was my first fiction. A comet visits our planetary system, and with dire results. Poe wrote in a more exalted vein his Colloquy of Monos and Una, and Jules Verne was at his best in his Off on a Comet. I had the temerity to sell my story for five dollars, and it duly appeared, ten years later, in a West Philadelphia journal, *The Telephone*. I have it in my desk with other disjecta membra. When The Star, by Herbert Wells, appeared I realised how clumsy was my pitiable invention. The English author puts Poe and Verne in the shade with The Star, the supreme cosmical tale. But anyone who could write fiction on a day when the hinges of the nethermost abode were singed had the call of the inkpot. I hadn't. I disliked writing principally because of the pothooks and hangers involved. Invention least of all troubled me. My handwriting had become "standardised." I indited leases, wills, and engrossed mortgages and real-estate deeds. Mr. Wilson was a notary public and conveyancer, and the old-fashioned methods of searching for clear titles in the Recorder of Deeds office prevailed. I had lots of fun in the Recorder's office, over which presided a jolly stout gentleman named F. Theodore Walton. His son, lovingly known as "Pud Walton," belonged to our gang of youngsters, lawyers "en herbe" and statesmen in embryo. Many mornings I spent over big leather-bound tomes bearing the cryptic letters F. T. W. (F. Theodore Walton's initials). Now, a title insurance gives you a title while you wait. This shoe-black part of the profession —as we called it—no longer exists.

I grew accustomed to the smell of parchment and carried a green baize bag (full of sandwiches and fruit). It looked so professional. Occasionally, not often, I was admitted within the charmed circle of a court-room and watched the legal wheels go round. Years before I saw Twitchell, the murderer, at the bar, and also Probst —a farm-hand, who had slaughtered an entire family of nine or ten. The Police Gazette was proscribed reading, but we contrived to see it. I remember "Bill" Mann, the public prosecutor, also General Charles H.

T. Collis. I became familiar with the procedure of gen-ral practice. I asked Judges for a delay, and my voice buzzed and thundered in my ears. My prime achievement was the day of the great Jay Cooke failure, when apparently the heavens of finance were tumbling into the Delaware River. Ellwood Wilson, Jr., contrary to the advice of his associates, precipitated that historical bankruptcy by setting off a tiny squib. A town and building association, of which he was part parent, had deposited its entire funds with Jay Cooke and Company. This was during the year 1873, if I am not mistaken. Armed with a subpœna I boldly entered the office of Pitt Cooke, a brother of Jay, and presented him with a summons to show why the five hundred dollars of the Freehold Mutual Company—or some such title—should not be returned to that important corporation. I was told that this subpœna set off the mine that blew up the banking house of Jay Cooke and Company. How true this is I can't say. I only know that I was scared blue and shivered in my skin even when the dignified banker thanked me as he accepted service. But I felt myself the guilty one, not he.

Mr. Wilson's associate was Henry Galbraith Ward, a handsome young lawyer from New York, where he is to-day on the bench of the Supreme Court—Appellate Division. Judge Ward took me in hand at once. Daily he put me through my paces, and my sleight-of-hand memory didn't deceive him. He would say: "Define!" and I was forced to define or be sent back to the neglected page. I realise now he was studying me. He was the willing recipient of my half-baked enthusiasms, and one day he advised me to become a musician. But

steady piano practice was abhorrent to me. Yes, dazzle
an audience, but to prepare for that pleasing event—
ah—the shoe pinched too hard. And then a new crisis
had declared itself—fine clothes. What Carlyle called
the "dandiacal" spirit inflamed my very bones. Those
pernicious collars of Heide Norris had undermined my
Spartan soul. I became a dandy. No pattern in colour
or design could be exaggerated enough. Finally one
morning when I appeared in a snuff-coloured suit, baggy
as to trousers, and preposterously cut away in the coat,
Mr. Ward spoke to me paternally—I don't think he was
more than twenty-two years old. He argued the case
of taste *vs.* tastelessness. Clothes, like manners, should
be unobtrusive. It was Walter Pater's "tact of omis-
sion" in the concrete (a phrase, by the way, that Oscar
Wilde calmly appropriated). I listened and my mood
was chastened. I have often thought of Judge Henry
Galbraith Ward when I revelled in a purple prose-panel.
My temperament has always inclined to the excessive,
the full-blown, the flamboyant. That clothes crisis is
common to hobbydehoys. I was infatuated with Ouida,
the heavy swells in *Punch.* Anthony Trollope filled me
with pangs of envy. His longest novel, The Way We
Live Now, and the young aristocrats of the Bear Garden
Club, Dolly Longstaffe, and the others, seemed ideal.
Those fleshpots of Egypt were not subtle, yet they flooded
my little firmament. With a chum, Charles Sloan, I
contemplated setting up a trap, a dog-cart, and even the
price, six hundred dollars, for a second-hand affair,
didn't daunt us. Chestnut Street was transformed to
Piccadilly, the Park to Rotten Row. I was badly bitten.
I only read English fiction, preferably Guy Livingstone.
I recovered from this attack of snobbish measles by the

aid of music—that universal solvent, as Henry James calls it. But London was my dream-city then. Paris came later. Dickens had fed my fancy until I saw a Dickens character behind every tree. My favourite promenade was along the Delaware River water-front, as far north as Port Richmond. How I revelled in the ships, the smell of tar and cordage, not to speak of the brackish water! It was all in the tonality of London, and, need I add, that when I first visited that mighty city in 1878 I was disillusioned? Continued residence brought back the enchantment. I still see London through the spectacles of Dickens, Thackeray, and Trollope. In the nineties George Moore gave us a new pair of spectacles, though much of the old charm had gone. Boston and Philadelphia are the two American cities that remind me of London; certain localities, be it understood. New York is so original that it is monstrous. A new cosmopolis, one that Stendhal, greatest of cosmopolitans and promenaders of souls, would have reviled.

About this period I laid the keel for a course of study upon which, if the ship had been built, I could have straightway sailed to the Blessed Isles of Knowledge. The faded red copy-book I still treasure wherein I wrote —yes, with legible hand—a scheme of reading that would have staggered Lord Acton, and a more omnivorous reader than he I do not know. All English, American, Italian, Spanish, French, German, and classical literatures were included in this vast undertaking. The mere transcription of the authors' names covered many pages, and, remember, I only selected the best. In English I was satisfied to begin with Chaucer, ending with Ruskin and Pater. Poets, dramatists, essayists, novelists were there, and subdivisions devoted to writers on special subjects: art, music, science. It was a five-hundred-feet book-shelf, this of mine, and at least five hundred and more authors figured on it; a Rabelaisian feast, a gluttonous and greedy absorption of all the world has thought and written. When I read of Lord Acton's proposed History of Ideas the plan seemed perfectly feasible to me. My ignorance was on a par with my ambitions, which were immeasurable. It is a glorious, if foolish, time when a young man feels that the earth and the adjacent planets are his oyster; that he must make love to every pretty girl; that he will be rich, famous, happy, immortal— phew! what moral headaches after this autointoxicated nightmare. What cruel awakenings at cold, drab dawn. Ah! Steeplejack, descend rung by rung your shaky ladder and bury in the darkest recesses of your heart the clouded visions seen from the spire of your church of dreams.

The epical list would edify even such a supercritic as Paul Elmer More. It properly began with Æschylus— or, was it Œsop? I followed the alphabetical order— and ended with Xenophon. I purged all the lists as time rolled on, reading all the while, as if some devil would catch the hindmost; technical books multiplied apace. Music and art predominated. It was my fate to enter many gardens of art and only by traversing the avenues of critical literature. The great epics were my constant companions—thanks to the judgment of my mother. She knew and loved the best, and if her passion for the life of the spiritual drove her to the reading of mediocre religious literature, her taste was never for a mo-ment led astray. This trait she had in common with Huysmans—she esteemed the piety of an author while detesting his style. Mrs. Craven bored and so did Eugénie de Guérin. Thus it was that I read and liked St. Teresa, St. John of the Cross, and St. Catharine of Emmerich. It wasn't a wide step from Dante's Inferno to John of the Cross's Dark Night of the Soul. I remember a friend of my mother's, an invalid, Mrs. Joliffe, long since in some paradise, I hope, so fervently did she long for it; she was a Second Adventist, and once when the "Second Coming" seemed nigh she put on her best night-gown, and in company with a band of pious geese she went on the housetop to be nearer the sky. She caught a bad cold, but her belief remained unshaken. She had a chart of tremendous significance over which I was allowed to pore. It showed the swarming hosts of Antichrist, which were to swoop down from the impenetrable wilds of Russia, devils with high cheek-bones, à la Tartare, though hardly a pleasing sauce. Most of us believe to-day that Antichrist didn't come from unhappy Russia, but then the Russian was an unknown factor, his country still a mystery. What fun that map of Armageddon was. My mother cautioned me against its apocalyptic denunciations, yet she admitted that some day the world would be bathed in blood, but the cross of Christ would conquer.

The curious part of my study-book is that I lived long enough to read and reread every book in the list. The original project was a five-year course—an impossible project; fifty years it has taken me. Once in a while I refresh my memory by reading my half-crazy programme. When music had gripped my vitals I did the same thing. I calmly played every piano study that I could lay my hands on, and lived to write a long chapter about my experiences. Now, I realise that while life is too vast to be compressed into any single formula, whether religious, philosophical, or artistic, universal wisdom has been distilled into certain books. All Christianity is in The Imitation of Christ, and the quintessence of secular wisdom may be found in Montaigne. No better gymnastic for the spirit is there than Plato, and woe to him that reads not the Bible—not alone for the style or the "quotations," but for the sake of his miserable soul. The classics, Greek and Latin, are what Bach and Beethoven are to musicians. Throw metaphysics to the dogs— unless you like a tortoise pace in a labyrinth and leading nowhere. Lock the door of your ivory tower and drop the key into the moat. But I am boasting. All those books did not make me wise. The lucid folly of love is more illuminating. George Moore once told me—it was at Baireuth—that after such writing as Flaubert's the young pretender to pen-victories had better sit on a fence and enjoy the fresh air and sunshine. I believed that the better part of wisdom was to stand on the sidewalk of life and regard the changing spectacle, the passing show, in a word, the disinterested attitude of an artist, enamoured of appearances, and the bravery of surfaces. It is the Hedonistic pose. But the street overflowed my tiny pavement, and I was swept into the moving currents, and that is a salutary happening for all save the elect, who may compass the life contemplative without becoming spiritually sterile. Bacon wrote that "In this world, God only and the angels may be spectators."

In the meantime my law studies were on the shelf. In despair I had been transferred by my parents to the law and conveyancing offices of the Hon. Daniel M. Fox, a distant cousin of my father. These offices were

at No. 508 Walnut Street, facing Independence Square.
I chummed with a young lawyer, Harry Hazlehurst,
and began to keep professional hours. Mr. Fox saw to
it that I was given much conveyancing work which I
had to copy in a clerkly hand, and his son, H. K. Fox,
helped in my studies. I frequented the Law School and
listened to young Dick Dale—who was to become a
brilliant advocate—plead a fictitious case before Judge
Sharswood, the great man himself, who was kind enough
to further the cause of our education. He was a modest,
reticent man, whose judgments were well-nigh infallible.
The younger men worshipped, yet stood in awe of him.
His influence was profound. I almost took an interest
in the abstract questions which he posed.

A friendship with a young man about this time made
the law more human for me. His name was Wickersham; Samuel George Woodward Wickersham. He
lived across the street from our house—we had moved
down-town to Race Street before the Centennial—with
his grandfather, George Woodward, a retired publisher.
From the windows of that house came the sound of
music-making. It was a cultivated family. Aubertine
Woodward played the piano like an artiste; George
Woodward, her brother, spouted Swinburne, the Poems
and Ballads, and from his lips the insidious music of
"Dolores" first fell upon my enraptured ears. Young
Wickersham had a hard row to hoe. His grandfather
was wealthy, but he believed that a young man should
be self-supporting. So his grandson, after graduating
from Lehigh University, proposed to study law. "Well
and good," said this shrewd old ancestor, "but how do
you propose to live in the meanwhile?" George—or
Sam, as we called him—knew that he had a roof over his

head, but as he was of a singularly independent disposition, he settled the question by mastering telegraphy, reading law during his leisure hours. I can see him in his little telegraph office at the general post-office, Chestnut Street, tapping the key, studying Spanish, German, and French. Carefully apportioning his time, he contrived to work twenty-five hours a day; at least, that is what we told him. His punctuality became notorious. As the evening Angelus rang at the Cathedral on Logan Square my father would take out his watch and say: "Sammy is due," and sure enough he would turn the corner of Race and Seventeenth Streets before the bells ceased. As he didn't smoke or drink he had leisure when needed. He was my first example in the concrete of that awful word, efficiency. I didn't pattern after him, but I admired the manner in which he organised his life. If ever a man went straight to his goal it was young Wickersham. He had Herbert Spencer at his tongue-tip when other boys were reading Beadle's dime-novels. One day I went to see him for a chat during the luncheon hour, and I found him elated over the arrest and conviction of a swindler named Seaver. He had handled the case alone, tracing the operations of the fellow through the telegrams, and landed his man to the great relief of the postal authorities, who had despaired of the task. The subsequent career of Wickersham is history, political and otherwise. He passed his last examinations, went to New York, engaged in practice, a corporation lawyer, now of the first rank, and onetime United States Attorney General during the Taft administration. We wrangled like all young men, and I often heard him declare that for him the law would only be a stepping-stone to political power. He was not of a religious turn, but he espoused the cause of the Quaker, telling me that it was the one truly spiritual religion, without dogmas, superstitions, or sacerdotal flummeries, and invariably, I would reply: "A religion without dogma is a body without a skeleton, it won't stand upright." Now, the position is reversed. Mr. Wickersham is a good churchman, an Episcopalian, and I admire the Quakers. He reproached me for my faineant attitude towards life. Be up and doing! was his policy, and I would smile indulgently at his robust will and tremendous capacity for taking pains; above all, his intellect, which could assimilate the toughest problems, pulverise cobblestones, and macerate the arguments of his legal opponents; all those qualifications for a successful career seemed to me so much waste of time and energy. I must have been an annoying person to sensible men. I have wondered how all the kind people, who advised me then and since, had so much patience; their advice I could not, or would not, act upon. The other side of George Woodward Wickersham is rather astonishing. He has a well-developed æsthetic culture. He learned to love Black and White from studying my father's collection, and to-day he buys mezzotints and engravings. By his music he came naturally. I don't think he plays on any instrument, but he knows the tone-language after a long apprenticeship at his home. He looks the same to me as he did four decades ago, barring a greyer head. He is the picture of a grave Spaniard, an illusion that is not dispelled when he speaks the language, though he has the vivacity of an Italian. A traveller, linguist, man of the world, rich, famous, and erudite, I think Philadelphia has reason to be proud of her son, even if he was born in Pittsburgh.

Again I changed my law preceptor. New Year, 1878,
I went to the office of Attorney William Ernst, No. 727
Walnut Street. The building has not changed a bit.
Across the street were the offices of Benjamin Harris
Brewster and John G. Johnson. Again I became a
window-watcher of other people's doings, instead of
poking my nose into my own business, which was supposed to be the law. It was my last chance. Pernicious
were my activities otherwise. Another crisis had supervened, music, and I never got over the attack, never
shall until I die. A book had decided my vocation, St.
Martin's Summer, by Annie Hampton Brewster, sister
or half-sister of Attorney General Brewster. I had the
courage to speak to him about this book, and he was
pleased, I could see that. "Burnt-face Brewster," as he
was so charitably nicknamed, was a charming man with
a high, fluting voice, polished manners, and a flow of
profanity that stirred my young manhood to its centre.
I heard him curse an absent member of his family in the
form of a syllogism that made my spine freeze. He admired his brilliant, cultured sister as a matter of course;
all the Brewsters were brilliant and cultured. Doubtless
his deformity, a face from which fire had burnt nearly
all semblance of humanity, made his blasphemy more
impressive. He reminded me of a ghastly illustration
in Tom Moore's Lalla Rookh, a fanciful portrait of the
false prophet (Query: What is the difference between a
false or true prophet? Aren't they both fakirs?)
Like Wilkes, said to have been the ugliest man in England, Benjamin Harris Brewster used to boast that after
five minutes had elapsed he could make any woman forget his hideous mask. True, but they must have been
shuddering minutes. I was attracted by his ugliness.

As a pleader before a jury he was very convincing, though I doubt if he had the acumen of his next-door neighbour, John G. Johnson, or the persuasiveness of Daniel Dougherty.

Mr. Johnson was a heavy-appearing man, with seal-like mustaches, sullen expression, and slow but penetrating glance, who had a way of winning cases that made him the envy of his colleagues. He was not admired by his staff. I disliked his personality. Years later, I told him how he rather scared us, with his grimness, and he smiled. In reality he was very human. After I saw his pictures I forgot the bogie of Walnut Street. Boys are a queer lot. There was Mr. Brewster, a demon of irritability, but a born wheedler when he willed, and Mr. Johnson, never choleric, impassive, if anything, yet we young chaps gave our admiration to the uglier man. Mr. Wayne MacVeagh had an office in the same building as Mr. Brewster. I knew by sight all the heavy swells of the profession. I wonder whether they were as great men as people believed? Public men, like actors, live in an artificial illumination. I recall what Richard Wagner said of Bismarck and Van Buest; the latter had pursued the composer for his political opinions with unabated rancour; for Wagner was a political refugee since 1849. Political great men, so-called statesmen, are not great, they usually have mediocre intelligences, but are crafty, and flatter the people who are always greedy for praise, like collar-wearing dogs, averred the musician. They do more harm than good; in a few years they are forgotten, while a master-painter, poet, musician, lives on forever. The coin outlasts Cæsar, as Théophile Gautier properly observed. Not a novel assertion, this of the greatest composer of music-drama, but it contains more than a moiety of the truth. The great men of my day I've forgotten, Lincoln, excepted. But the busy little lawyers, the grave and learned judges, the pestiferous politicians with their incessant clamourings, their raising of false, stupid, dangerous issues—where are they all? Not a book, not a picture, not a melody did they bequeath to us, and so they are irretrievably dead. (This is extremely hard on those humbugs, the reformers.)

My restlessness increased, spiritually, physically. One might fancy that after all these seismic manifestations that at least a mouse would crawl out from my mountain in parturition. Nary a mouse. Only dissatisfaction with the universe, and not a finger lifted to set it right. I was the square peg in the round hole, that's all. According to ridiculous custom of the country I had been taken to a phrenologist, Professor Fowler, to have my bumps felt, my genius proclaimed, my share on the globe staked out. Phrenology, thanks to the labours of Spurzheim and Gall, was once believed in; its true relation to our knowledge of the brain being what astrology is to astronomy. But the superstition prevailed. Solemnly my expectant mother was assured that I had a capacity for anything if I could be persuaded to apply myself seriously—which I never could; furthermore, I had the centrifugal temperamant, not the centripetal. President Wilson has the centripetal temperament, or as he puts it, a "one-track mind." So has my friend, Mr. Wickersham. Both men concentrate. Colonel Roosevelt had the centrifugal cast of mind; evidently I have the same. I fly off with ease on any tempting tangent, also off my handle. The aptitude displayed by the Yankee for a half-dozen pursuits is the sign-manual of the centrifugal soul. It is pleasant to hear the whirring of its wheels though they serve no particular purpose. Thrashing the sea, eating the air promise-crammed, filling the belly with the east wind, fighting windmills—these are a few attributes of the centrifugalist. He is nothing if not versatile. His intensity lasts ten minutes. He is focal in consciousness, as the psychologists say, but his marginal subconsciousness is strongly obtruded. The sensory periphery is more masterful than the hub of his being. When Professor Fowler was told that my birthday occurred on the last day of January, he exclaimed: "The Water-Carrier," and seemed relieved. Sons of Aquarius, fickle, thirsty—not water —for knowledge, are the rolling stones that gather no moss. Now, that had always appealed to me—the non-gathering of moss. Precisely for that reason the rolling stone is more successful than its stationary brother who accumulates the moss of decadence. The centrifugalist is usually an optimist. All is for the best in this best of demi-mondes. The flowers of evil that blossom in the hothouse of hell become pretty pansies when plucked by a centrifugal poet. There are a lot more things I could tell you in defense of this nature, but these arguments made no impression on my parents, who were beginning to suspect that I was a shirker. I was, though my waking hours were stuffed with febrile gestures. If I had been a poet I might have replied to my critics that I was beating my luminous wings in the void, but, being neither Shelley nor Arnold, I shrugged my shoulders and watched the sky, hoping roast larks would fall into my expectant mouth.

Daniel Dougherty was consulted. "Mary," he said to my mother, and I, sulking in the background, "the

law is a jealous mistress, and if the boy doesn't like it
set him to something he does like." I mentally applauded this decision, though I wondered at the banality
of the quotation. I was at the hypercritical age, believing that no phrase should be repeated, an insane notion
that often afflicts "stylists." Mr. Dougherty was then
in the flower of his reputation, though he hadn't yet
made his famous speech nominating Grover Cleveland.
His trump card was oratory. He held most juries in
the hollow of his hand. His devotion to the Irish cause,
to my grandfather, James Gibbons, who had encouraged
his youthful ambitions, was unquestionable, although he
was worldly enough, as are all lawyers, to foresee that
the Fenian cause was a forlorn hope. As he possessed
tact he knew how to carry water on both shoulders, but
as a churchman his sincerity could not be challenged.
His relations with my parents were cordial, and despite
the changing years he was always "Dan" to them.
From what I have been told his legal erudition was
hardly profound; rhetoric, flowery and forcible, was his
forte. However, they never called him "Judge Necessity," as they did Judge Allison, or was it old Judge
Finletter? because "Necessity knows no law"—a venerable epigram that was moss-grown when I first heard it.
Daniel Dougherty, like so many men of Irish blood, had
the head and features of a Roman Senator. You looked
for the toga. Handsome, eloquent, scornful, his resonant voice still rolls and rings in the chambers of my
memory. His wife, his sons, his daughters are, like
himself, gone. The boys were school friends. Charlie
Dougherty was a long time at the Roman Embassy, and
in Paris beloved of newspaper men. For years he was a
correspondent from Paris.

My father's card parties were well attended. Mark

Wilcox, Michael Dohan, John and William Lucas, General Ruff, General Walker, Ferdinand Fetherston, editor of *The Evening Bulletin*, and other well-known men would play whist, old-fashioned whist, till the lights burned blue. Occasionally my father played a rubber at the Philadelphia Club, with General Meade, General Ruff, and General Walker—the latter a Rebel officer, and one-time adversary of Meade. I can see the old gentleman in high spirits preparing for these reunions, his wide-spreading collar, setting off a singularly attractive head. Rafael Joseffy after seeing him whispered to me: "He looks like a Magyar Magnate." I never saw one, but he did. Editor L. Clark Davis was a visitor. My mother admired his wife, Rebecca Harding Davis, a novelist, and mother of Richard Harding and Charles Belmont Davis. The Davis boys were friends of John Ruff, the son of the general. Many times we played together in the yard of the Ruff mansion on Filbert above Sixteenth Street. There would be John Ruff, Dick and Charlie Davis, my brother Paul, and, at intervals, Sam Wickersham. The Davis boys were then freckle-faced. Later Dick became a newspaper reporter, and, need I add, a figure in the field of fiction. I wonder if Charlie Davis ever recalls the Ruff yard and the fierce games in which pirates were heroes! Sam Wickersham didn't believe in pirates; he only believed in lawyers. But the clearest call of my life was sounding. Music began to fill my ears with its sweet importunings and I hopelessly succumbed. At last, that abominable inhibitory sign, "No Thoroughfare" vanished from my foreground and the pathway was shining. If I had known what I now know —but don't let us waste time in regrets. Music, the Conqueror, beckoned to me and up the stairway of art I

have pursued the apparition ever since—up, a steep
stairway, like one in a Piranesi etching, the last stair
always falling into space as you mount, I have toiled,
the dream waving me on. I shall never overtake this
dream, but with Sadak seeking the waters of oblivion,
in John Martin's design, I must mount till poor old
Steeplejack falls earthward (much to the relief of my
neighbours who have heard me trying to play the A minor
section of Chopin's Second Ballade for the last forty
years).

XIII

MUSICAL PHILADELPHIA

Philadelphia is a music-loving city. Its history proves the assertion. Opera in Italian has always had a vogue, and, like opera elsewhere, it is first fashionable, then artistic. Real music—that means orchestral—has a following there which is gratifying, though a local symphony orchestra they have not had so many years. Visiting orchestras with solo singers, pianists, violinists, and other instrumentalists, supplied our early deficiency. Honour is due to such pioneers as Michael H. Cross and Charles H. Jarvis—whose portraits in bronze adorn the lobby of the Academy. The Cross and Jarvis symphony concerts in Musical Fund Hall were in existence before the advent of Theodore Thomas and his orchestra. They were not financially successful, but much good came from them. Young folk enjoyed the classical repertory: Haydn, Mozart, Beethoven, Schubert, Schumann, Weber, and were well grounded when Thomas introduced modern music. And this was as it should be. At Michael Cross's string quartet parties on Saturday nights I heard the entire quartet literature. I was only a youngster, but I could hum the themes from any of the numerous Haydn quartets, and at one time, urged thereto by Louis Gaertner, I began to fiddle, hoping to master the viola parts. The original Cross quartet consisted of Carl Gaertner, Sr.—alternating with William Stoll—Simon Stern, second, Roggenberger, viola, Michael Cross, violoncello. At the age of forty, Mr. Cross took up the 'cello and played it in quartet. His teacher was Leopold Engelke, our vocal director at the Roth Academy. When Engelke or Charles Schmitz, a professional, took the 'cello part, then Cross played the viola. Sam Murray often played second, or else Billy Ware, an incredibly fat man who sported a linen duster Summer and Winter, indoors and out. A lovable personality his. Those were jolly nights of music-making. I usually stayed all night in Summer; the Cross home was empty.

Mr. Cross undertook my musical education. He was rather cynical on the subject, advising me to stick to the law, for, said he, the musician's life is a dog's life. He was truly a cynical man in all his views. His versatility was marked. I best liked his piano playing, though his technique was limited, but he had a singing touch, his taste was sound, his style clear and musical. He played Mozart in a limpid manner, and the Field Nocturne was his battle-horse. His organ-playing leaned heavily on improvisation. He was not a virtuoso on any instrument. He taught all; a chorus conductor of the Orpheus and the St. Cecilia, and organist at the Cathedral for many years. An all-round musician of the old school, disdaining specialists and virtuosi. Chopin composed music in a cellar he said and he preferred Kalkbrenner. But once in my presence, he called Sterndale Bennet "small potatoes," and I began to hope for his conversion to modern music. The truth is that in Philadelphia then Mendelssohn was first and the others somewhere out in the field.

His rival—for there was concealed rivalry between the two men—was Charles H. Jarvis, a piano virtuoso of the first rank—that is, in a school of playing long since obsolete. He had been technically grounded in Hummel,

and his delicate touch, pearly scales, and finished style
were unimpeachable. His musicianship was not so
broad in scope as Cross's but it was more thorough. He
was master of the keyboard, nothing else; he didn't
compose, conduct, or play on a stringed instrument;
as an organist he was merely a salary earner, but his
knowledge of the piano repertory from Alkan to Zaremb-
ski, if we put the matter alphabetically, or, say, from the
early Italians to Chopin, Schumann, Liszt, was astonishing. As a prima-vista reader he could have challenged
Saint-Saëns, though not of orchestral scores. He never
played without notes, telling me that some day von
Bülow or Rubinstein would break down in public. He
had not a musical memory, that was the reason. De
Pachmann never played concerto with orchestra without notes; he once had a bad smash-up in public. Jarvis
was not so musical as Cross. He was an intellectual
artist, not an emotional one. Tonal monotony was
felt by his audience before the end of his lengthy
programmes. The illuminating phrase never came, but
there was infallible technique and a flowing style. One
Summer he gave twenty private recitals at his residence
on North Nineteenth Street, devoted to the historical
development of piano music, and not only solo but
chamber-music, duos, trios, quartets, quintets, sextets,
septets, and octets—Onslow, Hummel, Fesca, Schumann,
Schubert, Beethoven, Mozart, Haydn. Carl Gaertner
fiddled first, as usual, and made up for uncouth method
and scratching by his enthusiasm and genuine musical
understanding. It was positively fascinating for me to
see Charlie Jarvis in his shirt sleeves, like his confrères,
ploughing through a mass of antiquated compositions—
fancy Onslow or Kalkbrenner, or the Ries piano concerto
in C sharp minor!—and with a vim that was stimulating.

At the Cross parties I heard the old string-quartet literature, the piano was seldom used; at the Jarvis recitals
all piano concertos—with string quartet accompanying—
from the Bach D minor to Henselt's in F minor, were
given in a finished manner, though profound interpretations were absent. Von Bülow was the piano god of
Jarvis, for Cross it was only Rubinstein. And Cross was
right. Years later, and shortly before his sudden and
lamentable death, Charles Jarvis visited me at the
office of the *Musical Courier*, then on Union Square.
His opinions of music and musicians had little changed.
He had spent several years abroad. He complained that
modern piano virtuosi banged too much, and he didn't
hesitate to condemn the so-called "orchestral" style.
Liszt and Rubinstein were to blame; the latter had a
marvellous touch, but he couldn't hold a candle to Thalberg in the art of singing on the keyboard. I heard the
same judgment from the lips of Georges Mathias of the
Paris Conservatoire, a pupil of Chopin, who declared
that Rubinstein butchered the exquisite music of Chopin.
Back to Hummel! cried Jarvis. With all my heart, I
said, but to play in the colourless, withal chaste manner
of Hummel, and to pass over as non-existent the modern
palette of tone-colour, with its varied range, its nuances,
its atmospheric pedalling—no, that would be impossible. You may set the clock back an hour but you can't
fool the sun. As a matter of history we have heard three
pianists who combined the purity of the Hummel school
with the iridescent colour-scheme of the moderns—need I
mention the names of Vladimir de Pachmann, Rafael
Joseffy, and Leopold Godowsky?

The violinist, Carl Gaertner (there was no "von" as a
handle to his name then) was an eccentric man, of vio-

lent temper, his heart, however, in the right place, but he was as vain as a peacock. He was a perfect example of the popular conception of a musician. He acted in a crazy fashion whenever he had an audience of even two; but he wasn't crazy, far from it. My mother, who heartily disliked his rude pranks, admitted his brains, Jewish brains she called them. Gaertner came to America about the same time as Carl Sentz, and was a drummer in the band. He studied the violin after settling here, and never mastered it. He often played out of tune, and his style lacked tonal suavity and facile technique. His vanity as a musician was only topped by his masculine conceit. A preposterous dandy, he thought he was irresistible with the unfair sex. When he strutted down Chestnut Street, he was, literally, the observed of all observers. No wonder. A waist pinched in—he undoubtedly wore a corset—his shoulders padded, a low-cut collar revealing too much neck, long floating hair, elaborately curled, surmounted by a graceless chimney-pot, invariably a crimson necktie, yellow kid gloves, trousers painfully tight, lacquered boots with straps—he was simply wonderful. Through narrowed eyes he disdainfully regarded the passing crowd. His contempt for Americans was true to type. Because Philadelphians refused to admire his scraping of the classics, though good-humouredly, mocked his affectations, therefore, we were pigs, blind to finer issues. So he fought on, and in the end did accomplish something. His zeal for good music found expression in his concerts given as a rule in the Foyer of the Academy of Music. I don't believe they were lucrative, any more than the Jarvis Soirées at Natatorium Hall, across the street. But they served their purpose. There, a small nucleus of

VLADIMIR DE PACHMANN
(1890)

RAFAEL JOSEFFY
(1886)

music-lovers were introduced to the best in musical literature. To be sure, the terrible old man fiddled like a demon, but a virile demon—oh! how he hated Sarasate and the whole tribe of "sugar-water violinists"—and stamped his foot so loudly that one night Rudolph Hennig, a true artist on the violoncello, warned him if he didn't stop, he would quit the quartet. It is a fact that in the Gaertner music studio there were three busts: Mozart, Beethoven—and Carl Gaertner's. How painful were our lessons. In company with Franz Schubert, already an excellent violinist, I stood a weekly browbeating that would have discouraged a Joachim. "Hein! you think you play the viola some day. Hein! A toy fiddle is what you ought to get, hein!" all this in a raging voice and with an accent that would have made him a hero at Weber and Fields'. He bullied poor Schubert who finally rebelled, though in a mildly sarcastic way. He told the old man: "When you learn to play in tune then I may learn something from you." We fled at once after this, pursued by stormy vows of vengeance. My father was informed that I played like five pigs, that I had better study that tin pan, the piano. The two sons of Gaertner were musical; Carl, Jr., on the 'cello, Louis, the violin, a pupil of Joachim and a far better artist than his father.

When Wilhelmj came to Philadelphia in 1880 he had as accompanists Max Vogrich, Hungarian pianist and composer, and Constantine Sternberg, a Russian piano virtuoso—and I think a composer of piano music worthy enough to be ranked in the same class with Scharwenka and Moszkowski. Perhaps he remembers the scene in the green room of the Academy, when Carl Gaertner pompously entered, gave his card to the giant August

Wilhelmj, and politely remarked: "If I played the Mendelssohn concerto as you did to-night, I would be hissed off the stage, as you should have been." All this in German. Wilhelmj, who had played like a god, remained impassive, called to his secretary: "Hans, show this gentleman the door." After that Wilhelmj could not play at all, according to his irate critic. But Gaertner met his match in Eduard Remenyi, who was the Liszt of the fiddle, technically. This little bald Hungarian Jew, who looked like a fat unfrocked priest, came to see us, on Sunday nights. A linguist, a travelled man of culture, he was always interesting. He was playing at the time at Männerchor Garden, at Franklin Street and Fairmount Avenue, kept by Robert Tagg, and I think down on his luck. Carl Sentz led these open-air concerts. Remenyi abused Brahms, in a public address, for stealing a Hungarian dance of his. We heard lots about Liszt and Wagner from him. It was true that he played in concert with both Liszt and Brahms. His real name, he told us, was Hoffman; Remenyi is Hoffman translated into Hungarian. "I am a born Roman Catholic, an Abbé," he avowed to my mother, and then winked at my father, adding in an undertone: "a Kosher Abbé." He looked it. He always fetched with him to any musical reunions two violins, a Stradivarius and a Guarnerius. He called one of them the Princess, which one, I forget. His tone was full, his style supple. With what head-wagging he would play his fiery version of the Rackoczy March or with what a sliding technique he would fiddle the D flat Valse of Chopin, a difficult feat, not alone because of the treacherous double-thirds, sixths, octaves, and tenths, but because of the dizzy speed and the ungrateful key of D flat. He was a master of masters, Remenyi; and his charlatanism was only a copy of Paganini's and Liszt's.

A member of an old Hungarian noble house, the De Vay—a distinguished prelate of the same family visited America later—turned up in the city, playing the violin in superlative fashion, and gambling away every dollar he earned in concert-giving. This Leonard de Vay had studied with Remenyi; and when he encountered his master he was embarrassed. He, too, had his violin, and with him was an extraordinary clarinet virtuoso, the E flat clarinet, a Hungarian named Matrai Pista (that is Peter Matus or Matrai). When my father saw De Vay face Remenyi, not shaking his hand, he whispered to me: "Look out, the fur will fly!" Luckily it didn't. Remenyi bowed and said a few welcoming words in Hungarian, but De Vay did not take his fiddle from its case. Matus opened the evening with a cascade of notes, a richly embroidered Hungarian Czardas, unaccompanied, which he naïvely confessed he had "made up" after hearing some gypsies play on their native Putzta. Remenyi was interested. He complimented the clarinetist—who was later with the Gilmore band —and as he had coached me in the piano parts of Wieniawski's "Legende," and Prume's "Melancholia," I was forced to accompany this very great artist. Remenyi played with passion and poesy. The climax of the evening was his tender interpretation of Schubert's "Serenade" which he delivered on his knees before my mother, who took his homage in good temper. My father was greatly annoyed, why, I can't understand, for Remenyi was all smiles, his tongue in his cheek. "Parcel of fools," was the governor's verdict when the party left. That night must have been one of wild revelry according to

the report of Matus. They went to some café and at
seven in the morning were quarrelling over a question
of technique. But in the evening Remenyi played in
his accustomed form at the Garden, while De Vay
eloquently held forth at a garden on Girard Avenue below Seventh Street.

As I said, old man Gaertner came off second best in
the tilt he had with Remenyi. (Remenyi was a bit of a
charlatan, but Gaertner was the bigger of the pair.)
One night, after the Hungarian virtuoso had finished a
Bach Sonata, unaccompanied—oh, yes! we listened to
Bach at open-air concerts in those benighted days—
when a hissing was heard. Remenyi bowed. "Will the
critic who hissed my Bach please make himself known?"
he said in his ironic manner. Immediately the only
Carl Gaertner arose, anxious to vindicate the musical
taste of the town: "You play Bach like a fool!" he
roared. Remenyi smiled. Then in a burst of generosity he tendered his violin to Gaertner, adding: "Perhaps I do, but will my critic show me how not to play
Bach like a fool?" He underlined "not," and the other
shrugged his shoulders and stalked out of the garden
followed by howls and jeers. Remenyi won that time.
The occurrence got into the newspapers, but Carl Gaertner never turned a hair. The only man who did succeed
in taking the starch out of his ludicrous dignity was a
young barytone, Max Heinrich by name, afterwards to
become a significant figure in the musical world. One
night, a wet night, after much music-making at the
Cross house, the party went in search of more refreshment, solid and liquid. An old hostelry stood at the
corner of Race and Sixteenth Streets and was kept by a

publican named Dunn. The place was noted for its fish-
cakes and musty ale. There, a certain convocation took
place, and during its progress, Gaertner said something
in praise of Germany. At once, Max Heinrich went up
into the air. He had escaped military duty in Saxony
and had become an ardent lover of our democracy. He
cursed the old Kaiser, he cursed Bismarck, and he made
so much noise that the lobby was broken up by Pop
Dunn, who didn't like rows on his premises early Sunday morning. Squabbling, the violinist and singer went
to the sidewalk to settle their differences. Although the
elder, Carl Gaertner was a powerful, deep-chested man
with muscles like steel, he would have made mince-meat
of the slender Heinrich if he could have reached him.
But Max knew better. Taking a glittering weapon from
his back pocket he pointed it at Gaertner crying: "Go
down on your knees and say 'To H-ll with Bismarck!'
or I'll shoot you through the gizzard." Scared, the old
man did as he was told and renounced Bismarck and all
his works. Then Heinrich shrieked with laughter. It
was only a metal shoe-buttoner, that pistol. In the
fracas some one lost his false teeth and there was much
rummaging and lighting of matches before they were
restored to the owner. But after that affair, Gaertner
hid his patriotism under a bushel.

In 1916, when Heinrich died, he was as implacable a
foe to his Fatherland, politically considered, as in the
middle seventies. He was as well-known in London as
in San Francisco as a singer of Schubert, Schumann, and
Brahms. With few exceptions I never met a man so
completely an artist as he. His voice was not remarkable;
a barytone with a low range; a "basso cantante," he
called himself. His tone was often hard, hollow, "gum-

my," is the exact word, and his enunciation guttural. He never mastered English, his pronunciation after many years' residence here and in England, leaving much to be desired, yet his musical intelligence, the emotional temperament, carried his hearers away, literally "on the wings of song." In his best estate his work in "Elijah" or any of the classical oratorios was unapproachable, and he had plenty of rivals in that field with more sonorous voices, Franz Remmertz, among the rest. But Heinrich outshone them all musically; the intensity of his dramatic nature transfigured his rather commonplace vocal resources. His versatility was best expressed in song interpretations. Such an emotional range and feeling for swiftly changing moods I have never heard with the exception of Marcella Sembrich and Lilli Lehmann. And remember that he had no personal glamour, in the sense of good looks, as had these women singers; his bold hawk-like profile, and too narrow face, were not particularly attractive, had he not such brilliant eyes which mirrored his evanescent moods. He was magnetic, light-hearted, generous, and I fear that he hung his fiddle outside the door, as they say in Ireland. Yet he was not only the "joy of the street and the sorrow of the household" but also a joy at home. A more loving and quick-tempered father I never saw. Happily married to a musical wife, Anna Schubert Heinrich, he lived every minute he could spare from his professional duties—and a game of pinochle—within his own four walls. In 1876 his little house with a garden in front was on Cherry below Twentieth Street. It is there to-day, Max, who was the father of at least eight or ten children, led the life of an artistic sybarite. His versatility was not confined to his music—he played his own accompaniments in an incomparable style—but manifested itself in painting. He was mad over landscape and animals. In the house, besides babies which sprawled everywhere, you would encounter a wind-hound, a flute on four legs, puppies of various breeds and a formidable Russian mastiff, broad of chest, with a baying voice that sent policemen scurrying round the block. A cruel beast. I often saw it jump from a second-story window to the lawn and nab a cat by the neck. Crunch! The cat's spine was broken. Max named the brute Bismarck. I asked him why, for I knew he hated the Iron Chancellor. "Because he kills so many cats," was the cryptic reply, followed by peals of sarcastic laughter. There was a Mephisto concealed in Heinrich.

And the birds. They were uncaged and owned the house. A spectacle for the gods was Max Heinrich, as stark as the day he was born, pipe in mouth, palette in one hand, brush in the other sitting in his half-filled bathtub painting an imaginary landscape, the easel stretched across the tub. "It's cool!" he would say, on one of those sweltering August mornings when other people's vitality would be depleted by such sultry conditions; he, on the contrary, was more noisy, more vigorous than ever. The joy of life! That he had as few have it. He tingled with vitality. He imparted his high spirits to his companions. The babies sat up and gurgled when he passed, the birds flew to his shoulder, the dogs barked. A happy household. His nervous wife would sometimes go outdoors to escape this truculent happiness. She was blonde, charming, possessing a divine patience, not only as a mother but as an artiste.

She sang musically. At Concordia Hall I saw her as Marguerite to her husband's Mephisto. She looked the part without make-up. It was as a guitar virtuosa, however, that she made her reputation. She mastered that difficult and "ungrateful" instrument, making it something more than mere string strumming. I have heard her play the A flat study of Chopin, the "Aeolian Harp" most effectively. The little menage didn't always run on oiled wheels, for Heinrich was a bohemian to whom regular hours were destructive of his own personal rhythms—which were many. He earned plenty of money and spent it, though his family came first. He sang at the Cathedral, where my mother had introduced him to Father Elcock, and on Saturdays he sang at the Hebrew Synagogue on Broad Street. He had all the brilliancy and versatility of the Jewish temperament; also a choleric nature. His theory was that if you couldn't do a thing at first throw out of the box—it was his own dicing simile—then you would never do it; which is pure nonsense. When he allowed me to play an accompaniment to his singing, if the slightest slip or stumble occurred on my part, he would slap my neck, not softly, and curse me for a sloven. He got over this irritable precipitancy with the passage of the years, and his art gained thereby in repose and mellowness. During the last decade of his life his singing was a thing of beauty because of its profound interpretative power and penetrating intensity. A dynamic man. He was the first artist I saw who borrowed from a music-critic; the other way round is the popular belief. Max asked H. E. Krehbiel, critic of the New York *Tribune*, for a five-dollar bill. He got it. His Cherry Street landlord was Joshua Gregg, the wool-man. Heinrich owed a month's rent. Gregg came to collect it. Max sang "The Heart bowed down by weight of woe," and the rent was remitted by Gregg, with tears in his eyes.

Oddly enough, he was only a Mendelssohn singer when I first knew him; and the old barytone repertory: Lortzing, Mozart, Marschner, and Abt, yes "Swallows Homeward Fly" Abt. We fought about the merits of Schubert and Schumann till he took them up, and it wasn't long before he was in love with the entire song literatures. At a time when Brahms and Robert Franz were rather patronised by critics, he sang both with sympathy. I always liked him better than I did George Henschel—who also played the piano—or the operatic Franz Wüllner. Heinrich, on a bet, studied and played Chopin's E flat Polonaise, at that time so exquisitely delivered by the crystalline fingers of Rafael Joseffy; and he also took up the violin for a year and played the second violin in Haydn's D minor string quartet. This, too, on a wager. Naturally, I was lost in the penumbra of this irresistible artist. Older by ten years, nevertheless he made a companion of me, calling me a "paleface" and reproaching me for not being man enough to take a drink once in a while (every ten minutes). But I was then austere. I had mapped out a plan of study from which plan I never swerved—at least for an hour or two. I was a bit of a prig. I didn't dissolve in the warm bath of these ill-assorted personalities. I preferred the companionship of Franz Schubert—a living human, not the composer—who was the brother of Mrs. Heinrich. The musical furore sounded in my skull. I had heard Rubinstein—and couldn't appreciate him (1873), but his Calmuck features, Beethoven-like head, and extravagant gestures fascinated me. His playing was velvet-thunder; that's the fantastic way I described it to myself. Twenty years later, when I heard this giant at his seven historical piano recitals in Europe, I took his true measure—a heaven-storming one. Von Bülow at the Academy and Annette Essipova at Association Hall, both during the season of 1875–1876, filled me with joy. The magic brew began its work. Never had the law seemed a drearier mistress. I thought of nothing but piano technique; my experiments in prestidigitation were transposed from cards and coins and the blossoming of conjurer's flowers, to the keyboard, to Mozart, Haydn, yes, even to Carl Czerny, the indefatigable chemist who distilled studies to grease weak fingers. Max Heinrich encouraged me. My father did not. As an experienced amateur he foresaw loose company, irregular hours, and the drudgery of teaching. He foresaw clearly. My mother, who had given up all hope for my priestly vocation, thought I might become an organist and play the Cathloic service "Ad majorem Dei gloriam." I had studied piano with little result when a child, and with an old German named Carl Rudolph, a hornist who had a marked sense of rhythm, a clear touch but no technique to speak of on the pianoforte. He could play dance music well, the old-fashioned kind; Strauss, the elder, Lanner, Diabelli, but Chopin was a sealed book to him. Once when I presumptuously played "at" the "Military Polonaise" the grey-haired teacher shook his head, saying: "I don't call that music." Later I went to another pedagogue, but he stiffened my wrists and fingers, and I quit him; besides, magic held my interest then. But in 1875 it was different. I heard the call and obeyed it, and have regretted doing so ever since—that is, when I look at my bank-book.

With Franz Schubert I traversed the entire land of literature for violin and piano; but my ambition excelled my technical ability. I was a "fingersmith," to be sure, but I needed a solid grounding in the essentials of the art, also fundamental brainwork, as Dante Gabriel Rossetti used to say. In my predicament I went to Michael Cross and frankly asked him to help me, telling him that later I would pay him for his instruction. My mother joined the conspiracy, my father being kept in ignorance and soon I was launched in midstream as a student of the piano. My music copy-book tells me the date, number of lessons, also the list of pieces undertaken. September 25, 1875, I began; I ended May, 1878. My first Sonata was the Mozart in D, the last Beethoven's opus 31, No. 3. To take lessons I had to be at the Cross piano at six A. M. He was an early riser. I sneaked out of the house, my music hidden in my coat, for fear of meeting my father—usually gone on his business before that hour. He was no doubt surprised at my activity but never suspected the cause. At nine A. M. I was at my desk in the office of Daniel M. Fox ready for the transcription of some dull will or deed of real estate. My leisure hours were devoted to music-study. I got along fairly well, though I had to unlearn lots when I went to other masters. Michael Cross was not modern in his treatment of the piano; furthermore, he gave his pupils more Mozart than Bach; he believed more in the lyric than the polyphonic. He played Bach, though I never heard his Bach on the organ; Mozart was his passion, and an admirable passion it is; but his pupils suffered for want of variety, just as the Roth scholars suffered from too much Latin. Jarvis should have been my teacher. He began with Hummel and

Bach. He believed in a sound technical apparatus, then
the music (if you had any in you) would take care of
itself. Cross practised the reverse. Music first, technique afterwards—all very well for a finished artist but
hampering to a student. Once, when I had played Mendelssohn's "Rondo Capriccioso" too glibly, he put me on
a simpler diet and banished finger-studies. Since then I
have gone to the opposite extreme and swallowed too
many technical studies with consequent digital indigestion. When you study piano, study with a pianist.
Michael was not a specialist. I remember Theodore
Thomas telling me years later that he found the choral
bodies trained by Cross remiss as to attack, intonation,
and rhythmic sense; all of which may have been an ill-
tempered slur of the great conductor.

Time fugued by. I became a slacker as far as the law
was concerned. I was always at the heels of Max Heinrich, or playing the bass in piano duos, Mrs. Heinrich
taking the treble. Musically, I owe much to that amiable and estimable woman. And I closely hugged the
neighbourhood where I might hear Mr. Jarvis play, or
the Cross string quartet. There were summer nights
when I leaned out of my window longing for music. I
could hear the soft strains from the back garden—we
were removed from the Cross music room by two houses
—and I dreamed and yearned, as only a lad love-sick
with art can yearn. Life stretched like a lyric ray of
moonlight paving the silvery waters of the future.
Nothing seemed impossible. All was permitted. I felt
an invincible force within my veins—the swelling sap!
Ah! Youth is immortal. But youth can't always foot
the bills. My father had to. The secret came out, and

he promptly paid my three years' tuition without grumbling. Michael was a life-long friend, a lover of engravings, too, and on his walls hung several masterpieces, gifts from my father. A cultivated man, Mr. Cross, the owner of a well-assorted library, in which I browsed for years, and a man who attracted friends; indeed, he was the object of friendships rather than friendly himself. He was self-contained, frigid at times, but could unbutton in the seclusion of his music-study. A high liver, he held the championship for disposing of edibles and liquids. The late Dennis McGowan, then at Sansom and Fifteenth Streets, told me that when Michael Cross was in his prime he would open a hundred and odd oysters for him at a sitting, and saw them washed down with tankards and tankards of "musty." But it should not be forgotten that he was a huge man physically, not so monstrous in size as Billy Ware, but of a Brobdingnagian presence and capacity. I envied him then; I envy him now. Apart from his annual attack of gout no one ever saw him the worse for all this. With a punctuality that was chronic he occupied his organ bench in the choir of the Cathedral and often played so expressively after High Mass that my mother would say to me: "Michael played as if inspired to-day," and when I repeated this he would reply, his eye twinkling: "Yes, at Van Hook's last night." He didn't mean to be cynical nor was he a materialist; but he knew the law of metabolism. He knew that rich food and fermented drink was a nourishment that might be transmuted into beautiful sounds by accomplished musicians. Plain living and high thinking is well enough for saints or philosophers but not for sinners or singers.

The Van Hook he referred to had a restaurant at the

northeast corner of Twentieth and Tower Streets. It
had a wide vogue. The proprietor was a handsome
blond man, hospitable as the night was long, and a
famous contriver of mixed drinks. But the glory of the
place was the cooking of Mrs. "Billy" Van Hook, then
a fair-haired, blue-eyed young matron with a fried-
oyster technique only second to Finelli's down Chestnut
Street. There were some connoisseurs who preferred
the Van Hook interpretation. Her chicken and lobster
salads, her deviled crabs were masterpieces in miniature.
It was not alone the artistic and musical crowd that
patronised the Van Hooks; club men from Walnut
Street found their way to the little restaurant, those
dashing young bucks, Jack McFadden and Al Hetherington, among the rest. But the Cross, Jarvis, Gaertner, Billy Ware—a marvellous virtuoso with the oyster-
fork—Max Heinrich party went to Van Hook's as to a
church. Max called it "St. Billy's" and Billy would re-
tort: "Not for too many bills"; he was easy in money
matters and when in hard luck he helped a fellow through.
He never had the reputation for terrapin enjoyed by
McGowan or Augustine, but Michael Cross always
swore that his most malignant gout was developed by
Mrs. Van Hook's terrapin. You must not suppose that
Schubert and I were intimately admitted in the sacred
circle; we were happy witnesses, contemporaries. I, as
a pupil of Cross, Franz as a brother-in-law of Heinrich.
But it was no Barmecide's feast for us. We swallowed
real food and drink while our seniors swallowed theirs,
and we saw some strange doings. Proving that time occasionally halts, I may add that the same Mrs. Van
Hook—more power to her elbow—still lives, cooks, and
has her being, in a restaurant, bearing her name, behind

the Custom House, where the oysters are fried under her surveillance and where (tell it not in Gath or Gotham) they taste as they did forty years ago. After that, don't speak to me about time, its whirligigs and caprices.

Strange to say, despite his marked dramatic aptitude and personality, Max Heinrich was not a success as an operatic singer. He was a member of the Metropolitan Opera Company, New York, for several seasons. I think 1887–1888, perhaps earlier, but with the exception of a fairly good characterisation of the Night Watchman in The Mastersingers, and other minor rôles, he did not shine in comparison with such acting-singers as Emil Fischer, Robinson, von Milde, or the mighty Albert Niemann. His art was essentially intimate, and destined for the smaller spaces of the concert stage, and not for the broader key of fresco-painting, which is the operatic. But give him a grand piano, a sympathetic audience, and he could make you forget all the gauds and chicaneries of opera, and the inartistic bellowing of opera-singers. He was a rare artist, Heinrich, and it is a peculiar satisfaction to his friends that his mantle has fallen on the shoulders of his daughter, Julia Heinrich, soprano, born in Philadelphia, educated by her father, an opera-singer in New York, as well as on the continent, but a concert-singer born. She is vocally better equipped than was her father, she has his musical memory and the special art of accompaniment. In the latter art, he drilled me for years, and even to-day when I support a singer at the piano I have a freezing sensation on the nape of my neck. It is the functioning of my memory-cells through association of ideas. My neck remembers the slaps administered by Max, as he sang, making an occasional parenthesis such as: "Chim, verdammte Esel! why don't you keep time?" And the "damnable ass" would bow his head to the anticipated blow. It never failed to register.

I have taken some pains to describe the man and my admiration for him. Yet, such is the irony of the years, the last time I saw him, several months before his death, and in company with Julia Heinrich, we disputed like a pair of old fools over trifling data. He had the rather unusual weakness of pretending to be older than he was, and he persisted in treating me as a child no older than I was in 1876; childish, withal, we called each other familiar, though not complimentary names. I was again "Chim" the "Esel," and secretly I was scared. There was fire in the eye of the old war-horse. The extinct volcano spouted again. I was glad to see such vitality. He said he was seventy-two years of age; he was only sixty-six. I told him so. He called me a liar. The joke was that his New York friends and admirers gave him an elaborate dinner on his seventieth birthday. I asked him why. He couldn't help smiling. His daughter smiled. We all smiled. And that's the last I saw of Max Heinrich in the flesh. He was one of the formative influences in my irregular life. Wild as he was, he steadied me, not because I took him as an example to be avoided —as my mother said I should; and as I did in the case of George Woodward Wickersham, whose concentration had something inhuman about it ("If Sam would only take a drink or smoke a pipe," his uncle would despairingly exclaim); but because Heinrich embodied all I admired as an interpretative artist. I dissociated the man from the singer. He dragged me with him everywhere; to the choir of the Cathedral, to the Broad Street "Shool," where I first heard the magnificent Hebrew

VICTOR MAUREL

MAX HEINRICH

cantillations, which, coming from an antique civilisation, Egypt, filtered through the ages to the ritual of Mother Church; an echo may be found in our Plain-Chant.

XIV

MY FRIENDS THE JEWS

"How shall we sing the Lord's song in a strange land?" I couldn't help recalling these words of the Psalmist, these and the opening, "By the rivers of Babylon," in which is compressed the immemorial melancholy of an enslaved race, when I heard Sophie Braslau intone with her luscious contralto a touching Hebrew lament, "Eili Eili lomo asovtoni?" at a concert. Naturally I believed the melody to be the echo of some tribal chant sung in the days of the Babylonian captivity, and perhaps before that in the time of the prehistoric Sumerians and the epic of Gilgamesh. Others have made the same error. Judge of my surprise when in a copy of *The American Jewish News* I read that the composer of "Eili Eili" is living, that his name is Jacob Kopel Sandler, that he wrote the music for a historical drama, "Die B'ne Moishe" ("The Sons of Moses"), which deals with the Chinese Jews. Mr. Sandler had composed the song for Sophie Carp, a Yiddish actress and singer. The "Sons of Moses" was a failure, and a new piece, "Broche, the Jewish King of Poland," was prepared. (Not alluding to Pan Dmowski.) It was produced at the Windsor Theatre in the Bowery. The song, not the play, was a success. Then the music drifted into queer company, for music is a living organism and wanders when it is not controlled. Finally Sophie Braslau got hold of it, and the composer, who was directing a choir in a Bronx synagogue, was astounded to hear of the acclamations of a Metropolitan Opera House Sunday night audience. His daughter had listened to "Eili Eili" and brought home the good news. After troublesome preliminaries "Meyer Beer," the pen-name of the musical editor of *The American Jewish News*, was able to prove beyond peradventure of a doubt the artistic parentage of the song, and Jacob Sandler is in a fair way of being idolised in his community, as he should be.

"Eili Eili Iomo asovtoni?" may be found in Psalm 22, the first line of the second verse in Hebrew. In the English version the words of David are in the first verse: "My God, my God, why has thou forsaken me?" And in St. Mark's gospel we read: "And at the ninth hour Jesus cried with a loud voice, saying 'Eloi, Eloi, Iama sabachthani?' which is, being interpreted: 'My God, my God, why hast thou forsaken me?'" (chapter 15, verse 34.) The exegetists and apologists, as well as sciolists, have made of this immortal phrase a bone of theological contention. Schmiedel, who with Harnack believes the words to have been uttered by our Saviour, nevertheless points out various details which prefigure the same things in the crucifixion—the just man hanging on the stake, the perforated hands and feet, the mocking crowd, the soldiers gambling for the clothes, everything takes place as described in the Psalm. Lublinski (in Dogma, p. 93) and Arthur Drews (in The Historicity of Jesus, p. 150) demur at the orthodox Christian conclusions of Harnack and Schmiedel. A beloved master, the late Solomon Schechter, disposed of the question in his usual open style. "The world is big enough," he has said to me, for both Jehovah and Jesus, "for two such

grand faiths as the Hebrew and the Christian." But he
saw Christianity only in its historical sequence, and not
as a continuator of Judaism; rather, a branching away
from the main trunk. If it had not been for Constantine, the world might be worshipping Mithra to-day, was
the erudite and worthy man's belief. Enveloped in the
mists of the first two centuries Christianity seems to have
had a narrow escape from the doctrines of Mithraism.
That Salomon Reinach practically admits in his Orpheus, a most significant study of comparative relig-
ions from the pen of this French savant.

Once upon a time I played the organ in a "shool," a
reformed, not an orthodox, synagogue; played indifferently well. But my acquaintance with the Jewish liturgy
dates back to my boyhood in Philadelphia, where I
studied Hebrew, in company with Latin. The reason?
My mother fondly hoped that I might become a priest
—the very thought of which makes me shudder now.
The religious in me found vent in music and my love of
change was gratified by playing the Hebrew service on
Shabbas (Saturday) and the Roman Catholic on our
Sabbath. Probably that is why I was affected by Sophie
Braslau's singing of "Eili Eili."

I have always entertained a peculiar admiration for
the Jews and Judaism. It began with the study of
Semitic literature of the Talmud, above all of Hebrew
poetry, the most sublime in any language, as Matthew
Arnold asserts in his comparative estimate of Greek and
Hebraic cultures. My dearest friends have been, still
are, of that race. Prejudice, social or political, against
the Jew I not only detest, but I have never been able to
comprehend. My early playmates were Jewish boys
and girls. I have stood under the "Choopah" (mar-

riage canopy) and have seen many a Bar-Mitzvah; even
sat "Shivah" for the dead father of intimate friends.
From Rafael Joseffy to Georg Brandes; from the brilliant Hungarian virtuoso that was Joseffy—whose father,
a learned rabbi, I visited at Budapest—in Pest-Ofen—in
1903, when he was eighty-four, an Orientalist, a linguist
with twenty-six languages, ancient and modern, at the tip
of his tongue—to Professor Brandes, the Danish scholar,
an intellectual giant, and a critic in the direct line of
Sainte-Beuve and Taine—both men I knew and loved.
Whether the Jew has attained the summits as a creator
in the Seven Arts I cannot speak authoritatively, although
the Old Testament furnishes abundant evidences that he
has in poetry. Disraeli (Beaconsfield), who liked to
tease Gladstone by calling him "Frohstein" and pointing
to his rugged Jewish prophet's features, has written of
his race most eloquently. I should like to quote a passage in its entirety; time and space forbid. But an
excerpt I permit myself the luxury of reproducing:
"The ear, the voice, the fancy teeming with combinations, the inspiration fervid with picture and emotion,
that came from Caucasus, and which we have preserved
unpolluted, have endowed us with almost the exclusive
privilege of music; that science of harmonious sounds
which the ancients recognise as most divine and deified
in the person of their most beautiful creation. . . ." He
goes on: "There is not a company of singers, not an
orchestra in a single capital, that is not crowded with
our children under feigned names which they adopt to
conciliate the dark aversion which your posterity will
some day disclaim with shame and disgust. . . ."
Lord Beaconsfield mentions Rossini, Meyerbeer, Mendelssohn as Jewish composers, and Pasta and Grisi among

the singers. Probably he had not heard Rossini's witticism uttered on his deathbed: "For heaven's sake, don't bury me in the Jewish cemetery!" Nor did Beaconsfield look far enough ahead when he wrote "dark aversion"—which phrase is wonderful. To-day the boot is on the other leg. It may be Gentiles who will be forced to change their names to Jewish. I could easily sign myself "Shamus Hanuchah"—leaving out the "lichts"— or pattern after the name Paderewski jokingly wrote on his photograph: "For Jacob Hunekerstein."

And I am ashamed to confess that I know Jews who themselves are ashamed of having been born Jews. Incredible! In Vienna I have seen St. Stefan's Cathedral crowded at the 11 o'clock High Mass by most fervent worshippers, the majority of whom seemed Semitic, which prompted me to propound the riddle: When is a Jew not a Jew? Answer: When he is a Roman Catholic in Vienna. But you never can tell. As Joseffy used to say when some musician with a nose like the Ten Commandments was introduced, as, for example, Monsieur Fontaine. "He means Brunnen, or, in Hebrew, Pischa. He is not a Jew, but his grandmother wore a 'scheitel,'" (the wig still worn by orthodox Jewish women). The truth is that among the virtuosi, singers, actors, the Jew holds first place. Liszt and Paganini are the exceptions, and Paganini could easily pass in an east-side crowd as Jehudah. As to the Wagner controversy, not started by Nietzsche, but by Rossini and Meyerbeer, who referred to Wagner as Jewish, that was settled by O. G. Sonneck in his little book, Was Wagner a Jew? but only after I had introduced to the columns of The New York Times Sunday Magazine in 1913 a book by Otto Bournot, entitled, Ludwig Geyer. Geyer was, as you may remember, the stepfather of Richard Wagner. Bournot had access to the Baireuth archives and delved into the newspapers of Geyer's days. August Böttiger's Necrology had hitherto been the chief source. Mary Burrell's Life of Wagner was the first to give the true spelling of the name of Wagner's mother, which was Bertz, which may be Jewish or German, as you like.

The Geyers as far back as 1700 were pious folk. The first of the family mentioned in local history was a certain Benjamin Geyer, who about 1700 was a trombone player and organist. Indeed, the Geyers were largely connected with the Evangelical Church. Ludwig Geyer, virtually acknowledged by Baireuth as the real father of Richard Wagner, looked Jewish (which proves nothing, as I have seen dark, Semitic fisher-folk on the coast of Galway) and displayed Jewish versatility. For that matter the composer von Weber looked like a Jew, as does Camille Saint-Saëns. When I ventured to write of this racial trait—much more marked in his youth— the French composer sent me a denial, sarcastically asking how a man with such a "holy" name as "Saint-Saëns" could be Jewish. But Leopold Godowsky, who was intimate with him, told me that he took his mother's name. As to Wagner, a little story may suffice. In 1896 I attended the Wagner festival at Baireuth. Between performances I tramped the Franconian hills. My toes hurt. Looking for a corn-cutter, I found one not far from the Wagner house. The old chap seated me in his doorway, probably to get better light, and as he crouched over my feet in the street I asked him if he had known Richard Wagner. "Know Wagner!" he irascibly replied. "He passed my shop every day. Many the times I cut his corns. Oh, no! not here, over yonder"—he jerked his head in the direction of Wahnfried. I inquired what kind of a looking man was Wagner. "He was a little bow-legged Jew, and he always wore a long cloak to hide his crooked legs." Enfin! the truth from the mouth of babes. This beats Nietzsche and his "Vulture" Geyer.

Not religion, not nationality, but race, counts in the individual. Wagner looked like a Jew. And there are many red-haired Jews with pug noses and light blue eyes. Renan in Le Judaisme has shown us how non-Jewish elements were in the course of time incorporated within the race. The Chazars of Eastern Europe are Jews only a thousand years old. Dr. Brandes in a confession of his views on the subject has said—in *The Journal for Jewish History and Literature*, published at Stockholm (*Teidscript for Judisk Historia*), and quoted by Bernard G. Richards in a capital study of Brandes—"from the fifteenth to the sixteenth year of my life I regarded Judaism purely as a religion." But when he was abused as a Jew then Georg Brandes felt himself a genuine Jew. Many a man has found himself in a similar position. Atavistic impulses, submerged, may explain why certain men, Gentiles, scholars, by nature noncombatants, have left their peaceful study, jeopardised their life, ruined their reputation, to battle for an obscure Jew, Dreyfus. Zola, of Greek-Levantine origin, perhaps Italian and Jew, was one of those valiant souls who fought for the truth. Anatole France, born Thibault, another. Count Thibault, at the time of the Dreyfus uproar, challenged the great writer who signs himself Anatole France to prove his right to that distinguished Roman Catholic name. That the gentle Anatole is the very spit and spawn of a Jew, as appearance goes; that since Heine (baptised a Christian) no such union of mocking irony and tender, poetic emotion can be noted in the work of any writer, are alike valueless as testimony. Nevertheless, many believe in this Hebraic strain; just as they feel it in the subtlety of Cardinal Newman's writing—he was of Dutch stock—and in the humour of Charles Lamb. Both Englishmen are authoritatively accredited with the "precious quintessence," as Du Maurier would say.

I have stood a lot of good-natured fun poked at me for my Jewish propensity. I can stand it, as there is a solid substratum of history for my speculations. Some years ago *The Contemporary Review* printed an article entitled "The Jew in Music," with this motto from Oscar Wilde's Salome: "The Jews believe only in what they cannot see." The writer's name was signed: A. E. Keeton. Not even the assertion that Beethoven was a Belgian is half so iconoclastic as some of the assumptions made in this study. "When Mozart first appeared as a prodigy before the future Queen of France, Marie Antoinette, she announced that 'a genius must not be a Jew.'" The original name Ozart was changed. Mozart was baptised. Which anecdote makes the scalp to freeze, though not because of its verisimilitude. Beethoven and Rubinstein looked alike; ergo! But then they didn't. In the case of Chopin he was certainly Jewish-looking, especially in the Winterhalter and Kwiatowski portraits. His father came from Nancy, in Lorraine, thickly populated by Jews. The original name, Szopen, or Szop, is Jewish. His music, especially the first Scherzo in B minor, has a Heine-like irony, and irony is a prime characteristic of the Chosen (or Choosing, as Zangwill puts it) race. But all this is in the key of wildest surmise. Wagner was born in the ghetto at

Leipsic; yet that didn't make him Jewish, any more than
the baptism of Mendelssohn made him Christian.
Georges Bizet was of Jewish origin, he looked Jewish;
but the fact that he married the daughter of Halévy
(Ha-Levi), the composer of La Juive, didn't make the
composer of Carmen a Jew. Neither religion nor nationality are more than superficial factors in the nature of men and women. Race alone counts.

Once upon a time I wrote a Jewish story, The Shofar
Blew at Sunset. Maggie Cline liked it; so did Israel
Zangwill. I preserve a letter from Mr. Zangwill telling
me of his liking. The story appeared in *M'lle New York*,
now defunct. It was afterwards translated into Yiddish, though it did not give general satisfaction in either
camp, Jewish or Christian. It revelled in the cantillations and employed as leading-motive the Shofar, or
ram's-horn blown in the synagogues on Yom Kippur or
the Day of Atonement. The scroll of the Torah also
appeared. But these liturgical references didn't offend;
it was my surprising denunciation of Jewish materialism
in New York that proved the rock of offence. I say surprising, for what is a Christian-born doing in another
field and finding fault? I'm sure I can't say why, unless that in writing the tale I unconsciously dramatised
myself as a reproaching voice. There was much in my
strictures of that son of Hanan who prowled through the
streets of the 'Holy City in the year A. D. 62, crying
aloud: "Woe, woe upon Jerusalem!" I remember that
I predicted because of the luxury of the American Jew
lofty Jewish idealism might be submerged in a flood
of indifference and disbelief. Prosperity would prove
the snag. In the heart of the Jew is the true Zion, not
in success nor in some far-away land. Naturally, that

didn't please the Zionists.   One professional Jewish journal said that I preached like a rabbi (Reb), but thought
like a goi.   The word "Chutzpah" was also used.   Yet,
wasn't I right?   It is the spiritual Ark of the Covenant,
the spirit of the law, and not the letter that killeth,
which should be enshrined in the heart of the Jew.
He may dream of Palestine, of its skies of the "few
large stars," a land overflowing with milk and honey;
but in the depths of his soul it is the living God
to whom he must go for spiritual sustenance.   God
the eternal reservoir of our earthly certitudes!   Schma'
Ysroel!

And now for fear that all this sounds more like a sermon than a sonnet—and I'm in earnest, not forgetting
that the lofty ethics of the Old Testament apply quite
as much to Christians as to Jews—I'll conclude with the
statement that the most Jewish composer I know of,
bar none, is Ernest Bloch, a Swiss musician residing in New
York City.   He has great gifts, abundant science, and an
inborn sense of orchestral colour and rhythms.   I heard
him conduct a concert at Philadelphia entirely devoted
to his own works.   I shall not soon forget the emotional
impression created by his "Solomon" for violoncello solo
and orchestra, interpreted on the solo instrument by that
splendid young artist, Hans Kindler, the first 'cellist of
the Philadelphia Orchestra.   It is a masterpiece.   But
the concert was too long;   there were colour and sentiment
that cloyed, and the beat of the composer-conductor
was not propulsive.   With Leopold Stokowski things
would have gone at a brisker tempo and would have been
charged with more vitality.   As the final note was sounded
a well-known wit and jurist, a Hebrew—if I say more,
Philadelphia will surely recognise the man—passed into

the lobby of the Academy of Music. He sighed. He said, with the self-mocking irony of his race: "Beautiful music, but another afternoon like this and I'll turn anti-Semite!" Selah!

XV

THE GIRLS

Race or religion never troubled me. Music was become my sole passion. I even ceased to envy Heide Norris his tailor, Williams Carter his good looks. I frequented places where musicians gathered, much to my mother's disdain. Not that I was dissipated. I had to sow my wild-oats after my own fashion. My liquid measure, as they say at the grocer's, was the envy of the gaugers. My father, who refused to see me in any but a humorous light, had called me "hollow-legs," changed that title for "copper-lined." He classed me as a human armoured tank. It was not flattering to a young man with a thirst for the infinite. I was always thirsty, and moistened my clay and my wits with equal facility. I asked him whether whisky wasn't more harmful than beer. His reply was prompt: "Beer is bellywash"—dear old Kensington phrase—"and in my day gentlemen didn't drink whisky, they drank brandy." I shuddered. It was true. During the first half of the last century, cognac was preferred to corn-whisky by people of taste. But to my way of thinking both are poisonous.

I have mentioned Williams Carter as one of the beaux; I must not forget those other beauty-men, Dr. John Taylor or Dr. Thomas H. Fenton; Greek of profile and admired of the belles who promenaded Spruce and Walnut Streets. Ernest Law was considered by feminine judges to be a model of manly form, and later Barclay Warburton

entered the "Greek God" class. And there were "dancing" Willie White, Charlie Sloan, and how many Binneys
and Biddles! The girls! I was an onlooker with an
eye on the Burton girls, Sallie and Carrie, the Junoesque
Bessie Tunison, and the much-admired Eloise Conover,
or the handsome Burrows sisters, our cousins. The
Carter girls were distinguished-looking in the indolent
Italian style, and there was the gypsy beauty, Lizzie
Evans, on Walnut Street below Tenth; and a slender
girl with large unfathomable eyes ("incessant eyes," as
poet Vance Thompson calls them), hair that Titian would
have gloated over, and features that may be seen in a
Greek medallion. I only remember that her last name was
English, and that I worshipped her from afar; the desire
of the stone for the star. (If I could remember her first
name I might give vent to another of my emotional
shrieks: Bertha! Elaine! Molly Bawn! and the rest.)
La crise juponnière had definitely declared itself. Music
was but an accomplice of the petticoats, and during my
seventeenth year—not sweet but simply seventeen—the
female planet arose on the rim of my soul and shone
serenely into my agitated consciousness. Calf-love had
begun its silly sway.

I have said that love is lucid folly, but it is fascinating
folly in the first quarter of its honeynoon. And no
matter the fun poked at the awkward age there is no
denying the single-heartedness of a boy's first love. A
girl is a madonna in his eyes. A jest made about her
turns his little sky black. Nor does it have to be a girl;
a married woman will do; married women are usually
the target for boyish adoration. I remember one wedded
lady whom I had honoured with my timid attentions (I
could never follow Stendhal's advice, a trooper's motto,

and make love to every woman I happened to find alone).
She was mysterious—Ah! how youth enjoys mystery—
and she impressed me as having married her husband as
an accomplice in some dark enterprise. Perhaps she
had. He was far from being the hateful husband brute
of fiction. To me he was quite affable, till one afternoon, as we drank tea I heard him ask the housemaid if
"that lightning-bug" was with his wife. I never went
back to her. I don't mind abuse, but the implication
of the lantern and its location—you have studied en-
tomology!—was too much. But there were plenty of
consolations: Bessie and Sallie and Adele, sweetest of
girls, who taught me how to walk, talk, but not to dance.
I was born with a Quaker foot. I often wonder what
girls see in hobbledehoys. They are, I know, a continual
source of amusement. I was. My dancing gave great
pleasure to the children; but as I could tinkle pretty
tunes for others to foot the mazy dance I was occasionally
rewarded with a bright look. Kissing was never attempted. I contend that a boy's mind at a certain period
is as pure as a girl's. (A pure girl, of course.) Youth is
pure just because it is youth, says Dostoievsky. Vague
desires assail him, at which he blushes, but for unadul-
terated chivalry, give me the average lad who blushes
when his mother tells him "Mamie is coming over to-night,
Jack, hurry, wash your face and don't forget to change
your collar." Forget to change his collar! Wash his
face, forsooth! With a Byronic scowl, which is not
missed by his sympathetic mother—and sneered at by
his cynical aunt—he stalks out of the room, and for a
full hour faces his glass, alternately admiring and dis-
trusting his pulchritude. The boy who doesn't make an
ass of himself over a girl is apt to miss out later in his

manhood. It meant something, the toga virilis of the Romans; at once a symbol of virility and sex-initiation.

But no love is comparable to the first love of a boy for his mother. It is the greatest romance in the world. It comes earlier with some lads than others, and it lasts till his death. My affection took a peculiar turn. I realised that the end of mankind was death. We are all condemned, as Victor Hugo said; but not our mothers. I was sure that my mother would never die. She was something so exquisite that she was deathless, and like the child in Wordsworth's poem, I could have obstinately repeated "We are seven," when I argued the matter with boys of my age. Their mothers might die, mine never. The illusion long endured. I shall never forget the afternoon that I climbed to the base of the dome of the Cathedral on Logan Square. From a window I saw my mother's terrified face, as I triumphantly waved a handkerchief. I felt like Ibsen's Master Builder in the tragic play. I was true Steeplejack. In the meantime my brother, John, without any fuss or feathers, calmly ascended the dome by a small ladder, invisible from the street, to the gilded globe and cross at the very top. He had a contract to fresco the church and re-gild the cross. It was all in the day's work for him, to me a victory; but when I descended and realised what a shock I had inflicted on the loving woman my conceit was dampened for the nonce. Another picture. Evening in the nuns' flower garden at Emmitsburg, Maryland. "L'heure exquise," as the poet so charmingly phrases it. In the soft slanting light of a westering sun, I see my mother slowly walking under a trellised path, her rosary in her hand, on her head a mantilla that transformed her into a Spanish dame of high degree. I was not more than eight or nine years old, but it was the first time that I consciously realised that she was my mother. She was the most beautiful creature on earth. The gentle nuns who moved along this enchanted garden were only phantoms. The one great fact was my mother and her calm intellectual features. It is the most vivid memory I have of her. With difficulty I summon up to my recollection meeting there the poet, George Miles, and hearing him discourse on his Pontius Pilate, his Truce of God, and of his theory as to the cause of Hamlet's irresolution. This theory he afterwards published, and the essay contains some plausible arguments; among the rest, that Hamlet, being a Roman Catholic, and a fervent believer, despite his surface scepticism, could not kill the King unshriven without doing violence to his conscience. As Hamletic theories go it is worth while.

I must add that while we had Jewish friends, I did not fail to associate with boys and girls of our own race and religion; the Barrys, the Raleighs, the Sullivans, Dohans, Wilcoxes, McGlenseys, Doughertys, and other Americans of Irish stock. Will Sullivan, the brother of John and James, was one of the handsomest young men of our set and possessed a nature transparent and lovable. Yet, when it came to spooning, I sought pasture elsewhere than among our crowd. My first grand passion was a cousin, but she jilted me for my younger brother. Then a certain Annie and a Theresa loomed large. Annie was short, plump, materialistic; Theresa wore long curls, had large eyes, an empty gaze, and a saccharine smile; in short, she was a girl of the sort that girls detest. Sly, was the epithet applied to her by Annie. Neither one cared a rap for me, but each was determined to beat the other. I played a fatuous Paris to their rivalry, but when I attempted to award the golden apple—meaning myself—they at once became close friends and gave me the cold shoulder. For weeks I ruminated, not without bitterness, on feminine treachery, and even went so far as to consult my mother. She bade me not put my trust in princes, and quoted Wolsey's speech: "If I had served my God," which seemed to me to be superfluous. It is Lincoln who is credited with the wise and witty axiom: "You can fool all of the people some of the time, and some of the people all of the time, but you can't fool all the people all the time." He might have added: But you can fool yourself every time. Self-illusion is the staff of life, the bread of egotism. I am not precisely a determinist, yet I believe our characters are immutable. I have always fooled myself, and successfully, up to a given point, then the disillusionment is accepted as a necessity. It had to come, I would say, seeking consolation in the shabby snare of fatalism. The petticoat mirage found me easiest of victims. It was years later I discovered that in the land of tone may be found the Elysian Fields. My mother's delicate warning fell on deaf ears, and when my father mocked me "beware of the girls!" I retorted with the elder Weller's advice to his son "beware of the vidders Samivel!" I knew it all before I was out of my teens. The omniscience of youth is both the pride and despair of parents. My craze for the girls was no doubt an illustration of Henry James's "manners observable in the most mimetic department of any great menagerie." But boys weren't monkeys nor girls parrots then, as they seem when life sets such things in truer perspective.

I have never suffered from the Time illusion. The past or future did not exist. It seldom does for the young. I have always had the delusion of free-will. There is only the present. That long shining corridor of Time did not invite me to traverse its eternal leagues. Carpe diem! When I read in Henri Bergson's philosophy—thrice-subtle French Jew—that "Time is both tough and resistant," I rejected the idea, fair as it is to the abused concept Time, always playing a minor rôle when in company with its brother, Space. Not even metaphysical Time is resistant. I can't divest my consciousness of the notion, naturally an empirical one, that Time is the glittering crest of a moment, not one of a series of beads strung out through eternity. Eternity is Now. Live in the present—which passes like a flash of lightning. I suspect that Walter Pater and his famous conclusion to the Studies in the Renaissance had much to do with my crystallisation of this worship of the present. My present didn't mean the actual; far from it. A cuckoo-cloudland was for me the present. I had neither hindsight nor foresight. With David Thoreau I could have cried: "Thank God, they can't cut down the clouds," possibly substituting "girls" for clouds. And petticoats stray in where fools fear to enter. Girls are ever wise; so they appeared to me. At each hour of the day I said, with Faust: "Stay, thou art so fair!" And they stayed, that's the funny part of it. They jeered at me, but they remained companions. I recall a dark-skinned, black-haired girl who was nicknamed Portuguese Annie. She was a nicely behaved miss of seventeen and one of those apathetic flirts. She never regarded you except from a great height, unless another girl became too friendly, then, hawk-like she would swoop down on her

innocent prey—meaning my lamb-like self—and carry
him away to her fastness, there to be dropped into the
next nest of her indifference. She piqued, did Portuguese
Annie—why Portuguese, I never found out; perhaps because she was Irish. I met her of rainy nights in Fairmount Park. We went around the Reservoir. At times
we sat on wet benches, an umbrella lifted, her cloak
about us. When the guardian of public morals shooed
us away we sought another bench, and potential pneu-
monia. What was our conversation? I've forgotten.
Probably chaste and silly. One night as we walked
about Logan Square, a lame man hobbled in front of us,
then he limped to our rear. A spy? A relative! I
warned Annie. She didn't recognise him and he so
manœuvred that I couldn't. At the advanced hour of
nine we separated—and forever. The reason I never
saw her again was a simple one. That lame man was
my elder brother playing detective. At home he warned
me that I was a sentimental ass. I openly admitted it.
There was other balm in Gilead. The charms of Portuguese Annie had begun to pall. The Eternal Feminine
led me upward and on.

Not far from Logan Square there was a mysterious
mansion occupied by two men, possibly brothers, though
they did not betray any family resemblance, and one of
the most beautiful girls on our perambulating bone-yard
of a planet. The entire neighbourhood of boys said she
was peerless and I soon chimed in. Through the inter-
mediary of her brother—he turned up from somewhere—
we were introduced, and I called at discreet intervals—
every afternoon between five and six. They were foreigners, Swiss, I think, and their drawing-room was
decorum personified. I can't tell how it was managed,

but each boy had his solo, or rather duo, interview with
the lovely Clarisse. I called her Monna Lisa because
of her delicate hands and slow, cold gaze. She could out-
stare a wooden Indian or a brass monkey, and when she
condescended to drop her disdainful eyelids, we shivered
in ecstasy. We adored her, and quarrelled over her like
a pack of hungry hounds about a live goose. Our leisure
was spent in discussing her mysterious family. No one
knew them, knew their business, except that at five
o'clock their solemn hospitality was bestowed upon the
elect. We, the ganders, were the elect. Hot love was
made to this madonna. We tried to arrange meetings
outside. In vain. I never saw such admirable team-
work. We were brethren united in a noble cause—to
carry off Clarisse from her home and marry her, not all
of us, only myself—and every chap said the same. Boys
have monstrous fancies. We believed that girl perse-
cuted by her loving father and uncle, though she was
serenely happy. We made up to her gawky brother,
bribing him with cigarettes, fondly hoping for a gleam of
light on the dark enigma of the household.

He never vouchsafed us this illuminating ray of hope.
The plot thickened. Other boys came into the net.
Every now and then we were not admitted, though we
saw our nut-brown maid in the bay-window on the second
floor, presumably leading on another brave knight to
destruction. We descended so low in the moral scale
as to spy upon the house after dark. By climbing the wall
of the Quaker graveyard opposite, we could, at the risk
of our unworthy necks, peer into the lighted rooms.
We never saw a thing; the curtains were always drawn.
Time passed. Clarisse remained the Marble Heart of our
despairing fancy. Suddenly her family moved. A sign

"to let" froze our overheated blood. Where did they
go, this charming, mysterious family? Alas! no one ever
discovered. But we discovered ourselves, when, one
evening in conclave over pipes and gingerpop, we frankly
bared our hearts. Every man Jack present had proposed
marriage to Clarisse (not one was more than eighteen),
and had been accepted. At least ten of us admitted the
soft impeachment. We reviled ourselves at the outlay
in engagement rings. Each chap outdid the other in
his effort to make himself the king-pin of ridicule. I
fear there were unshed drops in our tear-ducts, we were
so desperately gay. When I say that we all popped the
question, I must omit George Wickersham, who had remained a critical onlooker. "If I ever marry," he assured us, "I wish at least to know the lady's last name!"
George didn't approve of matrimony in the dark. I
fancy the solution of the "mystery" was only a widower,
endeavouring to marry his daughter to the best advantage.

That chapter closed I began another one—but stay!
These memoirs are not intended to describe my sentimental education. Any man could write a book of many
pages and call it My Love-Life (or Vita Sexualis, as the
psychiatric jargon goes). It would sell like hot cakes
on a wintry night. Consider George Moore's Memoirs
of My Dead Life—the unexpurgated English edition!
When I anxiously consulted my editor as to the inclusion
of the love element, without which existence is like an
addled egg, he tersely replied: "Be interesting, and if
you can't be interesting, be careful!" But then one
can't be careful and interesting at the same time. Many
a woman has come to shipwreck in attempting that im-

possible task. You can't have your cake and swallow it. So I shall desist from further recital of my salad loves, except to add that on the boards I had three passions: Adelaide Neilson, Mary Scott-Siddons and Teresita Carreño, and, as these three women ranked as the most beautiful of their day, I had half the town assisting me in my worship. Carreño, in particular, with her exotic colouring, brilliant eyes, and still more brilliant piano-playing, was like a visitor from another star. One night at a Gaertner concert she wore a scarlet dress, and a rose coquettishly placed in her raven-black hair drove the blood from my heart (probably pumped it too fast). I shall always remember this thrice-charming —and thrice-married—woman and great artiste, in the scarlet mists of my memory. When I told her later of my folly she naïvely answered: "But you foolish boy, why didn't you send me a bouquet of red roses, then I should have known that you admired me." The worst trick that fate plays on us is to let us know too late how near we grazed happiness.

XVI

MUSIC–MADNESS

Every girl has her day. I couldn't forever feed on sweetmeats. My musical studies were satisfactorily progressing. I knew because I never opened a law book and also because of my début as a pianist in company with my chum, Franz Schubert. Together we played Grieg's first Sonata for violin and piano (in F, opus 8) and a Sonata by Ries. Franz played the slow movement from the Mendelssohn Concerto and Wieniawski's "Legende," and most musically. He was a skilled fresco-painter, but I think he should have stuck to music. I followed with the "Loreley" by Seeling, and some Schubert pieces. As we were not paid for our services, it being a benefit concert—on Franklin Street in a small hall somewhere near Poplar or Parrish Streets—we were warmly applauded. There were no press-notices, luckily enough. It was my first, and with a solitary appearance in Paris, my last appearance in public as a pianist. The world of music has lost nothing through my resolve not to wear my musical motley on the concert platform. But I have worn it in print too often. We must, all of us, eat our peck of dirt. However, Schubert and I continued to play music in private. At the Academy our seats were in the top gallery, better known as the amphitheatre (entrance, 25 cents). When last season I saw the line stretched along Locust Street patiently waiting for the doors to open, and then a wild rushing up-stairs to be rewarded by the tones of Jascha Heifetz's magic fiddle, it was easy for me to forget the forty odd years when we

also stood there, good or bad weather, hoping to get a
front-row seat, or when Theodore Thomas conducted his
wonderful orchestra. With Alfredo Barili I heard Joseffy
play, and Theodore Ritter—with all three I studied later.
My first visit to the Academy began when the Majiltons,
or was it the Hanlon-Lees, acrobats extraordinary? Little
America, a Japanese child, astonished with his aerial
flights. Ole Bull, Vieuxtemps, Sivori played their fiddles;
but it was Thomas that I best loved. The orchestra,
the synthesis of instruments, cured me of my operatic
mania. The symphony, with its reasoned narrative in
tone, is the epitome of music.

The Mercantile Library, on Tenth Street, where it is
to-day, had me as a daily visitor. It was there I began
my browsing in many fields. Like an animal I instinc-
tively sought the food my system demanded. I was like
a horse let out to graze. I must have had an appalling
appetite for printed matter. I would, in the absence of
an English book, read any foreign language, although
I didn't understand it. There was something friendly
and inviting in strange letters. Hebrew intrigued my
fancy. To-day I can make out the meaning of headlines
in a Yiddish newspaper, thanks to that one-eyed ex-
rabbi's lessons. I had the good luck to read the "new"
English literature of the seventies and eighties. The
poets enthralled me. Swinburne, Dante Gabriel Rossetti, William Morris, Matthew Arnold, Clough, Patmore,
and the Alfred Tennyson of that period, as well as George
Meredith as poet, and a host of minor singers such as
Gosse—his "On Viol and Flute"—Arthur O'Shaugnessy,
Austin Dobson—delightful reading—and even the extravagant Theophile Marzials. The essayists, Arnold,
Pater, George Saintsbury—who first wrote of Baude-

laire—attracted me. But the pre-Raphaelitic movement left me indifferent, especially the painters. I had sufficient art training to recognise the gimcrack mysticism, preciosity and woful lack of expert brushwork in the productions of the Brotherhood. Think of Woolner as a sculptor! A mediocre modeller who wrote "occasional" verse. Rossetti is a musical poet; as a picture-maker he is an imitator; the hand is his, but the voice is the voice of the Italian Primitives. A pretty colour scheme, a sentimental attitude towards mediæval religious faith, and drawing that is "papery." His sonnets will be read when his painting is forgotten. A visit to the Grosvenor Gallery is a disillusion. Watts is another mediocrity despite his poetry. His paint is "woolly," his design obviously "eclectic," that is, not original. Edward Burne-Jones has a thin vein of poetry, but his wan allegories seen in the cruel light of this century are feeble dreams. I like better the honest but uninspired realism of Ford Madox-Brown. Albert Moore is decorative, Leighton pasticcio, and Holman Hunt with his "Light of the World," is a sacred bore. The one strong man, John Millais, didn't long remain in the movement. His artistic lungs were too big to respire in that morbid marsh air of mysticism and faded eroticism. I had begun to enjoy the Barbizons, but the French Impressionists I knew little about, yet there they were, only a few miles across the Channel bringing the pure light of heaven into the dingy, musty atmosphere of Academic art; while the pre-Raphaelites, their faces turned towards the fifteenth century, were indulging in various insincere poses and hysterical contortions, thus thinking to set back the implacable clock of time. London was then artistically as far from Paris as if it were Pekin.

To catch the first glow of a rising sun is a pleasant experience. Swinburne was new, Wagner was new, Manet, Monet, and Rodin were new. I was happy in being born at such cross-roads of art. I watched all novel manifestations across the water. George Eliot had just published Daniel Deronda, and while the waning of her popularity dated from that fiction, over here she was at her apogee. I admired her, still admire her, but wouldn't give up Charlotte Brontë or Jane Austen for her. Indeed, I would rather read the critical writings of her companion, George Henry Lewes, with his lively Jewish imagination, capital memory, and splendid workmanship. His Life of Goethe, despite some omissions, is better than the pretentious three-volume biography of Bielochowsky, and where is there a more succinct summing up of the historical aspects of philosophy than Lewes furnished us. His coda, a veritable challenge to idealism and its exponents, still remains unanswerable. On the last page (789) of The Biographical History of Philosophy, he asks: "Have we any ideas independent of experience?" The answer is always a negative. The latest champion of idealistic absolutism—despite William James and his Pluralism, it is idealism—Henri Bergson may wriggle as metaphysically as he pleases— and as a phrase-maker he is an artist, but he can't evade that question of George Henry Lewes without imperilling his shaky lath, plaster, and cobweb edifice. The essay by Lewes on Actors and Acting is a classic. Nevertheless, George Eliot had a touch of genius and her mate had not. He was supremely clever, nothing more.

The Mercantile Library was a trysting spot for enamoured youth. There I saw the girl with the medallion

features and Titian hair; there we had encounters with
the old Cerberus, Donigan, who only did his duty as a
doorkeeper in keeping the lobbies clear and suppressing
laughter. We thought otherwise. We loved to romp,
raise a row, and drop books. I can evoke the absorbed
expression of Mr. Edmands, the librarian, which would
modulate into pained astonishment when our gang talked
too loudly in the reading-room. After we were ejected,
which occurred at least once a month, we would shake
our fists at Donigan, and go across the street to Dooner's,
there to swagger before the bar and sip soda-cocktails,
as harmless as buttermilk. What men around town we
were! Popular concerts conducted by Sentz, or Mark
Hassler, or Wolsieffer always saw us. I made the acquaintance, through a school companion, young Shaw,
of his brother-in-law, Siegfried Behrens, an admirable
conductor of opera, as well as a scholarly musician. I
think the Shaws lived on Locust Street. A Sunday
morning treat was to go in company with my father to
High Mass at St. Augustine's Church, to the choir, there
to hear Henry Thunder, Sr., play the organ of which he
was a master. His pedalling made me forget the divine
service. There was a bass in the choir named Winter-
bottom, a friend of my father's, who always saluted him
as Summertop. The association of Thunder and Winter-
bottom set me to speculation. With Laurence Sterne's
Slawkenbergius I believed in the fitness of names. I
have mentioned Alfredo Barili. He taught me. He was
a finished pianist of the French school. When he first
played Chopin's B minor Scherzo for me, it acted like
catnip on a feline. I rolled over the floor. The music
made my nerves naked. I play the tragic, morbid composition now—yet can never rid myself of the initial

impression. Later S. L. Hermann and Anthony Stanko-
witch guided my musical studies. What these three
young men thought of me I never knew, but I do know
that they were exceedingly forbearing. The sad sequel
is that with all my striving I only attained mediocrity
as a pianist. Any young conservatory miss can out-
play me in glib fingering. Yet, music is a consolation,
an anodyne, like religion. It keeps off the deadliest
beast that lurks in the jungle of life, the beast I stand
most in fear of—ennui. Many are driven to monotonous
labor by ennui. Its presence is a pathological symptom.
If this be true then all animal creation from man to
beetles, is sick in spirit. I've seen dogs yawn from bore-
dom; yea, even the flowers droop when weary of life.
Art has been my escape, and my native laziness was
surmounted by the terror bred of ennui. Making money,
love, playing games, are but so many forms by which
to escape the oppressive monster, and also to create the
illusion of progress. To fill in the seemingly intermina-
ble interval from womb to tomb, man invented politics,
money, wine, cards, war, love, and religion. (Satan
Mekatrig is personally interested in several of these inventions.)

A certain Christmas, I've forgotten the year, I was considered, by such inexpert authority as my parents, to
be capable of handling a church organ. My nervousness
was pooh-poohed as stage fright. Finally I ceded, but
only after severe pressure. Midnight Mass at Christmas
Eve had been temporarily abolished by Archbishop
Wood; a Mass with music at 6 A. M. taking its place.
Without a day's warning, I was asked to "substitute"
for the organist at the church near Moyamensing Prison.
I went to bed early, spent a sleepless night, anticipating

a breakdown at the organ, and of being chased from the choir. Shivering, I arose at four o'clock, swallowed a pot of coffee to keep up my courage (and to prevent the heart leaping out of my bosom) and proceeded to board a Tenth Street horse-car. It took about an hour to reach the church—I can't recollect its name, though I shall never forget its interior—and when I arrived in the choir it must have been a half-hour too soon. The place was chilly. I "gloomed" around, tried the little organ and its two banks of keys, and was wondering what Mass I was expected to play without rehearsal, when the soprano appeared. It was Madame Sauvan, a friend of my mother's, who proved my saviour. She picked out either Concone's or Bordone's Mass (?)—very easy to read, and she gave me a welcome hint about the voice of the celebrant priest, who sometimes deviated from pitch. The worshippers straggled in, the choir arrived, the Mass began, and my knees as well as my teeth started to chatter. (Didn't you ever have chattering knees?) I plunged into the music ahead or behind the singers. My tempi were erratic. Madame Sauvan beat time for me and steadied my nerves. There was no pause for a sermon and the solemn service smoothly progressed. I had to accompany the reverend Father. In the "Pater Noster" he intoned the "Et ne nos inducas in tentationem" a half tone flat. I vainly scrambled from the key of G to F sharp. There followed a distinct series of dissonances that would have made Richard Strauss or Stravinsky envious. I peeped into the telltale mirror hung over the organ manuals which enables the organist to watch the movements before the altar. I saw one movement and I grew pale. It was the indignant side glance shot at me by the priest. He blamed me for his singing off-key! If he had shot me I should have died with a martyr's aureole and a heavenly smile on my lips. Cold as was the morning, I sweated. I fled after playing the "Adeste Fidelis," so disconsolate was I over my blundering. It is the prime duty of an organist never to allow the congregation to overhear flat singing on the part of the clergy. To do that is to commit the sin against the holy ghost of music. Madame Sauvan told my mother some weeks later that I did as well as could be expected, which truly feminine expression left me more dubious than ever as to my success. When I wrote a horrible and blasphemous short story—though I still can't see the blasphemy—entitled, Where the Black Mass was Heard (and translated into French by Remy de Gourmont) I utilised as a background the choir of this church; also the crypt of St. Joseph's Church in Willing's Alley. This tale was not admired by those clergy of the diocese who read it, yet in it I only affirmed in unmistakable terms what is preached from every Roman Catholic pulpit, i. e., the existence of a personal devil, the demon of mid-day who goes abroad like a lion seeking whom he may devour. I had been reading too much Huysmans and his description of the Black Mass in that astounding novel, Là-bas, but my yarn—which is not included in my Melomaniacs or Visionaries—is individual and devoid of the erotic element. Remy de Gourmont wrote me a letter of congratulation when the story appeared in M'lle New York, declaring that my invention was as vivid as Huysmans. The mistake I made was merely a matter of taste. I should not have used St. Joseph's as the spot where my particular devil showed himself, horns, hoofs, and hide, although he hangs around churches, as is well known in theological circles.

I have dwelt on religious matters too much, but only to prove that my vocation, despite my pious environment, was not a priestly one. I often follow with my eyes some young priest and shudder at the idea that I might have been persuaded into taking orders and with what doleful consequences! There but for the grace of God go I—John Wesley's words—I say. To me the most melancholy apparitions in this vale of Armageddon are a disfrocked priest, an ex-vice-president, an ex-dramatic critic. (There is no such thing as an ex-music-critic; a music-critic never stops criticising. Even on his death-bed he would criticise the tone-production of Gabriel's last trump.) Religion has given an emotional colouring to my modes of thought. It has been called a crutch for lame minds by Huxley; it is really a spiritual anodyne. Mankind demands some superstition—to give it a Voltaire's name. "Ecrasez l'infâme!" he wrote, forgetting that belief in the impossible is an organic necessity, and not sacerdotal dupery. Without vision people perish. Montaigne, Anatole France, made of their scepticism the smiling religion which their souls craved. We all worship something; usually ourselves. There is a wilderness in the heart of every human. And the arch-devil ennui hides behind the trees spying his chance. Mother Church knew this when she devised her elaborate ritual, her consoling sacraments, her future rewards and punishments. The void is filled. Man, ever credulous, spends his life earning a living and dodging the devil. Eternal activity is the price of sleep. I am chronicling all the small-beer of my uneventful life because I am afraid of the twilight that sets in during the lonesome latter years. The personal pronoun which I am forced to use, and abuse, but serves as a peg upon which is hung the loop of my narrative. I am not a grandfather, but I have reached the age of dissent. In youth we rebel, in old age, we dissent. Thackeray wrote: "Youth goes to balls, old men to dinners." So please be patient with my anecdotage. Presently we shall be in Paris.

XVII

JIM THE PENMAN

Annie Hampton Brewster wrote the book that set me off on another tangent and helped to decide my future occupations. It is called St. Martin's Summer, and was published by Ticknor & Fields, Boston, 1866. It is out of print, as is her musical novel Compensation, the latter superior to the Charles Auchester kind of musical stories. Miss Brewster was for years Paris Correspondent of the Philadelphia *Evening Bulletin*, and was succeeded by Lucy Hamilton Hooper. She went to Rome and wrote letters to the same newspaper that revealed her generous culture and critical sensibility. Writers of her calibre were as rare then as they are now. As Havelock Ellis says: "The exquisite things of life are to-day as rare and precious as they ever were." St. Martin's Summer is a book composed of loosely-strung chapters, a mere thread of a story connecting them. There are travel pictures, criticisms of art, literature and music, keen aperçus, and a catholicity in taste that is refreshing in this age of specialisation and Gradgrind "efficiency." The times were more spacious, the dilettante was still in existence—dead as the dodo bird now—and life a pleasanter affair. To be sure, there were wars and rumours of war, and politics and Cad Stanton, Dr. Mary Walker, and the mysterious case of Charlie Ross. There were also cultivated men and women who saw life steadily and as a whole. Miss Brewster was one of them. A convert to the Roman Catholic faith, her tact saved her from excess in zeal. I admit she was occasionally sentimental, and that her judgments were not always sound; but she introduced me to Stendhal, and to a group of writers, not so cynical as Stendhal, to whom I owe much gratitude, Chateaubriand among others. The Centennial Exposition and the Brewster book set ringing the alarm bells in my conscience. Europe was bound to see me soon.

A victim to suggestion—the Higher Snobbery, I fancy it should be called—I discovered Walt Whitman after reading the admirable essay by Moncure D. Conway— the uncle of General Peyton March on the distaff side —in *The Atlantic* (?), and as I followed that grand old iconoclast in many of his views, I became a Whitmaniac about in the same time that Swinburne, William Rossetti —the brother of the painter-poet—and John Addington Symonds sang the praises of the Camden bard; also at the same time that William Winter, dramatic critic of the New York *Tribune*, and poet, the "Weeping Willie" of Charlie McClellan, attacked Leaves of Grass. Walt disposed of Winter thus: "Now, there's Willie Winter, miserable little cuss." Swinburne had penned his dithyrambic praise of Whitman in his study of "William Blake" and compared that master of lyrics to the American yawper. A poor enough comparison, for in Blake there is lovely music, while in Whitman the chaff almost smothers the wheat. Possibly the Prophetic Books of Blake and their windy ramifications suggested the comparison; certainly Swinburne was unhappy in that, as later he permitted himself to scold Whitman like a fishwife (that is, the fishwife of Daniel O'Connell). He said Whitman wrote poetry as would

a drunken apple-woman. (I quote from memory.)
Again old Walt "called the turn." As reported by Horace Traubel, he remarked of this sudden change in the
critical attitude of the poet; "Swinburne—ain't he the
damnedest simulacrum!" Simulacrum in this case is
almost too good to be true. That exquisite poet and
prose stylist, Alice Meynell, reached the same conclusion in her Hearts of Controversy, about Swinburne;
she doesn't even believe in his foaming passion.

After reading that Shelley lived on fried bread I
upset our kitchen by frying bread and writing verse
under its greasy inspiration. That, and my short-lived
Whitman worship, are indices of my weather-cock temperament. And with Walt there was a more personal
reason. I was in love with a dainty miss who weighed
two hundred pounds. She literally oozed health, and
was sentimental, withal; most fat girls are. Together we
read Children of Adam, and when I showed her photograph to Walt one hot afternoon in Camden—1877—
the good old soul sympathetically said: "She will be a
mother of ten, at least," appraising her, as he would a
brood-mare. He saw men and women as fathers and
mothers, and his preoccupation with sex, above all,
with maternity, caused Edmund Clarence Stedman to
write in *The Century* that there are other lights in which
to view the beloved than as the mother of one's future
children. However, Walt was right. He represented
the violent recoil from the New England school in whose
veins flowed ink and ice-water. His bombastic patriotism, his delight in cataloguing the various parts of the
human body was but a revolt against the nasty-nice
puritanism of his day. It's a dull reading for us now,
accustomed as we are to the poetry and fiction of ladies

with triple-barrelled names. In the seventies when
Moncure D. Conway pleaded for a fair hearing, Walt
Whitman's name was anathema. In company with that
same fat girl I took him to all the concerts I could. He
usually scribbled, but enjoyed the music as he enjoyed
life, seemingly through his pores. He was as receptive as
a sponge. And he was one.

Then the pen fever seized me. After that Sunday
afternoon hailstorm of which I wrote I went into the
street and ate my fill, as if it were ice-cream. Pneu-
monia, coupled with typhoid fever, followed, and it meant
one year indoors for me; it spoiled me completely, for I
had only to emit a hollow cough and my school was
over for the day. Boys are worse humbugs than girls
—and that is saying a lot. I slipped around the curve
of least resistance, and each experiment was only the
search after a softer spot to nestle in. I was like a cat.
I wanted my place in the sun, and with a Dickens' novel
and an apple (or ten apples) I was perfectly content to let
the world wag on. The vagabond spirit of Whitman followed the trail of the gypsy. Much later, when Walden
and A Walk to Wauchusetts fell into my hands, I realised
that in David Thoreau a true American is incarnated, and
not in Whitman. And the prose of Thoreau. What an
artist! After the word-wallowing of Walt who wrote
neither prose nor poetry, the incisive sentences, the swift-
moving paragraphs, the nutty Yankee flavour are singularly convincing. A mystic, he writes not in the clear-
obscure style of Emerson, but with the precision, the con-
cision, and the light, dark from excess of brilliance. "I
hear music below; it washes the dust of life, and everything I look at." "The pine-tree is as immortal as I
am, and perchance, go to as high a heaven, there to

tower above me still." Walt, who suffered from a mental indigestion, brought on by MacPherson's Ossian, Emerson, and Thoreau—R. L. Stevenson first pointed the debt he owed Thoreau—never clarified his mental processes enough to write as well as the man of Walden Pond. He has no more sex—though he loudly advertises his virility by hanging his banner on the outer wall—than Thoreau, whose early and unhappy love-affair—she married his brother—made him a stoic. He is more tonic than Whitman, and I say this, well remembering the fact that in my obituary of Walt I slopped over most uncritically.

I repeat, pen and ink and paper beckoned me to that swamp from which no penman ever emerges. My old joke, so old that it is decrepit, that once a newspaper man, always a cocotte, is not without a shade of truth. I had made foolish and extravagant attempts at fiction: The Comet, The Velvet Tree, The V-Shaped Corsage, and criticism had to come next on the roster of my destiny. I needs must write about music or burst. I began with the Charles H. Jarvis Classical Soirées in Natatorium Hall. My friendship with Leander Williamson, who, with his brother, John, was in the editorial department of *The Evening Bulletin*, led me to make some experiments. I showed them to him. "All right," said Leander, "bring them to me at the office and I'll see that they go into type." Ferdinand Fetherston was a friend of my parents and, as publisher of the newspaper, in company with Mr. Peacock, I had my way cleared, though it was Leander who gave me my first lift. The Jarvis concerts invariably took place on Saturday nights. I had free admission because of the Jarvis friendship. I usually reached the hall before he did. On Sundays I laboriously

carved out an article. Dr. Lambdin and Mr. Bunting
were then the principal music-critics. I read them with
fanatical fervour; but I also read Berlioz, Dr. Ritter, the
husband of Fanny Raymond Ritter, and Franz Hueffer.
Critically, New York didn't exist for me; Boston did in
the shape of *Dwight's Journal of Music.* I possessed the
critical vocabulary before I knew my scales. After
passing under the revision of my mother the "story"
was ready. How well I recall my halting heart as I
climbed the two or three stories to the office of *The Bulletin.* Leander would ask me if I were ill or only frightened. "It's those stairs," I would reply. It was stage
fright, all the more ridiculous because I was paid nothing
for my work. It was worth nothing. On Tuesday, my
little pair of paragraphs duly appeared. I, at least, read
them; so did Mr. Jarvis. Michael Cross merely smiled,
his funny bone being tickled by the idea of this putting
the cart before the horse, writing of an art instead of first
mastering it. But the method hath precedents. I saved
these notices and I find that they read like the regulation
bone-dry critique, with its spilth of adjectives and its
amateurish omniscience. I had horse-sense enough to
avoid too many technical terms, and the criticisms that
read the most reasonable are those in which the news
element predominates. But the critical values! Oh!
Moscheles and Kalkbrenner were treated with the same
consideration as Beethoven and Schumann. Max Heinrich often sang, always the best music. Emil Gastel was a
frequent "guest," as were Mrs. Darling, Leopold Engelke,
Massah Warner, and Richard Zeckwer. I again heard
the call. I determined to both play music and write
about it. "Qui a bu, boira!" With the emerald of
Antoninus I could have said: "Whatever happens I

must be emerald!" I determined to be a musician and a littérateur. "Gosh!" said my boy friends.

I went in the Summer to Bryn Mawr, then a sketch of its present prosperity. I remember the day the Wheeler house was finished and with old Sam Clemens, the builder, I put the little tree on the ridge-pole of the roof. I saw Walter Damrosch conduct a chorus in the wings at the concert of his father, Leopold Damrosch, at which "The Damnation of Faust," by Berlioz, was sung. I recall trudging after every parade that I encountered, with Beck's military band at the head. Beck, a German, was then the Sousa of Philadelphia. He was the father of James M. Beck. I began to watch the pageant of life. I asked Leander if I might write of fires, dog-fights, or drunken men. He said yes. Unknown to my father, and absolutely shirking further law study, I began reporting for *The Bulletin*. Salary nil and unattached. My enthusiasm might have led to a profitable connection if I had stuck to the game. I tried my prentice hand at everything. I reported lectures. I went to spiritualistic seances, and one Sunday night, at the corner of Thirteenth Street and Girard Avenue, I was thrown out bodily by an enraged "medium" whose wrist I held till the lights were turned on. As an amateur magician that kind of foolery was easy to expose, but the duped ones present had other views and I fled down two flights pursued by most unspiritual language. I was congratulated by Leander Williamson, who told me that if I kept it up a century or so I might become an editor. He jeeringly referred to me as the "boy-critic." I taught piano. I went into the house of bondage, where to the click of the metronome, the puling attempts of the pupil, and the irritable lead-pencil of the teacher was added the fear that no money would be forthcoming at the end of the term. And then my good mother, who thought piano teaching was a gay rigadoon, added to my list of pupils a half-dozen charity patients. I didn't much mind the extra burdens. But I did protest against the lack of talent I found among them. I went to Riverton, N. J., two days a week. That was an agreeable diversion; the trip, the pretty country roads, the cordial pupils— ah! what a nice lot of little girls I had. Their names sound like a rosary; Hattie Hovey, Ellie Earp, Josie Cook, Bertie Bechtel, and other children, who tapped the keys while their mothers complacently listened, occasionally rewarding me with home-made pie and milk. It was idyllic. I ate the pie and gave the milk to the cat. I must have been a "rotten" teacher, yet my pupils progressed. I had more important ones in the city; Miss Lillie Frismuth, of Chestnut Street, the Misses Lewis, of Pine Street, and Miss Dougherty, of Spruce Street. If I had stayed in the rut, to-day I might have owned a little home near Manayunk and commuted, and contributed to the *Musical Banner*, and despite the dustiness of my intellectuals might have been happy with a galloping gang of grandchildren. Qui sait?

About this time I met Theodore Presser, who, as everyone knows, has started musical orphan asylums, homes for reformed musicians, and sanatoriums for hands lamed by excessive use of the thumbs on the black keys. Then, Mr. Presser was a lean, hungry-looking man with his head full of half-crazy schemes; at least, they seemed so to me. He had started a musical monthly whose pulse, temperature, and respiration he watched as if it had been a chick in an incubator. And it was a chick of uncertain health. I wrote paragraphs for it; betimes, I spread my wings and flew to the editorial roost and sounded my little cock-a-doodle-doo. My salary was as ever, nothing; but Theodore let me splash about in his pond and I was contented. Many nights we went to the post-office there anxiously to open letters. What a hurrah of joy when a dollar bill was found for an annual sub-scription! Presser, who is the Henry Ford of Philadel-phia sheet-music, saw further ahead than I. *The Etude* has a subscription list that must make envious even Mr. Bok. Presser did it all with his canny Yankee patience and shrewdness. He knew that the daughter of the plumber, the daughter of the policeman, hankered after music, and he deliberately built a machine to cater to their needs. The curious part of it is that he really improved their taste. The most famous pianists con-tribute to *The Etude*, are read and inwardly digested. I am in hopes that if these "few lines may meet his eye" —as they say in manuals of writing made easy for servant-girls—that he will give me a bed for my old bones in one of his eleemosynary institutions. You never can tell. A music-teacher, a music-critic, an au-thor—the very gods fight against them in the heavens.

But matters were coming to a climax. If Miss Brew-ster had defined my wishes, given them pith and point, where great writers on whom I leaned did not, it was be-cause her book touched responsive chords. This con-tinuing explanation of mine must strike you as an apology for my native indecision, and, as Leslie Stephen says: "An apology sometimes is worse than a satire." Further to muddle my affairs was a disinclination to make money. My father often declared that if I saw a ten-dollar bill coming to greet me I would run away. I have changed since then. I like money. Who doesn't? I spend it, believing that it's bad luck to save. But to pass our interval between two eternities raking in gold is simply absurd to me. I have always worked for leisure to waste time. I know of some families, not bohemian in their habits, who are never more than a few dollars ahead during their lifetime. I am in that class, living from day to day on the industry of my pen. It seems ridiculous, and it is perilous. Life at best is a dangerous adventure, and I think that the modern gladiator should change the old formula and cry in the arena: O Death! those who are about to live, salute thee. Schopenhauer—who has been wittily described by Paul Bourget as "Chamfort à la choucroute"—argued that philosophers more than other men should have means ample enough to allow them leisure. It is time, not money, that is the true treasure of life. Our sole recompense is to have lived, but to have lived as we elect, not as the other fellow tells us to. Ay! there's the rub. And, as there is nothing so much to be feared as fear of fear, then money is the solvent. Without it you fear, yes, fear. I dodged my duties like the moral skulker that I was, not knowing then that the hawthorn must grow with the spirit of the triangle in it, else not be hawthorn; that the "honey-harp," the bee as Thoreau calls it, remains valiantly a bee till its final exit to honey-heaven. But I didn't moralise during the middle seventies. I roared like a serpent, and hissed like a lion—a clothes-line; and I avoided every opportunity where money might be acquired. I see now it was because of my absorption in a few ideas, which to-day I repudiate. The leopard does change its spots once in a while despite the adage.

Suddenly I decided that life held nothing so precious as Paris. To help matters along, I offered myself as a clerk in a piano house. It was the Chickering piano agency at the corner of Chestnut and Thirteenth Streets, where Wanamaker's now stands. Mr. William D. Dutton, still spry and little changed by the passing of forty years, was associated with his father, William H. Dutton, in the business. It was a pleasant wareroom. I arrived at 6 A. M., went to the basement, and two hours later, after my travail with finger exercises and Czerny studies, I was ready for the day's toil. It was light. Young Mr. Dutton, who had a flair for the artistic, played the piano with taste and possessed an excellent technique. His father, a handsome old gentleman with a fresh complexion, would say as his son played: "He studied the Hummel school. It's the only one." That is true; it is the only one in which to acquire pearly scales, but it is otherwise inadequate. When customers entered I had to accost them. Once I was showing off my paces on a second-hand instrument before a prospective purchaser, a woman, whose face expressed repugnance. Mr. Dutton supervened: "James," he suggested, "clean that case with the feather-duster. I'll show the lady the piano"; and he began playing Gottschalk's "Cradle Song" with a touch that melted her heart. She bought the piano. After she went away he said to me with a characteristic glance over his eye-glasses, "It all depends on the way it's done, young man. If your touch is too truthful with a shaky old piano you will never sell it." It was a grand lesson in worldly ethics for me. I never forgot it. And when I read Ibsen's statement that all truths grow old or stale after twenty years, I think of Mr. Dutton and his second-hand piano.

"Our America is here or nowhere," says the poet. We are the supermen. Why wait for another century to prove it. "You must live in the present, launch yourself on any wave; find your eternity in each moment." I hadn't read Thoreau then, but Irish-like, I determined to take the bull by both the horns of dilemma. I was like the poet's cloud, "which moveth altogether if it moves at all." I actually sickened for Paris. It was in 1878, the year of the first Exposition since the Franco-Prussian War, France was en fête. Best of all, Liszt was named honorary director of the Hungarian section at the Trocadéro. An impulse throttled me. Why not steal away between two days, sail to Paris, see Liszt and die? The Liszt cult was strong in our household. For my mother he was the Abbé Liszt, for my father a grotesque daddy-long-legs, or a centipede. His picture showed us one of those faces that had become hardened in the pitiless glare of the public glance. Nevertheless, he was a cult, and a cult, as has been wisely remarked, is always annoying to those who do not join in it, and generally hurtful to those who do. But, oh! to see him, to hear him play. I began to manœuvre. I sold my beloved books. I parted with my pictures. I scraped and saved and stared in the windows of steamship offices. It was to be a stealthy departure, an egotistic elopement, with a melancholy alibi of the soul. At last I was to "Drive a straight furrow and come to the true measure of man" (I had been reading Theocritus, his Hylas). To attain the necessary courage I became reticent, avoided my friends and family. Anyone with a half eye would have noted my nervous behaviour and watched me. That was precisely what happened. I packed my few clothes in a handbag and was caught in the act by my brother, Paul, who, always realistic, asked: "What's her name?" Art, I might have replied, but with Macchiavellian casuistry asked him in turn: "Who won the game to-day?" Finally, I boldly marched into the agency of the French line, and bought for $28 a ticket in the fourth class of the *Canada*, sailing September 25, 1878. There are some dates that are unforgetable. You may forget the name of your divorced wife; but your first ocean trip—never! (That is, if you are a person of sentiment.) I expected to make a "clean getaway," as they say in superior criminal circles, but I was balked, and by my own imprudence. Early in the morning—the steamer was to leave New York about 2 P.M. —I awoke my parents and told them of my plan. They consented with suspicious alacrity, after interposing the usual objections; my youth, my health (I had, still have, the constitution of an ox; knock wood!). It was settled. Rejoicing, I awoke my brother, who made comments unfit to print. At the Pennsylvania Railroad station, then at Thirty-second and Market Streets, a few friends saw us off—I was in the custody of brother John— Alfredo Barili among the rest. New York reached, I went on board. Ring down the curtain on old Philadelphia!

I have written enough to give you a fair idea of my mental and physical characteristics, so that you will judge the critic as he should be. This is the method suggested by Hennequin, of which I told you. A moral précis of the critic and a peep at his temperament, then much that is dark becomes light. As for the modesty of the method? Such a monster as a modest author does not exist. Perhaps one is mentioned in history, but he was so morbidly modest that he forgot to write his book. Therefore, accept my chattering as a thing to be expected. I am an optimist at bottom, with a superficial coating of pessimism, which thaws near a piano, a pretty girl, or a glass of Pilsner. Without hope it is impossible to achieve the hopeless. I believe that anyone who has sung a song of hope has his prayer answered; indeed, William James has said that no prayer is unanswered; when it is uttered the relief (liberation of nervous energy) is instantaneous. But I loathe the fixed grin on the faces of those cheerful humbugs, adherents of cheerful cults, pollyannas, and other bores. These people want you to be happy against your will. Time works prodigies, but the hypocrite never dies. "Les gros bataillons ont toujours raison," wrote Jomini, and this must be, not alone in the battle-field, but in peaceful life—charlatans are always in the majority, charlatans and imbeciles. I have spent my life in tilting at them, and at times I am afraid to look at the mirror.

Maeterlinck asks: "Are you of those who name or only repeat names?" I fear I am one of the repeaters. No man is a hero to his wife (if they have been married long enough), and I think that no writer should be a hero to his readers. It is an impressive pose—that of omniscience, or lofty morals. But a whited sepulchre is soon deprived of its whitewash. If a critic can't be human, then let him become a pedicure or a bugologist. Swinburne said: "I have never been able to see what should attract a man to the profession of criticism but the noble pleasure of praising"—and then he went out and slew his enemies (critics and authors) by the hun-dreds. He had the most vitriolic pen in England. It sounds magnanimous, but neither praise nor blame should be the goal of the critic. To spill his own soul, that should be his aim. Notwithstanding the talk about objective criticism, no such abstraction is thinkable. A critic relates his prejudices, nothing more. It is well to possess prejudices. They lend to life a meaning. For example, consider my eclecticism. In Edgar Quinet's romance, Merlin, we read of a visit made by the magician to Prester John at his abbey. This abbey is an astounding conglomeration of architectures—pagoda, mosque, basilica, Greek temple, synagogue, cathedral, Byzantine and Gothic chapels, minarets, towers, turrets in bewildering array. Prester John is a venerable man with a long white beard: "Upon his head he wore a turban with a sapphire cross. At his neck hung a golden crescent, and he supported himself upon a staff after the manner of a Brahmin. Three children followed him, who carried each upon the breast, an open book. The first was the collection of the Vedas, the second was the Bible, the third the Koran. At certain moments Prester John stopped and read a few lines from one of the sacred volumes; after which he continued his walk, his eyes fixed upon the stars." Of course, he stumped his toe against the actual, as do all mystics. Eclectic is my taste in creeds and cultures. And in cultured eclecticism may be found the shallows and depths, defects and virtues of our times. I am the child of my century, and can echo Mallarmé: "Hélas! J'ai lu tous les livres." But I had set my feet upon the trail of Bohemia, the fabulous "sea-coast" that lures most men. You may be as prudish as an oyster, as patient as a prostitute, as sober as a Judge (naturally a Judge who doesn't drink), but you shall not escape a touch of lunar folly when young girls sometimes with the seal of their solitudes see the moon in company with their sweethearts—little shocks without words, not by Mendelssohn; but it suffices for the lads to see the girls. My moonshine came from the Seven Arts; they are indigenous to Bohemia. Where is Bohemia? Is it a state, not of soul, but of the purse? Perhaps, again I was to discover it through disenchanting experience. Later I knew that there is only one way to become a perfect Bohemian; lead the existence of a sober sedentary bourgeois, with cobbler's wax on your chair, grease on your elbow, sweat on your brow, and, what the metaphysicians call the Will-to-Sit-Still. Then you may write a book, master music, or play on your intellectual instrument to perfection as Henry James puts it. But I hear the "all ashore" whistle. All aboard for Paris!

PART II

PARIS FORTY YEARS AGO

I

I'M AFLOAT

Behold me afloat at last on that good old tub, long since sent to the scrap-heap, the *Canada* of the Compagnie Générale Transatlantique, with my heart full of hope, my eyes turned eastward, my wallet not too heavy, and few clothes. My brother John took aside the chief steward of the quatrième classe and tipped him. A swift survey had told him that I was in for trouble, and perhaps, he thought it would open my eyes all the sooner to realities. That fourth-class on the outward-bound steamship politely masked its true name; it was the steerage, nothing more, nothing less. At the age of thirty I would have revolted at the smells, the dirt, the promiscuity, but youth swallows trouble and I was not disgusted. It was life. And I meant to live. It soon proved to be life, of all sorts. We slept in bunks, not beds, with no protection from the prying gaze of neighbours. Our steward rigged up a calico curtain for my couch, as if I were a girl. The men made rude commentaries. We were segregated; the women were across the corridor. When I read Stevenson's Amateur Emigrant I admired his art, though wondered at his dodging of disagreeable details. His description is rose-coloured. But a steerage, even the best, and the French Line was not so bad as the worst, is horrible. I confess when bedtime came that I was rather blue about the gills. The smell, a medley of bad tobacco, alcohol, unwashed bodies, vile breaths—phew! I must have been copper-lined and

213

riveted to stand the combination. Every port-hole was closed; we had struck a bit of rough water, and the wind was freshening. The gabbling died away. Lights were out. I clutched my pocketbook and fell into a doze. It didn't last, noises awoke me. The ship was pitching, and oh! brethren, what followed I shan't record, except one word—seasickness. I've crossed forty odd times and never have I been, in fair weather or foul, seasick. That night tried my nerves. I went on deck to escape nausea, and at once felt better. My nose had nearly proved me coward.

Next morning I sought the head steward and asked him why I was covered with little red spots. He at once explained that the salt air affected the blood, that —"but," I interrupted "the salt air doesn't run over the bed with legs, does it?" My crudeness made him blush. "Ah, Monsieur," he deprecatingly replied, "some things must be. The fare is cheap, and if you find certain other passengers, well—the company doesn't charge extra for their passage." It was now my turn to blush. I was drop-ripe in my verdancy, but the cynicism of this elderly person pained me. What a rascal he was. He plundered me of my five-franc pieces, whether in making change or charging for extras—tobacco, coffee. The wine was free. It was also poisonous. I ordered a better vintage —a vin bleu that rasped my throat, but I could get it down. When I saw the sea it was as flat as a temperance lecture, I was disappointed because of its wet monotony. I quoted Landor to help me out: "Is this the mighty ocean?—is this all?" Like the girl in the Stendhal novel who found love insipid, I felt like asking: "Is that all?" I wished for this same monotony a week later when we nosed into a gale that kept us under cover

for two days, swept a seaman into the water, and banged
things generally. Then I saw my fellow travellers without their daily posing. A ship is the same all over as
far as human nature is concerned. The first day I had
walked the decks, and was not held up at the various
barriers because I may have been better dressed than
my companions; but the second day out I was asked for
my ticket and peremptorily bidden to go to the deck
below. I resented the manner of the chap, who wasn't
precisely rough, but, as I thought, too sharp. Did he
take me for the cattle herded forward? I soon learned
that when you travel fourth-class you are considered
fourth-class, with all its implications. It was my first
contact with social distinctions. I didn't like it. The
third and fourth class mingled on the same deck, though
we ate and slept apart; second-class was almost aristocratic; first-class in the empyrean. After I had been
turned out of first-class I sat down on the second deck;
this time I was chased away, much to the satisfaction of
my fourth-class contemporaries. I was ignorant of rules,
but they thought I was putting on airs, and therefore de-
served a rebuke, but as I didn't attempt to play the disguised nobleman or reduced gentleman, I was soon received into the guild of dirt and poverty as if I belonged
there. I did. I was presently as unkempt as my associates. I sported a Scotch cap, went collarless, wore a
flannel shirt, and my hands and face did not shine from
soap. I defy anyone to keep neat in such circumstances.

The crowd wasn't a bad one; it was poor, and had
neither time nor inclination to wash. "Personal dirti-
ness is the real and permanent dividing line of classes . . .
there is no social equality between the clean and dirty.
The question of physical purity lies at the root of the

real democratic problem," wrote Havelock Ellis. Cleanliness is greater than godliness, and I have always noted that the more superstitious a religion the filthier its followers. What surprises me now is to remember with what ease I reflected the colour (a black and tan) of the society in which I found myself. There was the usual mixture. A dozen black-sheep, some members of good families, who left home in disgrace because of gambling debts or women scandals, and were returning in a still more disgraceful state. Then there were a half-dozen families who had saved enough to retire to their own departments in the provinces and live "en bourgeois," a dream realised. Two theological students on their way to Rome via Paris added variety to the personnel. I must explain that they, like the families I speak of, were in the third-class. Economy was their shibboleth. As I seemed fairly decent (I brushed my hair every day) I was admitted, though not without reservations, into the aristocracy of the steerage. Our voyage was not unpleasant; even in Hades good company counts. The early rising was the worst part of the day, the sleeping-quarters smelled to heaven; but once on deck life became bearable. That first breakfast, a bowl of coffee and a stale roll—how it went down! The waiting between meals was trying to healthy young stomachs. Soup, boiled beef, beans, a litre of wine and bread "at discretion"—I ate it by the yard—comprised the second breakfast; better was the dinner, a function as well as a "feed." We had a roast of some kind, fresh vegetables, and more wine; without that blessed wine the food would have gone begging. The promenade on deck was quite fashionable. I have many times since watched such perambulations from an upper deck; now I was one of

the dramatis personæ. We had no smoking-room, hud-
dling in the corridors when the weather was unfavourable.
Have you noticed that a war, a calamity, brings humanity
to a common level? What cared we if the upper-decks
looked down at us condescendingly! We were the real
passengers; the others only phantoms.

The "life of the ship" was also with us. Above decks
he is known as the "joy of the smoking-room"; sometimes
he is a "she." Our social hero was a suspicious scamp
in rags, a polylinguist, a cultivated man of the world,
unshaven, unshorn, with polished manners, and a tongue
hung in the middle. He gave himself out as a gold pros-
pector from the West, where he had staked out a claim,
but—inevitably—had been robbed of it by his evil partners while he was sick with fever. In fact, the old legend,
and related with such authority, such a profusion of
details, that he won our respect and was nicknamed the
"millionaire." He borrowed our cigarettes, our wine,
our loose cash. Had he not an uncle, a wealthy banker
in the Rue de Provénce? When our passage tickets
were collected he disappeared. I fancy he had bribed
the steward; certainly he was a stowaway. But he bore
a charmed life and only once did I see him discomfited.
He had made a jesting remark about religion to the
theological students, and found himself sprawling on the
deck; one of the pair, a husky Irish lad with a fist of
iron, had knocked the farceur down. A sadly black eye
kept him quiet for a few hours, and then he sought our
sympathy by pointing to the swollen pouch under his
eye and gaily declaring that he received it in a worthy
cause—"pour le bon Jésus-Christ"; but the students
were always on the other side of the boat when he ventured on this sorry witticism.

II

IN PARIS AT LAST

We entered the roads of Havre, October 6, and the next day we were in Paris. Havre detained us because the chief steward, with the "favoris," side whiskers, wished to show us that city. It was my first taste of French life. Everything seemed miraculous. Not only had I the "innocence of the eye" but an innocent palate; the native cuisine opened my eyes as well as my throat. Cookery, too, is one of the Seven Arts. The French have made it an art. We went to a gingerbread fair, an imitation of the fair at Vincennes, and sought our beds in a condition of inflamed sobriety. I remember leaning from the window of my wretched little bedroom and listening to a woman singing in the back alley. She had tears in her voice, and her voice was riddled by rum. I fell asleep in a fever of contentment which even the awakening in a chilly drab dawn did not dispel. After a bowl of onion soup, the regulation remedy, we boarded our train, third-class compartments. I had gone up in the social scale, had mounted just one rung on the ladder. Drizzling rain fell as we entered the Gare St. Lazare at five o'clock in the evening. Paris, after we had passed the bridge of the Batignolles, was not very attractive. Those high tenements—they seemed so in 1878 as compared with houses in Philadelphia—on either side of the railroad yards are still to be seen; each time I return to them I experience the same sinking of the heart. That first night in Paris left a bad taste in my mouth; perhaps

Havre had something to do with it. I had attached myself to one of the families, and after patrolling the grand
boulevard we found ourselves as far as the Boulevard
de Sébastopol. We had passed through the Rue St.
Lazare and, naturally, stopped for a "consommation"
at some café with tables on the street. The lights—
electricity was coming into use, the Jablochkoff lights on
the Avenue d'l'Opéra set the fashion—the cleanliness of
the establishment, the bustle of the waiters serving
thirsty people, who had fresh coloured faces, much impressed me. Even then I noted that the nation had
made eating and drinking human. Sociability was ra-
tionalised. The drunken man abounds on the globe
but less in Europe than elsewhere.

Exhausted by the terrible noise, the horns of the big
buses, I followed in the wake of my comrades. There
were halts, hesitations, and tentative sallies into cheap
hotels. We all had an address "highly recommended,"
and argued at corners while I, like one of those dogs that
follows a mob till it falls, sat on my valise and patiently
waited. Gendarmes were consulted and politely showed
us various lodging-houses. This amiability on the part
of policemen set me to wondering. Not a trace of hos-
tility or surliness. It was "Monsieur, par ici! Monsieur, par là!" as the men of our party wrangled with
their wives. My French I had already discovered on
shipboard was not the language spoken in France. I
understood the general meaning of a phrase, which I
persisted answering in a loud voice. Our business was
settled by the diplomacy of a hotel proprietor who saw
that to a dozen souls he could make concessions. He
diplomatically invited us to a drink, claret in bottles
this time, and the ladies said that he was "très gentil."

He was. He was also a common or garden variety of swindler when we paid our bills a day later. I, in particular, was a lamb led to the shearing. My wool was depleted. Confused, raging, I said a few things to him that astonished my companions, who understood American profanity. Come, come, that's too strong! The game isn't worth the candle. Perhaps we are in the wrong. Paris is much more expensive than in 1860! Thus I was pacified by one of my friends. The French stuck to their countrymen. I had been robbed, petty larceny of the meanest sort, but, after all, what could I expect? I was only a Yankee! Thoroughly disgusted with the crowd and the surroundings, I paid the bill, hailed a fiacre, and drove to Drexel, Harjes & Cie. I had definitely ruptured with the fourth-class and had become a bourgeois overnight.

I found letters at the bankers'. Well-dressed people read newspapers in the waiting-rooms. The place wore a hospitable air. I was with my own race once more. My letters filled me with joy. Philadelphia became the pivot of the planet. I saw my family through the sentimental haze of years; twelve days' absence seemed a century. Best of all, for I was a pragmatist, was the command of the Philadelphia Drexel house to pay me a certain sum, not much, but a "magot" as they say. My mother, I knew, had been active in this matter. I've forgotten my first evening spent in Paris with the immigrants, but I do know that when alone, I went to the Jardin Mabille, on the boulevard. I can boast that I saw the last of that famous establishment though it was dull diversion. During the Second Empire it had entertained the world with its wickedness. I searched with the ardour and curiosity of a green youth for that same wickedness. I only attended its obsequies. A dozen fat, stale, and unfair women pranced around to the noisy music of a band. Offenbach was still in vogue, but it was like corked champagne, this music. The men dancers looked like professionals. The Latin quarter masquerade wouldn't have deceived even a reader of that bogus bohemian romance, Trilby. But Trilby was unwritten, I was young, and presently I was sitting before the buffet drinking expensive vintages in company with an accomplished young lady, of at least forty-five, wearing a blonde wig and a professional grimace. I paid for the refreshment, "Garçon, deux bocks!" and my accent was so outlandish that M'lle Claire—her real name, she solemnly assured me—forced me to repeat phrases so that the waiter might join in the fun. Wicked! Why, the dear old aunt wasn't as wicked as a village-pump. She became maternal and confidently told me that as a fool and his money are soon parted, I had better go home to my mamma. My vanity wounded, I took her advice, tipped the waiter, ordered a fresh beer for Claire and, bowing in my best Gallic manner, I hastily went away. I looked back as I turned the corner. The lady, the waiter, the lady cashier at the desk, were staring in my direction. They were not jeering. I must have impressed them as something so indescribably provincial that they held their breath. And I, who fancied myself "rigolo" with my Scotch cap, velveteen coat, flaring necktie, low collar, baggy breeches! Wasn't I the picture of a Latin quarter student or artist? I had read Henri Murger's Vie de Bohême, and believed myself the real thing. Alas! Claire and the greedy waiter didn't agree with me, and my guardian angel being "on the job," I went to my hotel in an irritable humour. But I had seen the historical Jardin Mabille, had spoken to one of its houris, and instead of dazzling wickedness, I had been sent away with a sermon in my ear. In this individual case Lecky was right when he called the harlot the protector of the home.

The next morning not feeling in the least like a "brand plucked from the burning," I went to the friends of my parents. They had made a fortune in Philadelphia, first in the sewing-machine industry, where Mr. Lefevre found himself an associate of George W. Childs. He was one of the early fashionable dressmakers of the town, and his imported Worth gowns brought him fame and money. In 1878 he returned with his wife—an adorable Frenchwoman—and children to Paris and lived up in the Quarter of Europe, which is at the top of the Rue de Rome, and close to the boulevards, Batignolles and Clichy. I was received with open arms. Letters had evidently preceded me. My education was taken in hand and I was not allowed to speak English, so I spent the day mumbling my Broad Street Academy French. Mr. Lefevre, one of those natty Parisians, white-bearded and insouciant, who are gay at four-score—he wasn't much over sixty—first showed me the town. But he was less interested in the architecture, statues, the Louvre, or Cluny, than in the passing crowd. He was a seasoned inhabitant and registered many nuances for me in moral and physical Paris. I learned not only classes and masses, but salient characteristics of the day and night life. We went all over the city. I became a cockney, a "badaud." I knew both sides of the river, the exterior boulevards, the faubourgs. Above all, I became intimately acquainted with the interior of churches. The Lefevres were religious. Every day I was trotted to church, and

as every other day is Saint's day in France, I often went
to High Mass. At first it was St. Augustin, then the
Trinity. I compromised on a chapel in the vicinity, St.
Marie des Batignolles. I hadn't come to Paris for its
piety. The enforced visits, confessions, and other commendable practices were irksome, in the end, and I rebelled. The Lefevre family moved to the country, and
I was left to my own devices, though I gladly visited
them at Villiers-le-Bel, on the northern railroad. Madame Lefevre was solicitous about the state of my soul;
she had promised my mother to look after me, when, if
the truth be told, my soul wasn't worth the powder to
blow it to Halifax. I kicked over the traces and determined to "live my own life," as they say in Ibsen plays.
And a nice mess I made of matters.

III

THE MAISON BERNARD

As I only had a small allowance I could not live where I should have lived. It was Mr. Lefevre who found me lodging in an old barracks on the Rue Puteaux, No. 5, off the Batignolles boulevard. It was kept by a dwarf hunchback with flaming eyes and tumbled hair. The house was not inviting in aspect or cleanliness. I was assigned a small chamber on the top floor, fifth story. The room barely accommodated a bed, wash-stand, armoire, the glass of which filled me with pride, my modest clothes, and a tiny upright piano, made by an Alsatian manufacturer, I think Kriegelstein was the name. Later a second-hand stove was bought and I was in daily danger of burning the house down when I made a fire—really a big smoke and a roaring sound of flames for ten minutes. I ranged my few precious books on the sill of my solitary window. I looked over a garden, and the usual array of chimney-pots. The climate was then, as it always is, abominable in Paris. Gay Paris is a figment of fiction writers. The gaiety is in the hearts of the inhabitants, not in the leaden skies. The cold of winter is more penetrating than ours, because it is damp, because the sun seldom shines, because houses are not heated as in America. Rain is the daily programme. Fall and winter are always wet. Spring is the best period, for summer, notwithstanding the popular belief to the contrary, is hot, sticky, and uncomfortable, all the more so since baths are for the well-to-do. Forty years ago this was the rule. The old apartments had no conveniences. I paid the munificent sum of fifteen francs a week for my room, and as my income didn't go higher than five francs a day I hadn't much left. Indeed, a period of hardship set in. I was to learn the exact value of five centimes, and how to make that amount go as far as possible. I forgot to say that bed-linen was not included in my weekly rental. The landlord, whose name was Bernard, was an Alsatian, and lived in the house. He supplied wine and table-board to his lodgers. At first I ate at cheap restaurants, gargottes, places frequented by coachmen, workmen, or in wine houses where for a fixed price you were given a copious bouillon—I don't think the Duval establishments were then in existence—boiled beef and carrots, one potato, and a big bottle of cheap wine for the sum of one franc. Those were not expensive times. France was rapidly recovering from the shock of the war with Prussia, and prosperity filled hearts with hope.

In my new home there was an old couple, the Grandjeans, he a retired functionary, living on a small pension, she, after a half century of petty economies and married life, a brave and devoted wife. They had one pleasure left. On Sundays they dined "en ville" with their son and his family. They were very proud of him. He, too, was a government employee, who bid fair to tread in the snail trail of his father. One thing disquieted the worthy pair. Their son had two children, the regulation number of a French household; it was the prospect of additions that made the grandmother unhappy. "Ah! Monsieur," she would say to me on the landing when we got our water-supply, "my daughter-in-law is again a troubled woman." Another mouth to feed. I was duly sympathetic. On Sundays they would mount the long flight of stairs at nine o'clock, and I could tell from their upward march whether matters had gone awry. Please don't think I was a Paul Pry, "snooping" about my neighbours' affairs; the truth is I left my door open to get more liberty, as I was in narrow quarters. I usually finished dressing in the hall. When I played more than ten hours a day on the tinpan piano, I was reminded that other people had their rights by a volley of old shoes, or loud cries of "get out," and such expressions of displeasure. I was too superior, too absorbed, to bother with these unmusical persons. The Grandjeans were politer. Madame told me that my practice made her dream of the siege when the Prussians bombarded the city. I thanked her.

I went on long walks with her husband, who escorted me to the Panthéon, the Invalides, the Tuileries, all the public buildings and monuments. One afternoon, after I had seen the reparations of the Tuileries, I asked how long it had been before the Prussians evacuated Paris. "Ah! young man," and he mournfully shook his venerable hand, "the boches didn't do all that mischief. I regret to say it was our own people, the communards."

Music was my chief pleasure. Hunger was also a focal-point in my consciousness. I was not in actual want, and with the exercise of a little prudence I had enough to keep the wolf from the back door; but he gnawed at my vitals, and not boasting Spartan fortitude, I was usually famished the last week of the month because I spent my allowance too soon. I ate so much at the little wine house that the woman who ran the place insinuatingly said: "Monsieur perhaps is suffering from a tapeworm." It was merely a delicate hint that I must not exceed my privilege of more than a yard of bread at a meal, a thing difficult to do; Paris bread in long sticks is appetising. Those few days of the month, how they tested my stomach! I could have gone to the Lefevres, but the railway fares cost too much, and then I had a few sparks of pride left in me. I repeated the words of Turenne, but they weren't very filling: "Thou tremblest, carcass!" Many afternoons I remained in bed with a heavy volume of Chopin's music on my stomach. It was a lazy equivalent for the belt strapped in. I had my chocolate, I smoked and I read. An unsatisfactory proceeding this one full meal a day, yet I worked, walked, was fairly content. Youth! The hunchback proprietor was kind. Occasionally, after I had paid my rent with approximate punctuality, he would invite me to déjeuner at noon, a royal feast. I never refused him. At his table I met a queer crew, chiefly Alsatians. German and French were spoken without prejudice, barring the provincial accent. There were a half-dozen couples, young people, who, not securing their parents' consent, had left home with their sweethearts and lived in Paris until they reached the age of twenty-five, when they could marry. And some of them did. No one was scandalised. They were all hard-working, fairly sober, and the men had the courage of their concubines. "We are too poor to marry," one of them, a house painter, informed me. They were devoted to their partners, and the monotonies of married life were much in evidence. Even in the atmospheric adulteries of the Henry James novels one may trace the platitudes of matrimony. To all intents and purposes these peasants, transplanted in Paris, were as securely bound together as if church and state had been invoked in the matter.

But after I had lived a winter with them I detected

rifts in their domestic lutes. Papa Bernard was married to a midwife who conducted her establishment across the Seine. She promptly appeared at dinner time, seven o'clock, possibly to look the boarders over. She had a ferocious eye for business. Her husband was henpecked; there was a reason. Every afternoon he had a habit of disappearing. I would keep house, enjoying the snugness and warmth of the dining-room where there was a battered upright piano. After the maid-of-all-work, a disreputable young female, would clear the table and go to her cupboard, there to wash the dishes and troll out some obscene song she had heard in company with her little soldier while walking around the fortifications, I would play to drown her voice. Bernard, after enduring the noise, would take off his wooden sabots and in his slippers would steal up-stairs, first placing an index finger on his nose in a significant way, as one should say: Watch, wait, tell my wife I've gone out! Once the midwife came in unexpectedly. Luckily, I was not there. The row that ensued must have been terrific. One young couple left the house the next morning. I feared to ask the reason. M. Bernard also drank.

But I didn't always dine luxuriously. I continued to rove and forage, and as that noble American institution, free-lunch, was unknown, I had little to spare when rent day arrived. One night a fellow-lodger took me to the Halles, the central markets, and after a tour through the labyrinths, which Zola faithfully describes in Le Ventre de Paris, he showed me a trick that I shall never forget. We found ourselves behind one of the halls, with a dozen vagabonds, one in shabby evening dress and top-boots, but bare-headed, mostly human wrecks,

drunkards and outlaws from society. They were in
jolly mood, evidently cognac of the worst sort was in
their veins. They were hungry. Like a band of wolves
we watched a big cauldron over a fire, in which sim-
mered a mass of meat and vegetables, the scourings of
the butcher's block and huckster's droppings. Fire and
water are purifying, and this indescribable olla-podrida
fumed and bubbled and sent to our nostrils a most tempting odour. A human hog in rags stirred the pot-au-feu
with a baton fit for a wash boiler. As he stirred he
hoarsely chanted: "One cent a try, one cent only."
The trial was this: as the whirling mass tossed up fragments of flesh, hunks of fat, potatoes, or carrots, you
jabbed at them with a long wooden fork, and what you
prodded on the prongs was yours. Only one cent. It
would have been amusing if it hadn't been horrible.
The gambling instinct, as well as hunger, was appealed to,
and the low price proved an irresistible combination.
I found it so. I speared like my neighbours and had
fair luck, a lump of veal, which I ate with good appetite.
No bread. No wine. These we found across the street.
I never returned to this slop-bucket lottery.

It wasn't necessary, my prospects were decidedly
brightening. I sent a letter to the Philadelphia *Evening
Bulletin*, and it was printed through the intermediacy of
Ferdinand Fetherston. It was dated from Paris, November 14, 1878. The banal letter of a young writer,
beginning: "Paris! beautiful Paris!" with lots of gasps
and exclamation points. These weekly letters lasted till
the following summer. They were edited by my mother,
who wrote a pure, flowing English, as her writings tell
me. I was in the torturing grip of Carlyle then, and my
contorted prose shadowed his excesses. My mother

warned me against this aping of a great man's style, and,
no doubt, would have approved of Matthew Arnold's
advice to Frederic Harrison: "Flee Carlylese as the
very devil." I didn't and concocted tortuous phrases
to my heart's content. Newman was upheld as a model
of grace and limpidity, but it was too early for the great
cardinal and prose-master. However, there was no great
trace of the fuliginous Carlyle in these letters. To be
frank, I think I wrote with more simplicity than now.
Life has intervened. The same preoccupation with the
arts may be found, also the same speed, vocabulary, and
lack of sequence. We change less than we think, and the
child is sometimes more sincere than the man. The
best thing about this new connection was the five dollars
it brought with each contribution. Twenty-five francs!
And remember that four decades ago in Paris, this amount
almost equalled twenty-five dollars in purchasing power.
I was a nabob when my monthly cheque arrived. I
would stroll into Drexel's after a glorious banquet con-
sisting of Chateaubriand beefsteak—the French are loyal
to their poets and celebrities, not to mention war vic-
tories; think of La Pompadour, of Madame Récamier,
Sauce à la Marengo, Mazagran of coffee—this from a siege
in Algiers—and other soups, gowns, corsets, and desserts
—washed down with Burgundy, together with radishes
and butter, Brussels sprouts, cheese and Mocha. How
I swaggered home and boasted of my déjeuner! I gave
up the cheaper restaurants and ate at the liberal table of
Papa Bernard, where I was received with the peculiar
consideration accorded newly-acquired riches.

IV

MADAME BEEFSTEAK

Then I fell in love. Not a novelty, but each new girl creates that illusion. It was hardly a "grande passion," this infatuation, only the reactions of two young persons thrown together at a common place, a Parisian table d'hôte. Contiguity breeds familiarity. I sat next to a handsome girl of twenty, a girl who had been a bonne. She wore the white cap of a servant, and behaved with the utmost circumspection. She lived in a hall-room on the floor below me, and had as a companion a nasty yapping dog which she petted and called "P-paul" after Paul de Cassagnac, then in the public eye as a publicist, politician, and duellist. P-paul hated me. I loathed the brute, which sat on the lap of his mistress at table. Whenever I spoke to the young woman I heard a growl. Nevertheless, I talked and she listened, fascinated by my fluent and fearful French. An intimacy followed. She was the only unattached female in the house. Of her antecedents I knew little. She told me that her baptismal name was Coralie; that's all. M. Bernard would slyly smile at us, the boarders took our friendship as a matter of course. Yet we never met except at the midday-breakfast and at dinner. Even Mother Bernard, with her beak of a bird of prey would regard us with a shrewd eye. Heaven knows why! She may have been anticipating future events. So platonic was my intercourse with Coralie that when I innocently invited her to hear a little music—sitting in the hall, be it understood, as my room wasn't large enough for two—she refused rather testily I thought, telling me that M. Bernard was very strict regarding the morals of his household—the infernal hypocrite!—but couldn't we take a little promenade some afternoon? Now, suspicious reader, you must not imagine anything wicked. Those guilty asterisks * * * much admired by novelists and suggesting naughtiness, I shall not use, for the reason that we never promenaded. It wasn't necessary. I disliked her animal, and the only time she went out of doors was to give P-paul necessary exercise. Her eyes—Coralie's—were large and like hard-boiled eggs. She had a well-shaped head, regular features, scarlet lips and tiny ears. Small ears are the shepherd's warning morning or evening. In a woman they spell selfishness, and a selfish man should never marry a woman like himself. This I told myself as I looked at Coralie. Uselessly, for I lost my head and made love to her. My tactics were simple. I had observed her fondness for rare beefsteak, an unusual taste in a Frenchwoman. I treated her every day to beefsteak. It went on my bill, and the bone belonged to the dog. Soon I paid for her déjeuner, but halted there. She hinted at hard luck, at dinners not within the compass of her purse. I was obdurate. Had I not grazed starvation? All went well till spring. Then I experienced a surprise.

The family had nicknamed her Madame Bifsteck, because of her carnivorous propensity, and by consequence I was called Monsieur Beefsteak. The dog remained plain dog till his next sausage—karma. With warmer weather my stove became an impediment; because of it I was forced to put on my shirt in the hall. A burst of generosity made me offer it to Madame Bifsteck. Her eyes shone like glorious lamps. I was assured that she loved me. I paid for another rare steak. We were almost happy. And then came the disagreeable surprise. One evening, after dinner, as we sipped our liqueurs, a burly coachman entered, whip in hand, and saluted the company. A swift exchange of glances. "It's her husband," some one whispered to me. "Le mari!" that name consecrated by melodrama. My Coralie's husband! Horrible. He was nearly seven feet high, weighed two hundred and fifty pounds, at least, wore the capes and glazed high hat of his profession, and also the professional red mug. He was drunk, indeed, was never sober, and odd to relate, when he opened his mouth to speak, I expected to hear a rich Irish brogue, so much like a Dublin jaunting-car driver did he look. But he spoke French mixed with the argot of the quarter. An awe-inspiring creature. I had been sitting with my arm around the waist of Coralie, having lulled the jealousy of P-paul with a bone. Unostentatiously I withdrew this incriminating arm when I learned the title of the stranger. What! Had my Coralie Bifsteck fooled me all along? Oh, grass where is thy greenness? Oh, beef where is thy price? I didn't have an opportunity to ponder the situation. The big devil looked at me and to my terror strode—yes, he had plenty of stride—towards me. "Ah, Monsieur Stove, it's you? Embrace your papa, young man!" He held me in a grip of steel. Mr. Stove! What did he mean? I had been saluted as Beefsteak, never as Stove. His bear-like hug nearly smothered me, I was hopelessly outclassed from the start. The audience tittered, but soon became silent. It was to be serious! Suddenly after a volley of objurgations, I was tripped up and found myself across his knees, and next to his "wife." She placidly stared, like a cow in a thunder-shower. Then I was ignominiously spanked, spanked as my father never dreamed of spanking me. The family roared with laughter. The Bernards only smiled. It was a joke! This M. Stove was such a funny fellow! At the word Stove ("la poêle") the gaiety redoubled.

I didn't feel much like a hero when I was set on my feet, my hair mussed, my eye blinking. But I hadn't seen—how could I, face down?—the series of winks bestowed on the spectators. M. Bifsteck, to give him a name, was as jovial a pirate as one could meet cruising about that most adventurous of seas, the streets of Paris. We became friends before the evening ended. I forgave his horse-laugh (also professional) and his coarse unpleasantry, but the attitude of his "wife" disgusted me. She was no longer Madame Bifsteck, only the slave of the man who paid her lodging. She nestled to him, provocatively staring at me. No use. The spell was broken. All's unfair in love or war; but her unfairness went a step in the wrong direction. Much cheap claret was consumed. The "cocher" kissed me on both cheeks. I preferred the spanking to the odour of onions and bad brandy. The next morning I missed my wallet and one hundred francs. I didn't feel particularly well and this loss sent my heart down into my boots. I raised the roof. I threatened to call in the police. Then it came to me that I had hidden with preposterous caution the money in the closet where I found it. I apologised in customary fashion to Bernard, and over our cordials he told me that the coachman had suspected his partner after my gift of the stove. Beefsteaks didn't count. It was the riotous extravagance manifested by that cheap stove transaction. I was advised quietly to change my address. This suited me. The city was warm. I was weary of Coralie—suddenly—and the next day I was en route for the country. Coralie insisted on accompanying me to the Gare du Nord, holding my hand, and at times, when P-paul permitted, tenderly patting my head. She had the limpid, luminous eyes of the born liar, yet she was simple and confiding. It wasn't her husband that worried her as much as her jealous dog. Whenever I tried to kiss her he snapped at my nose, did this canine guardian of the household honour. A kill-joy, a hateful hound, he barked to the very last when, with streaming eyes and to the evident approbation of railroad porters and boys, we kissed our farewell. Dear Coralie! Dear Madame Bifsteck! We were once young and loving. Beefless days must have overtaken you! Perhaps you married your drunken coachman. Adieu! But I hope that infernal P-paul went to his dogged reward.

V

THE WHIRL OF THE TOWN

Paris is a beautiful book, a book of ivory, gold and irony; a book that stirs the soul as it stirs the senses. Paris is a cloaca, the lupanar of the world where the vilest meets the vile. Paris, like Rome, gives you precisely what you bring to it. I have never had patience with the people who call Paris the City of Pleasure, as if it were not also the City of Work. Every aggregation of humans has its so-called pleasures, painful pleasures for the most part. Paris is simply the capital of the civilised world, and must pay the penalty for its preeminence. It is the modern Scarlet Woman in the eyes of ignorant prudes, and Montmartre is one of the Seven Hills of vice. But on Montmartre is enthroned the Church of the Sacred Heart. God's hired man is working without wage in Paris as in London or Pekin. In 1867, in the gardens of the Exposition, when Glory and France were synonymous, and to the music, cynical and voluptuous, of Offenbach and Johann Strauss, the world enjoyed itself, as it enjoyed applauding Renan's latest book, or Theresa's vulgarity; amused by Ponson de Terrail's fatuous indecencies while speaking in the same breath of the philosophical anarch, Joseph Proudhon. Bismarck and the Prussians seemed far away. Babel or Pompeii? The tower of the Second Empire reached to the clouds; below, the people danced on the edge of the crumbling crater. Jeremiah walked in the gardens. He was a terrible man, with sombre, fatricidal gaze, eyes

in which were smothered fires of hatred. His thin hair
waved in the wind. He said to his friends: "I come from
the Tuileries Palace. It is not yet consumed. The
Barbarians delay their coming. What is Attila doing?"
He passed. "A madman!" exclaimed a companion to
Henri Lasserre. "He is Ernest Hello." It was the im-
passioned polemist, prophet, and patriot. The disquiet-
ing figure is evoked of that son of Hanan, who prowled
the streets of the Holy City, in the year 62 A. D., crying
aloud: "Woe, Woe upon Jerusalem!" The prophecy
of Hello was realised. Attila came, Attila went. Seven
years later I saw his handiwork, and the handiwork of
the Parisian Bolsheviki of 1871, the Communists and
those hags of hell, the pétroleuses. The Red Virgin,
Louise Michel, was still living, and in the faubourgs,
memories of the burning and sacking of the city were
green, and memories, I am sorry to say, grateful to many.

But in 1878 there were compensations for the sadly
afflicted people. The Exposition was a rallying-point.
It was the first public expression of liberation since the
war. Paris breathed. Paris smiled. An enchanted city
for me. Each street had its history. Fresh from the
Centennial Exposition I could make comparisons. In
all that pertained to invention, to machinery, to the arts
industrial, Philadelphia led, but in the gracious arts,
painting, sculpture, music, and architecture, Paris was,
as ever, peerless. (I loathe this word, it sounds like a
baking-powder advertisement, yet I can think of none
better.) Peerless Paris! I discovered that my patriotism, at best a tender plant in my native hothouse, had
suddenly pushed strong sprouts. For the first time I
really saw our flag; my heart beat as it blew from the

Trocadéro. The American Section filled me with pride, but I spent most of my time in the art Salons. In Philadelphia we had raved over the huge panoramic canvas of Hans Markart, "The Triumph of Caterina Cornaro," the art of the theatrical scene-painter. In the Trocadéro were assembled all that was exquisite in contemporary art. And at the Louvre I completed my education begun in Black and White, with colour hitherto sadly neglected.

Jules Grévy was the political idol of the day. His face was to be seen in every shop-window. Gambetta shared honours with him. I remember one cartoon entitled "The End of a Bad Dream," depicting Grévy and Gambetta clasping hands, while in the background Marshal MacMahon and others are seen flying away. Gambetta, one-eyed, as Jewish-looking as a rabbi—he had been called Jew, though I noticed that many men from the South are Jewish-looking; Alphonse Daudet, for example, whose real name was David, a true meridional—and burly and bourgeois I saw Victor Hugo, who had ascended the final ladder of glory awaiting only the apotheosis of death, which came a few years later. I saw him a half-dozen times, a commonplace old gentleman with a white clipped beard, and the inevitable umbrella of the prudent Parisian citizen. He usually rode on the top of an omnibus, and was always saluted by bared heads. "It's M. Hugo, great poet," whispered a conductor as the great Frenchman nimbly mounted to the impériale. This fighter, who had helped with his mighty pen the downfall of that stuffed-dummy Emperor and bastard Bonaparte, Napoleon III, was not forgotten by his countrymen. His eyes alone proclaimed the fire of genius. They burnt in his head like lamps. I was not so lucky as George Moore, who shook hands with Turgenev, or as Henry James, who knew the lovable Russian novelist; but I once saw him, as I saw Guy de Maupassant at the Café Sylvain across the street from the new opera house. Guy was as burly then as Gambetta. He was sipping a bock. A more uninteresting young man you couldn't encounter in a day's walk. My most cherished recollection is the glimpse I had of Gustave Flaubert, huge, a veritable Viking, with the long, drooping mustache of a trooper, and big blue eyes in a large red face. A magnificent man. He was hurrying through the Rue Saint-Lazare, possibly on his way to the gare and Rouen. My old friend M. Grandjean, pointed him out, but while I had read Madame Bovary, the sight of Paul de Cassagnac, swaggering behind Flaubert, arrested my attention. The duellist and notorious politician was surrounded by a flock of sycophants who owned the sidewalk. Solitary, his brain filled with dreams, Flaubert went his way.

The reigning painters in 1878 were Meissonier, Carolus-Duran, Bouguereau, Jules Lefebvre, Cabanel—whose Venus painted with a brush dipped in soft soap may be seen smiling on a couch of sea-foam at the Philadelphia Academy of the Fine Arts here—Léon Bonnat, Paul Baudry, Laurens, Delaunay, Henner, Gérôme, and Henri Regnault; all men of the Institute, though the unhappy Regnault, his life lost through a spent bullet during the last days of the war at Buzenval, was considered a violent rebel. However, his "Moorish Execution," and his "Salome" reveal him as a conventional Orientalist. But the others, they ruled artistic Paris. Edouard Manet, Claude Monet, and a few brave men had exhibited at the Salon des Refusés in 1867 an invention of the Emperor, who, stunned by the clamour, instituted this gallery of the refused, as a sop to the cerberus of rebellion. In 1877 there had been another show that had scandalised Paris. Manet deliberately defied criticism with an exhibition of his own canvases for which he wrote a catalogue and a challenge. Whistler later imitated him. Official art frowned. Traces of this frown I found when I visited Julian's school, or the ateliers of Gérôme and Bonnat. The way I found myself in the very thick of art student life was through the good graces of Milne Ramsey, a young Philadelphia painter, in the atelier, I think, of Bonnat. He had married Miss Ruff, a daughter of my father's old friend, General Ruff, and it was at his hospitable studio that I met some of the young artistic Americans in Paris. Edwin Blashfield, W. H. Lippincott, Charles Sprague Pearce, Herman Hynemann, Henry Thouron, Van der Kempf, a sculptor, Thomas Healy— who at Rome had painted Liszt—Frank Moss, Loomis, and Helen Courson, who painted animals. Not Manet, but Bonnat was my man, and, with Gérôme, seemed to be the acme of vital progressive art. The portrait of Thiers is a solid work, after all, beside which the febrile, hasty, abridged statements in the Manet portraiture appeared thin and shallow. Yes, I confess it without a mea-culpa that the Impressionists repulsed me by their glaring, striped brushwork, ugly subjects (I fancy that it was there the shoe pinched, my eye having been fed with the beauties of the Italian schools) and their boastfulness. Manet in particular was an object of curiosity. His colour appealed; but his faulty technique, after the neatly finished surfaces of Meissonier or the creamy nudities of Lefebvre! I see it all now. The official painting of that time was not so bad as the new crowd pretended it to be. Other days, other palettes. Bonnat was

SALVINI
(1880)

GUY DE MAUPASSANT
(1880)

not a genius and Gérôme should have begun with modelling instead of ending his career chisel in hand. His
talent was more sculptural than pictorial.

Nevertheless, there was plenty of power, felicity of expression, and genuine craftsmanship in this much abused
group. After thirty years, and after revisiting the Louvre
or the Luxembourg, I find the Impressionists as old-
fashioned as the Fontainebleau group; yes, even the
Pont-Aven School, headed by Gauguin and Van Gogh,
is dating. The truth is that the time factor is grossly
overestimated. Good art in 1500 or 1830, or 1867 or
1918, remains good art. A Corot is a thing of beauty,
particularly his much-neglected figure pieces. The natu-
ralistic movement had for its true father Gustave Courbet—a romantic canvas is his " Funeral at Ornans," romantic and black as a Muncaczy. Monet was the first
Impressionist. Nietzsche said the first Christian and
only Christian died on the Cross. Claude Monet was
the original Impressionist, notwithstanding his debt to
Turner and Watteau; the Watteau of the "Embarkment
for Cythera" in the Louvre. The rest patterned after
this individual painter whose myopia made him see his
landscapes blurred. Manet, much influenced by Velasquez and Goya, followed Monet, while Edgar Degas,
strictly speaking, did not belong to this group, which had
been given the unhappy title of the Batignolles School.

Atmosphere was the valuable contribution of the Impressionists to art. I didn't know enough forty years
ago to feel the current of fresh air that swept through
Parisian ateliers. And the gorgeous hues of the new
painters. What courage they had, and how they were
jeered at. I remember going to a minor show by major

artists on the Boulevard Clichy somewhere, in company
with William Lippincott and Pearce. What fun we had
with the comical smears of Pissarro, Renoir—Mon Dieu!
think of it, Renoir, a painter of genius—Sisley—the most
exquisite of them all—and Monet. I blush as I write this.
I liked Boudin, one of Monet's earlier masters, yet couldn't
trace the logical development of his pupil. It was not
till the spring of 1885, and at the exhibition held in the
Durand-Ruel Galleries then on Fifth Avenue at Thirty-
sixth Street, that a great light broke in upon me. No
doubt my eyes had been unconsciously trained by the first
pictures seen in Paris. Now, the Caillebotte gallery in
the Luxembourg seems antiquated. The men of 1830,
too, are for the most part stale. Théodore Rousseau—
the biggest of the group—is blackening, Jules Dupré is
greasy in colour and sloppy in sentiment. Diaz is sensuous in colour, Monticelli in his best estate is richer,
while Daubigny, despite the high prices he fetches, is
often obvious. Corot has lasted. The followers, Har-
pignies, Breton, Jacque, and the rest need not concern
us. Painting has its fashions and fluctuations. I am
chiefly concerned with the fact that Meissonier seemed
then a more finished painter than Manet; perhaps he
was so finished that he was lifeless, his metallic style
crushing the vitality of his figures. Manet gave his
generation a new opera-glass with which to view the passing show. He was the great colourist of his epoch, though
not so big a personality or temperament as either Dela-
croix or Courbet. I fear that I have always been a re-
actionary, witness my present admiration for such dear
old-fashioned classics as Stendhal, Ibsen, Strindberg,
Karl Marx, Nietzsche, Max Stirner, and George Shaw.
Archaic? Yes—Noaharchaic.

Carolus-Duran made a deep impression on me, with his velvet jacket, lace collars and cuffs, dark, handsome head, and eyes sparkling with diabolic verve. He looked as he painted, a much more unusual combination than is believed—brilliant and attractive. I know now that he plays second fiddle to Alfred Stevens of Brussels, in quality and design, but he did knock us out with his virtuosity, which his pupil, John Singer Sargent, inherited. Gandara among living painters has the same clever knack, the drawing-room touch; never great art. Gérôme was a severe man, chary of speech, interested in paint-problems. Bonnat I liked, hail-fellow-well-met, yet always the dignified master, a rather difficult pose to maintain. Thomas Couture I saw in his home at Villiers-le-Bel, on the road to Ecouen. The admired painter of "The Romans of the Decadence," with its bacchanalian attitudes, its official scheme of composition and hot colouring, was then failing in health. He had outlived his reputation. An amiable invalid, happy with his wife and daughters in his villa and generous gardens, he told me some things of his contemporaries. He despised Manet, "a painter without talent, vain of his missing tail, like the fox in the fable." Couture painted some pretty pictures, notably the boy blowing soap bubbles, hanging in the Metropolitan Museum, New York; but he was obsessed by the grand manner. He longed to be a second J. L. David. And he was not. He died shortly after in 1879. My passion for the landscapes of Claude Lorraine and J. B. Poussin was justified by the architectural design of Poussin, and the tenderness of tone still surviving in Claude. They are masters despite the newcomers.

VI

BOHEMIA'S SEA-COAST

I went often to the Café Guerbois on the exterior boulevard, where I saw Manet, Degas, Desboutins, but not Monet. My acquaintance with the visionary Villiers de l'Isle Adam began at this café. Writer of prose tales, an improvisor at the keyboard as well as before a table, he fascinated me. I have written of him at length in the first chapter of The Pathos of Distance, called The Magic Lantern, and critically considered him in Iconoclasts. Villiers was a fabulous creature. Dream and reality were so closely woven in his consciousness that he never seemed quite awake or sleeping. Whether he drugged or not I can't say, but he was the greatest liar I ever met, and I have met many—being a newspaper man. Only—Villiers was an artistic liar. He told improbable stories, always figuring as the hero, that would have made Baron Münchausen blush. His magic lantern, for instance, which I recorded, is one of his splendid inventions. He was an accomplished monologuist, and needed but a vinegar-cruet as an audience, his fellow-man failing; but fellow-man seldom failed. When Villiers had money he paid for the entertainment, and if poor, which was the rule, he still paid for others' food and drink by improvising stories which were promptly gobbled up by his good friends, who lost no time in pawning the stolen goods at the nearest newspaper office. He was a gold-mine, this marvellous magician, Villiers de l'Isle Adam. But Joris-Karel Huysmans and a few

intimate friends had to look after his funeral expenses.
Perhaps there are a few Americans who remember his
tale, The Torture by Hope, as Poesque as The Pit and the
Pendulum. He loved Poe, and wrote a novel with
Thomas A. Edison as hero. The Eve of the Future, it is
called, and is the grotesque story of an artificial woman
made of steel springs, who loves a man. Perhaps if he
had heard an Edison phonograph with all its horrors,
he might not have put the inventor in a book, for he was
a fanatical lover of music and an intimate friend of
Richard Wagner. He it was who told me of Manet's
famous witticisms. Manet before a picture of Meissonier, "The Charge of the Cuirassiers." "Good, very
good," exclaimed the painter of Olympia—not then in
the Louvre. "All is steel except the breastplates."
Meissonier was furious when a kind friend carried the
mot to him. Alfred Stevens had said that Manet
"drank the beer of Haarlem" after seeing his "Le Bon
Bock," which is unmistakably derived from Frans Hals,
and Manet waited for his revenge and got it when he
saw a picture by Stevens portraying a fashionable young
woman in street dress standing before a portière, which
she is about to push aside to enter the next room.
Manet noted an elaborately painted feather duster—
Stevens was a master of still-life—which lies on the floor
at the feet of the lady—"Ha," he ejaculated, "she has
a rendezvous with the valet-de-chambre!"

Villiers wrote a five-act play entitled "The New World"
for which he won a prize of ten thousand francs, and a
medal of honour. The prize was offered to the French
dramatic author "who would most powerfully recall in a
work of four or five acts the episode of the proclamation
of the Independence of the United States, the hundredth

anniversary of which fell on July 4, 1876." It was hissed
at its production in 1883. There were only six presenta-
tions at the Théâtre des Nations. It is unreadable a
second time. The poet was not a playwright. He was
of noble family, an ardent Roman Catholic, and a Dia-
bolist; one of those Catholics like his friends, Barbey
d'Aurevilly and Paul Verlaine, of whom their coreligion-
ists were not precisely proud despite the devotion expressed in their writings to the church. One of the
witty epigrams of Villiers is worthy of Voltaire. After
a character of his Bonhomet goes to heaven the Almighty
greets him: "Well, Bonhomet, when do you propose to
drop the mask?" "After you, Seigneur!" responds the
cynical Triboulet, slayer of swans at midnight and professional idealist at large.

I have spoken of Franz Liszt and the almost irresistible
influence his legend had upon my youthful imagination.
He was like the mountain in the Arabian Nights; all the
ships with their little musical Sinbads were dragged out
of their course and ended by clinging to him as does iron
to a magnet. I had no plan, only to meet him, hear
him play. I have elsewhere related of pursuing an old
man with white hair, groggy nose and warts in abundance;
it was on the Rue de Rivoli. He was sitting in a fiacre.
I chased it for the length of that very long street. Was
it Liszt? I couldn't take my affidavit that it was.
There were many old, white-haired men in Paris; also
groggy noses—Liszt was a celebrated cognac absorber—
and wearing warts all over their faces. I haunted the
Exposition, especially the Austro-Hungarian section. I
never saw him, but one evening in the concert hall, I
heard Nicolas Rubinstein play the first Tschaikovsky

PAUL VERLAINE

After woodcut by Paterne Berrichon

piano concerto, the very composition he had derided under the nose of Peter Illitsch a few years previous at Moscow. It was not a novelty for me as I had heard von Bülow play it in the Academy of Music, Philadelphia, either in the autumn of 1875 or early in 1876. B. J. Lang, of Boston, conducted the orchestra and things were soon at sixes and sevens; the solo performer was white with rage. The playing of Nicolas, the brother of the mighty Anton, did not stir me, but it was of crystalline purity and impeccable as to technique. His style was more finished than Anton's. But the passion, and that nameless something we feel, rather than call, genius, he did not possess. Poor Tschaikovsky, who had been abused by both brothers for the workmanship of this B flat minor concerto would have smiled if he had heard the interpretation of Nicolas. Rafael Joseffy was at this time associated with Tschaikovsky in the Moscow conservatory, of which Nicolas Rubinstein was director. He it was who first told me of the mysterious taking-off of Nicolas, who did not die from too much wine-drinking, but was murdered by a jealous husband, and with a sand club, in the same manner as L. M. Gottschalk in South America. The piano virtuoso, Emil Sauer, a pupil of Nicolas, hints at the occurrence in his autobiography, My Life, but Joseffy gave me the details. Struck in the milt by a sand club, which leaves hardly a perceptible bruise, the unlucky pianist agonised for weeks; he even was transported to Paris, but he failed to get relief, and died stupefied by morphine. There are many matters that never get into the newspapers. Tschaikovsky's death was another. Cholera or suicide?

I was refused at the Paris Conservatoire de la Musique, then in its old quarters, Rue du Faubourg—Poissonière.

Ambroise Thomas was musical director, a soured man
whose "Mignon" remained his one success. "Hamlet,"
even with Lassalle singing the title-rôle, was a joke, Shakespearean and otherwise. My examination was set down
for November 13, and I had been prepared for its rigours
by going to church daily for a week. Old man Lefevre
saw to that. But if, as Napoleon said, God is on the side
of the heaviest battalions, he must have sided on that particular day with the greatest technique. I didn't have
a show. I was too frightened to play a scale evenly.
My entrance on the stage, before the jury, was greeted
by an exclamation from Madame Massart, née Masson,
"Quelle barbe!" alluding to the blond fleece on my
sawney chin. I had a sweet fluffy beard. Was I not a
Bohemian in Paris? Velveteen coat, Scotch cap, open
shirt. Oh! what a guy I must have been. Once I attracted the attention of a distinguished visitor in Paris,
though no stranger there, Albert, Prince of Wales. He
stood in a jeweller's shop on the grand boulevard, exam-
ining something sparkling. It was near the door. I
stared in. No doubt I looked like a hungry person. I
wasn't, but the Prince didn't know it, and putting a
spray of diamonds in a case into his coat pocket he came
out of the place broadly smiling at me, and his sole companion, a handsome young chap, joined in. I did, too.
Later at Marienbad (in 1903) I saw the same equerry of
King Edward, the Hon. Captain Ponsonby. But the
Conservatoire! To tell the truth I am tired of retelling
that old tale. Suffice to say that with all my "pull" I
was turned down. I had asked Lucy Hamilton Hooper
to get me a letter from General Fairchild, who was either
the American Minister or Consul General. I've forgotten which. Mrs. Hooper had been Paris correspon-

dent of the Philadelphia *Evening Bulletin,* and was the wife of Robert Hooper of our consulate. This letter, so graciously given me, was presented and did something, for it got me admission to the piano class of Georges Mathias, a pupil of Chopin, not indeed to play, but to listen, a very important act in the study of music. I became "auditeur" for a short period, and also had the advice in private of M. Mathias, a charming old gentleman, who told me more about the personality of Chopin than all the books on the subject. Chopin was a human being, after all, and neither an angel of light nor a demon of darkness. Like many another man of genius —or business—he was very irritable. His tuberculosis and neurasthenia made him impatient, poor suffering man. The Sand affair was over when Mathias had studied; Chopin did not die from the parting with Sand, but from the *liaison* itself. Sand never spared youth. Yet she, too, must have had tempestuous times. Her invalid had his daily tantrums. She loved her liberty. He didn't like the idea that she entertained men even at her home—also his—during his absence. That was the chief cause of the rupture with Liszt. I hinted at it in my book on Chopin. The worst side of the brief adventure was that Sand piloted Liszt to Chopin's own apartment, who, on his return, found the place in disorder. He never forgave either Liszt or Sand. It was an ignoble episode. To my surprise, I learned that Frédéric was fickle. He had a new affair every day. His parting from George was partly brought about by indifference on her side, and wholly through the devilish intriguing of her sweet daughter, Solange, who made open love to Frédéric, so as to give her mother pain. Most writers balk at this too Gallic situation (to be found in novels, and in Maurice Donnay's play "L'Autre Danger"). But Madame Waldemar Karénine, Sand's Russian biographer, does not. The combination of consumption and George Sand would have killed Casanova.

It must not be supposed that the seamy side of Paris interested me. I never worked under such a forced emotional draught as in those few years. I felt that my parents might send for me at any moment, and I didn't waste time. I had set high standards for myself. It was to be a crucifixion on the cross of art. Goethe's advice, which I had read in Carlyle, to live in the good, the true, and the beautiful, did not seem too difficult. Walter Pater, who owes more to the sage of Weimar than is generally supposed, had assured us that success in life was "to burn always with this hard gem-like flame, to maintain this ecstasy," a counsel of perfection, but one that might also lead to a mad-house. "Failure is to form habits . . . not the fruit of experience, but experience itself is the end." Well, I failed to form habits, yet I am no nearer success, hedonistic or worldly. And William Blake with his suggestion that the road to wisdom is through the valley of excess, did not work wonders with me. Havelock Ellis points out that spiritual excess is meant by the great English poet, mystic, and designer. Perhaps. In either case, headaches, moral and physical, are bound to follow. I was aflame with enthusiasm that like stubble burnt out in a trice. I never climbed so many perilous steeples as in Paris. I wished to be shown all the splendours of earthly wisdom. I longed for the glory that was Liszt's, and the grandeur that was Rubinstein's. After eating horse meat while waiting for the arrival of heavenly consigned parcels from the infinite, I became a cultivator of "res-

taurant fat," as Robert Louis Stevenson says; and R. L. S.
was at Grez, near Fontainebleau in 1879. I had rather
have met that uncanny Scotch youth or George Moore
than Flaubert or Turgenev. But fate willed otherwise.

I was a regular frequenter of the Pasdeloup Sunday
afternoon concerts in the Cirque d'Hiver, also of the Châtelet concerts. Jacques Pasdeloup conducted the Winter
Circus affairs. His real name was said to be Jacob
Wolfgang. But he was Parisian born, he wore whiskers and waved a wand, that is all I recall of his personality. Colonne and Lamoureux drove him out of the
concert field a few years after I heard him. As an orchestra the Pasdeloup could never compete with the
band at the Conservatoire, technically the most polished
in Paris. I listened to much new music at the Sunday
popular concerts, amongst the rest Rimsky-Korsakoff's
symphonic legend, "Sadko." And heartily hissed it was.
A minority in the audience, to be exact, the students in
the top gallery, applauded, and fisticuffs ensued. I
usually left the Boulevard des Batignolles after my mid-
day breakfast, traversing the Quartier de l'Europe, till I
reached the Rue de Rome, down the slope of which I
swiftly descended to the Gare St. Lazare, where I switched
through the Rue St. Lazare, to the grand boulevard, via
the Rue de la Chausée d'Antin, and down the boulevard
to the Cirque d'Hiver, a long walk, there and back, even
for my young legs. Invariably there was a battle to
reach the gallery—fifteen cents admission—and secure
front-row seats. Once on the Rue de Rome I saw the
blond-bearded Manet with Stéphane Mallarmé; both
lived in the European quarter; in fact, the Latin quarter
was not so popular with painters or writers then as the

more commodious, better-lighted studios along the boulevards des Batignolles or Clichy—really the same broad
street. The last time I was in Paris—1914—I walked
up the steep Rue de Rome and visited my old home on
the Rue de Puteaux, expecting to find another building.
But there it stood, shabby, like the entire block, while
across the narrow street was the yellow wall enclosing the
forlorn garden with the same dusty trees. I asked the
lady of the house, the concierge, if she remembered Papa
Bernard. I risked the question because she was over
eighty, and evidently an old inhabitant of the quarter.
Miraculously, she remembered him. She had been in his
service before my time, and later lived in the same street.
He had remained at No. 5 for a few years, then he had
moved up the Boulevard Clichy. After that—a shrug
of the shoulders. And his wife, the estimable sage—
femme!—ah! that predacious beak of hers, and her
prowling ways!—"Monsieur," responded the brave
woman, "he had so many wives."

Feeling as if I had peeped into a dark, dirty, old well,
I tipped her and resumed my excursion down the boulevard. Even that deformed dwarf had his compensations.
At the Comédie Française, I saw a revival of "Ruy Blas."
"L'Assomoir" was dramatised and produced early in
1879. The actor who originated the rôle of Coupeau,
the drunken roofer and husband of Gervaise, actually
died in delirium tremens. He had become abnormally
thirsty playing the rôle of a drunkard. The winner of
the grand prize in the lottery, 125,000 francs, was a
tanner named Aubriot. Clotilde Kleeberg's piano playing charmed me. She was a cousin of the painter, Herman Hynemann, of Philadelphia, I met her again at
Baireuth, in 1896. She remembered her début at the

Pasdeloup concert. I heard Miolan-Carvalho at the grand opera, also the tenor, Talazac. Camilla Sivori, one of the rare pupils of Paganini, played at the Pasdeloup matinée. He was very old, and his tone was small, but he was an artist. He had appeared in Philadelphia, as had Henri Vieuxtemps, and while the memory of the Belgian master is vivid, I can't clearly recall Sivori there. The original Carmen, Galli-Marie, I heard, but not in the Bizet opera. I don't think the work was given at the Opéra Comique while I was in Paris. It was not the enormous failure generally supposed. Philip Hale has dispelled that myth; nor did Georges Bizet die of a broken heart over the supposed fiasco. Like Alfred de Musset, he died from too much absinthe. Zola I saw and Daudet. There was no thought of Paul Cézanne in those days, but Barbey d'Aurevilly still promenaded, lace cuffs, clouded cane, corseted, and hair flowing like the mane of a Barbary mare (I never saw a Barbary mare, but suppose the animal has a mane).

Anna Bock was another débutante in 1879. She came from New York and had studied with Liszt. I heard her at the Salle Pleyel, where, in company with Leonard, she played Beethoven's Kreutzer Sonata for piano and violin; also some Chopin. Frédéric Boscovitz, another Liszt pupil, a Hungarian and cousin of Joseffy, gave several concerts at the Salle Erard. He was familiar to me as I had attended his daily recital at the Centennial Exposition, where he had charge of the Steinway section. The Marie Tayau string quartet numbered among its members an American girl from New Orleans, Jeanne Franko, the sister of the conductors and violinists, Nahan and Sam Franko. She is still playing in New York. Marie Tayau was a violin talent. Miss Franko took the second violin in the quartet. Louis Diémer played the E minor Chopin piano concerto. I didn't admire it. It was like most French Chopin interpretations, precise and chilly. Only Slavs play Chopin to perfection. Think of listening to Berlioz, his "Roméo et Juliette" at a concert du Châtelet! Colonne conducted. At the opera the director was Halanzier. During one week I heard "Der Freischutz," a ballet, "Yeddo," "Faust," and "Robert le Diable." Catholicity in taste! "Fatiniza" was also produced. I chiefly remember it with Jeannie Winston at the old Chestnut Street Theatre, Philadelphia.

Honoré Daumier died in 1879 at the advanced age of seventy-seven. He must have been pickled in alcohol, but, unlike Monticelli, that evoker of gorgeous landscapes, the great caricaturist, still greater painter, did not touch absinthe. He loved brandy. It didn't hurt his art, nor did absinthe hurt the art of Ziem, who lived to be ninety, but the poison killed Monticelli. It was simply a survival of the fittest tank. Daumier's modesty was proverbial. He was a close friend of Corot and Daubigny. One day Daubigny introduced him to a rich American picture dealer (are there any poor ones?) and warned him not to ask less than 5,000 francs for the first picture. This he did. The American paid the price, then begged for more. Daumier showed him another canvas. How much? The artist was perplexed. Daubigny had said nothing about a second picture. Embarrassed, he replied, "500 francs." "Don't want it," said the other. "I don't like it as well as the first; besides, I never sell any but dear pictures." Daumier delighted in repeating this rather doubtful story. But a witticism of his was afterwards appropriated by Jemmy

LILLI LEHMANN

ADELAIDE NEILSON

CALVÉ AS CARMEN

Whistler. Emboldened by his encounter with the American dealer, Daumier had asked a wealthy amateur 50,000 francs for a beautiful picture. The man looked around the shabby atelier and then at the artist as if he had been an escaped lunatic. "What, Monsieur! for that little canvas, 50,000 francs?" "My posthumous price, Monsieur!" proudly responded Daumier. The picture was one of his Don Quixote and Sancho Panza compositions, and its posthumous price was double what the painter had asked for it.

One afternoon as I was leaving my palace in the Batignolles an open carriage drove to the door and out jumped my old friend, the scarecrow of the steerage on the steamship *Canada*. He really had a rich uncle living on the Rue de Provence, and had learned my address at Drexel's. He carried a large bouquet which he effusively offered to me, as if I were a prima donna. Naturally I was embarrassed, but the concierge was impressed. The young man was again on Easy Street and no doubt had wheedled his banker relative into a grand generosity. What could I do but accompany him, breakfast with him at "Les Trois Frères Provençaux," still on the boulevard, and take a ride to Auteuil? There were other items, too, but I've forgotten them; suffice to add that I never saw him again, my friend with the rhetorical rags. He had called merely to dazzle me; and he did.

At a benefit for the yellow fever sufferers in New Orleans (September, 1878), I heard Camille Saint-Saëns at the piano for the first time. In company with his pupil, Madame Montigny-Remaury, he played his own arrangement of the trio from Beethoven's E flat Sonata, opus 31,

No. 3, for two pianos. He also gave with finesse his G
minor concerto for piano and orchestra. Joseffy alone
outshone him in the scherzo. In this hall of the Trocadéro, and in 1896, I heard Harold Bauer play the work.
And in that same season I went to a concert in the Salle
Erard which celebrated the fiftieth anniversary of the
first public appearance of the composer, who refuses to
become venerable, even in 1919. He played in
public there in 1846. I have listened to much of his orchestral music in Paris; too much, for his range is limited, though his resourcefulness is remarkable. With
the years his playing has become dry; in 1878 it was
scintillating. A piano touch, like a voice, loses its fresh-
ness, its tactile sensibility. Von Bülow was always dry,
but his intellectual power dominated his audience.
Saint-Saëns, a protégé of Liszt, wrote interesting music,
significant, though not original music. He is an eclectic.
His "Déluge" at the Pasdeloup proved a deluge of
notes without a Mt. Ararat of a melody to perch upon.
His opera, "Etienne Marcel," produced at Lyons, met
with fair success. Patti and Nicolini were at Nice.
Nicolas, her second husband, better known by his stage
name Nicolini, won favour in America. I heard them
in "Aïda." Aunt Adelina wasn't Aïda for a moment,
but how she warbled in the Nile scene. Her trusty companion, Mlle. Bauermeister—not Mathilde of Metropolitan Opera House memory—wasn't an admirer of
Nicolini. Too many husbands spoiled the vocal broth,
she grumbled. One night when the tenor was on the
scene, Patti asked the faithful Bauermeister his where-
abouts. "He is out there whimpering before the footlights," she grimly replied. Not such an unfair criticism,
as Nicolini did indulge in the "voix larmoyante,"

so beloved of Italian tenors. Fancy my hearing Alfred Jaell, the fat pianist, who gave up playing because his arms could no longer reach the keyboard when his stomach became a balloon. He played with neatness and musically. His wife, Marie Jaell, composed. Her piano playing was broader than her husband's waist; withal lacking in unction. Colonne conducted the "Damnation" of Berlioz—as well as of "Faust"—and I wondered why people went to hear Miolan-Carvalho, as Marguerite Gabrielle Krauss was more impressive. There was a composer in vogue named Leon Vasseur. "La Timbale d'Argent" made Offenbach sit up, but "Lé Droit du Seigneur" did not, though the book was naughty and mediæval, setting forth a certain immemorial right of the lord of the manor (see Blackstone on Free-Soccage and Knight Service).

Théodore Ritter, then cher ami of Carlotta Patti, was a popular favourite. He boasted a technique that made him king-pin of Parisian pianists (his real name was Bennet). Only François Planté excelled him in polish. Planté to-day is over eighty, yet gives the illusion of youth. His photograph was sent me recently by Isidor Phillipp, the director of the Conservatoire piano classes. How he could play the Mendelssohn Concertos! Alkan was another technician. Terrifying are his studies. I never heard anyone play them except Charles Jarvis and Edward McDowell. Ritter at the keyboard playing the slow movement of the Beethoven "Kreutzer Sonata" with the first violins of the Pasdeloup orchestra, twenty in number, was more novel than artistically stimulating. But the pianist was always sure of a recall after he had played his own arrangement of the Bizet Minuet from "L'Arlésienne." At the Académie des Beaux-Arts, Massenet was nominated to fill the chair left vacant by the death of François Bazin. Massenet won favour with his "Les Erinnyes," music for the antique tragedy. He was adored by the pretty ladies. Sybil Sanderson was not yet in Paris, and his fashionable operas not born. Théodore Dubois and his "Le Paradis Perdu" was well spoken of; Dubois is a genteel composer, politely saluting the classics. I liked much better Benjamin Godard. Laura Donne played with the Tayau quartet. "The Youth of Hercules," symphonic poem by the clever Saint-Saëns, was produced at the Pasdeloup matinée. Novelty, as it was, it was not hissed. Et patiti et patita! I might go on for years and not exhaust my reminiscences of musical Paris. But there is a time for all things, so let us talk about Worth, the emperor of dressmakers.

M. Lefevre, an old customer of the famous master of confections, introduced me to M. Worth at his historical atelier in the Place Vendôme. He was an Englishman aged forty-five or fifty years. His procedure when "composing" a toilette has been imitated by every male dressmaker in the business. I didn't see him in action—that might have made me uneasy, as his fair and fashionable clients were often forced to imitate the humble onion as to peeling—but he was amiable enough to give a list of the gowns composing the trousseau of her Imperial Transparency the Grand Duchess Anastasia of Russia. (Where are those virginal Muscovites of yesteryear? In Siberia?) And I printed the contents of this trousseau in my weekly letter to *The Evening Bulletin*. Imagine me writing: "A ball dress of pink tulle, satin trimmed with garlands formed by a fringe of orange blossoms." It was fair reporting and served to train my eye for the operatic stage, where costume counts more than sing-

ing. After Worth, I was ready to interview the Pope—
which I actually did in 1905. Benjamin Godard's new
Symphony-Drama, "Tasso," was liked. Victorien Jon-
cières had a not too flattering reception with his grand
opera, "La Reine Berthe." This Bertha, though royal,
had big feet, which in comic opera might have been enjoyed. In April, 1879, Emma Thursby made an unan-
nounced début at the Pasdeloup and achieved an Adelina
Patti triumph. She had sung at the Châtelet between
acts in "Le Désert" by Félicien David; but it was at the
Cirque d'Hiver that she caught the ear of the town.
She sang the well-known introduction and aria from
Mozart's "Escape from the Seraglio," followed by the
Proch Variations. The critics called her "the American
Nilsson." In Mozart and Bellini she was mistress. Her
voice was pure, she sang in tune, and her musical taste
was admirable. The American colony rallied around her.
Thursby was celebrated for a month, and then it rained
or snowed. Paris forgets as easily as New York or
Buxtehude.

I saw Charles Gounod at a Clotilde Kleeberg concert.
An interesting, romantic head. A young barytone, Jean
Lasalle, appeared in Massenet's "Le Roi de Lahore,"
and won his audience. His voice was fruity in its rich-
ness, his presence picturesque. The next time I met him
was twenty years after in New York and with the two
De Reszkes. He made one of that celebrated trio of
male singers at the Metropolitan Opera during the vocally
splendid consulship of Maurice Grau. David's Ode-
Symphony, The Desert, was revived by Colonne at the
Châtelet in March, 1879. It was my first hearing and
the Orientalism was delightful, that same colouring which

has since become cloying in so many compositions from Meyerbeer to Bloch. In painting it is become an abomination. Even Fortuny, that incomparable master of sunshine and jewelled apparel, palls because of it. Moscheles called David's "Desert" "Frenchified," but the Bohemian virtuoso was not a judge of the exotic. I found it fascinating. The stormy fugue in the Simoon episode, the chant of the Muezzin from the mosque minaret, and the tone-painting in the departure of the caravan, chorus and orchestra, was then the last word in musical realism. What was my surprise to learn that "Le Désert" had been sung by the Musical Fund Society of Philadelphia a quarter of a century or more before I heard the work in Paris. Poor slow old Philadelphia!

The churches of Paris often saw me in their interiors. I scoured the left bank as well as the right of the Seine, looking for them. Across the river I first heard Plain-Chant sung as it should be; better sung, in fact, than at St. Peter's in Rome, as I was to find out in 1905. St. Marie des Batignolles was my parish, but I went often to the services at St. Augustin or the Trinity. I attended a genuine midnight Mass at St. Augustin on a bitterly cold Christmas Eve, the compensation was the little feast of wine, rilettes, bread and butter, which follows in the household of any self-respecting Parisian; he does not have to be pious. Rilettes, minced pork, I liked. It tasted like scrapple, that Pennsylvania product so ancient that the memory of man runneth not to the contrary. I was too busy, also too poor, to experience the Parisian "vice" in quest of which good Americans travel thousands of miles. Of all the deadly dull spectacles, commend me to the Moulin Rouge or the Bal Bullier. When one is young it's another matter; but one must be very young to enjoy the high kicking by a lot of plain Janes, deficient alike in art or underclothing. The French girl "on the loose" is not lovely, though Paris orders that sort of thing better than in London— where the halting march of the female mob in Piccadilly Circus is the dreariest picture in the world. There was more fun in the impromptu dances at the barriers in the suburbs. Poor working girls, clerks on a lark, workmen in their shirt-sleeves, art students and their Mimi or their Aglaë, all furiously footing in the abandonment of a dance the elementary music made by a screeching cornet, a rasping fiddle, with the brassy sonorities of a piano as a background—there was a joy of life not to be found at such mournful professional gardens, the Jardin de Paris, the Folies Marigny, those slaughter-houses of love, where, as Huysmans wrote, love is slain at a stroke. Yet the American, green as grass, whether he hails from Manhattan or Manitoba, accepts the stencilled humbuggery of the boulevards and Montmartre as the "real thing." Life has its terrible revenges on those who flout her in youth. One of them is vice for the middle-aged in Paris.

I studied with commendable diligence. My daily average of piano practice was seldom less than six hours, and it often ran up to the ridiculous number of ten and more. No wonder my neighbours complained. No wonder they manifested their irritation by throwing solid objects against my door. Unmoved, I played on. What did I find to play during so many hours? Whence came all the music? I practised innumerable finger exercises. I had Bach, Beethoven, Schumann, Chopin; Brahms was to be in the foreground years afterwards. I need not add to this list. It is sufficient to fill a man's waking hours till his last croak, isn't it? I have been

warned about my refusal to play cards. I can't play, I
don't like cards, nor yet billiards, chess or checkers.
What will you do with yourself when you grow old if
you don't play cards? I'm old now, though hardly
tottering, and I never touch cards and I have plenty to
occupy my mind; Nor do I golf; that last refuge for
the afflicted on whom old Uncle Uric has left his acid
visiting card. I play Bach in the morning. I read Browning before breakfast (to cheer me up, a poetic fillip) and I
play other music whenever leisure allows. Piano playing, modern, not the old-fashioned finger touch-and-go-
method, employs every muscle in the body. It is also
an intellectual exercise of the highest character, besides
liberating an appreciable quantity of emotion. To play
the instrument in even a mediocre manner a mediocrity like myself demands a lifetime. Hence if health,
wealth, and the neighbours permit, I hope to keep at my
music for at least a half century more.

Horse flesh is dynamic food; it was still eaten in humble households, but it finally proved unpalatable. I
knew it was horse because of the taste and colour, and
as it was cheap, though not nasty, I ate it, glad that it
wasn't dog. I became restless. Spring was with us, a
French spring, not the rainy, blustering weather which
invariably appears in America at the beginning of the
vernal solstice. The sun flooded the boulevards. Birds
sang in the Parc Monceau. The little tables in front of
cafés overflowed into the street. At street corners violets
made their début of the season. The caressing air, the
sparkling humour of Parisian life had never seemed so
delectable. Yet all beckoned me to the country. While
my attendance at the classes of the Conservatoire had
been punctual, the place was stuffy and the conglomera-

JORIS–KAREL HUYSMANS
The Last Phase

tion of noises that assailed the ears as we entered the courtyard made my nerves revolt. M. Mathias was kind, but my admission must have been irregular. I was not an "official" pupil, nor yet an "official" auditor. I called on Théodore Ritter at No. 13 Rue Taitbout, but after playing for him the Bizet Minuet, his simplified version, he sent me to Leopold Doutreleau, whose home was on the Boulevard Clichy, No. 34, as my address book tells me. I studied with M. Doutreleau, both piano and harmony, and as my lessons were bi-weekly I struck my tent, shipped my piano, and with my inconspicuous baggage went to Villiers-le-Bel, nine and a half miles from town on the Northern Railway. You pass St. Denis en route.

This village of Villiers rambles over the countryside and was about three hundred years old, and contained two thousand inhabitants. It is now an important suburb, rich in villas. In the adjoining Ecouen there is the Château of the Montmorenci, built during the Renaissance, given to the Condé family by the original owners, and later sold to the Prince de Joinville. The Revolution transformed the historic edifice into barracks. A lawsuit followed after the Restoration, which resulted in the Joinvilles getting the worst of it. They removed the stained-glass windows and the altar from the private chapel to their other residence at Chantilly. But in the church near the château there is still to be seen a beautiful window which, so I was told by the village curé, was whitewashed during the Revolution to hide it from the iconoclasts of '89. The Montmorenci castle was in excellent repair when I visited it in 1879, and it was approached through a superb park avenue of trees a half-mile long. This château and the villa of Thomas Couture, the painter on the Ecouen highroad, were the chief attractions. The station of the Northern Railroad is two miles from the village and, like many French stations, bears two names: Villiers-le-Bel-Gonesse. A tram brought you to the main street. There was a Mayor, a little fat fellow, probably the grocer, and the only place of refreshment for man and beast was kept by a peasant named Bouty. I lodged with him, one flight up, in a long, low building, cool during the hottest days, as the floors were flagstone and the walls whitewashed. A bar did not exist beyond a sideboard. There were a few tables, and the establishment literally shone with cleanliness. My piano was ensconced in my bedroom, which was also my living-room. It was barn-like in dimensions. Therein I slept, played, read, ate my meals, when I didn't eat in the café on the ground floor. The cooking was good, the fare abundant, claret of quality only cost eight sous a litre. Remember this was forty years ago. Life was gay and I was satisfied.

I recall the late afternoon I arrived as if it were etched on my brain-cells. There was a careless sky with a few large clouds rhythmically clustered. The sun, possibly tired of staring at our mud-ball, endeavoured to evade the cosmic time-table and set before its hour. Gentle veils of mist were accomplices in this surreptitious retreat, yet on the clock second our parent-planet vanished. Bands of birds flew nestward in palpitating triangular patterns, and oh! the melancholy draperies of the willows. You looked for the harps of Babylon. The air grew chilly. I was glad to reach the hospitable doorsill of the Bouty auberge. The immense presence of the moon was like a silver porthole in the sky. My first sunrise

was memorable. In the east, it was a fanfare of
brass; it fairly filled the heavens with its furious rever-
berations. My habits were exemplary. (I escaped to
Paris twice a week.) The Lefevre family lived hard by
in their villa. As I have already related, I saw the master
Couture, and struck up an acquaintance with a pupil,
John Dunsmore, a young painter from Cincinnati.
There was an artistic couple in the neighbourhood, the
Shearers from Reading. When I met Shearer we discussed Lauer or Barbey and their wholesome home brews
more than we did the Barbizon School. But the name of
Millet was one to conjure with. Couture, who naturally
would admire the Poussins, had said that Millet was a
genius, unschooled, yet a genius. Isn't it lamentable,
this "unschooled"? I never heard from his lips an opinion on Corot. The forest of Montmorenci was near, but
the country was not so interesting as Grez-sur-Loing, or
the Fontainebleau forest. However, I was more devoted
to music than landscape. I accompanied Dunsmore on
sketching tours, but the events of the week were my
weekly visits to Paris. I had relinquished the lecture
course at the Sorbonne. Outdoors beckoned me, and I
loafed and invited my soul to drink and smoke. I was
a cigarette-smoker, cigars came much later, and the pipe
is still to come. Coffee, too, was a dissipation. I drank
it in bowls, black and strong. It never kept me awake.
To-day I work on tea without cream, and it is the most
propulsive stimulant to writing. De Quincey called it
the beverage of the intellectual, but that is a vain saying,
so is the much despised barley and hop brew. But
beefsteaks, omelettes, chickens—where do they taste
better than in the French provinces? Not forgetting
the generous wines! Was I homesick? Not in the

least. Philadelphia was a penumbra on my consciousness. No doubt I should return, letters were hinting at
the horrid probability, but I determined to put off the
tragedy as long as I dared.

The professor who lectured in the philosophy classes
at the Sorbonne was a mild, hairy, absent-minded man
who remainds one now of Monsieur Bergeret in the four
novels of Anatole France's Histoire Contemporaine. His
name I've forgotten, but his philosophy, a rehash of Victor
Cousin, an eclectic thinker, I do remember. It was
harmless and antiquated, the thought of this school, quite
in key with the precepts of art inculcated at the Beaux-
Arts, or the venerable pedagogic methods of the Conservatoire. Official art and literature in Paris are, of
necessity, antipathetic to novelty. Yet Balzac and Zola
tried to enter the French Academy; Balzac for the glory,
Zola, as he naïvely confessed, because the coveted chair
and palms would increase the sale of his books. These
contradictions puzzle. Certainly a central and invested
authority in matters artistic and literary is to be commended. Matthew Arnold believed in the Institute; but
so many wild flowers of genius bloomed in the field and
never could have been transplanted to the dry prim-pots of
the Academy that one's belief is confused when confronted
by such a cloud of witnesses. The big men in French
literature and art were not officially welcomed; even there
within the walls they would have prospered the same if
they had not knocked for admission. Genius comes not
by compulsion.

In the Salon of 1879 were pictures worth visiting.
There were Degas, and his pupil, Mary Cassatt—one of
the distinguished painters of America, a Philadelphian,
and the sister of A. J. Cassatt. There were Raffaelli, and

the sculptor, Bartholomé, whose monumental tomb in Père-Lachaise, was a starting point for Saint-Gaudens, and the tomb he executed near Washington. I first saw Mesdag's marines, that cordial old Dutchman whose gallery at The Hague is so rich in modern French art. Fantin-Latour was hung; Whistler owes much to him. Gustave Moreau, whose alembicated art so fascinated me at the Moreau Museum in 1900, showed several canvases. Flandrin I disliked. Puvis de Chavannes, his "Prodigal Son" and "Jeunes filles au bord de la mer" were on view. Gustave Doré was a disappointment, his "Orpheus" revealed his incompetency as a painter, original as are his designs (and a word might be said for John Martin, the English mezzotinter, whose apocalyptic imagination in his biblical plates influenced Doré). Jean Gigoux, a painter who was in intimate converse with the wife of Balzac, when he was dying in another room—you think of George Sand with Alfred de Musset and her Pagello at Venice—exhibited several mediocre canvases. (Read Choses Vues, prose by Victor Hugo, as to the Balzac scandal, since vigorously denied by Gigoux.) Cabanel's "Birth of Venus" picture—not the easel—at the Philadelphia Academy of the Fine Arts—an allegorical panel with nudes. The Venus looked like an inflated balloon. Roll, Lefebvre, Bouguereau, Duez, Van Beers—his portrait of Sarah Bernhardt, then in the plenitude of her power, a golden voice at the Français—and the entire official list were represented. Around the corner, figuratively speaking, were Monet, Manet, Pissarro, Sisley, Berthe Morizot— the greatest woman painter of France and probably the greatest in history, for what were Judith Leyster or Vigée-Lebrun in comparison? and the sister-in-law of Manet. Guillaumin, Caillebotte, and Zandomenechi were painting, but not recognised — which was the luckiest thing that could have happened to their art. Degas was in the official Salon because of the rectitude of his design, but not because of his original vision or his disconcerting subjects; chiefly race horses, ballet-girls, and ugly women washing in attitudes both batrachian and serpentine; of the operatic voluptuousness of Cabanel there was no trace in his work. Like Flaubert, Edgar Degas had the eye of a surgeon; he dissected, did not comment. We look in vain for a suggestion of the prurient, or the diabolic lustfulness of Félicien Rops. The humans of Degas are vital charts created by an analytical intellect. Cerebral, not emotional. And he was a master painter, a classic before he died.

At the Salon des Indépendants, in 1880, the revolutionists had their revenge. Impressionism reigned and Paris sniggered. The Durand-Ruel Galleries were a rallying-point for the rebels. Caillebotte was a difficult dose to swallow, but you had to or offend the others, just as to-day Cézanne must be accepted, else you are an obscurantist. But there can be no comparison made between the patient genius of Aix-en-Provence and the amateur who bequeathed to the Luxembourg that precious acorn of impressionistic canvases which finally grew into a towering tree; now a tree whose shade is become baleful to students, as is the poisonous Manchineel tree in "L'Africaine." Forain and Raffaelli in the first flush of their exciting and truly Parisian art were a treasure-trove. Forain had studied with Gérôme, but soon left him for Manet, where his satirical talent burgeoned in a congenial atmosphere. Mary Cassatt was a force. I saw the portrait of Edmond de Goncourt, brushed by Bracquemond, which had the hard relief of a Holbein.

(I was present at the obsequies of the subtle French prosateur and amateur of exquisite art in Paris, 1896.) What prose-master has, in a style, deliberate and personal, pinned to paper such ephemeral sensations, and the most fugacious of nuances, as the Goncourts? Degas is their antilogue in painting. And compared with Claude Monet, what official painter of his time could touch his Mozartean serenity of mood, or his landscapes drenched in rainbow mists! His "Gare des Batignolles," afterwards hung in the Luxembourg, was the first attempt to deal with a certain joyless phase of life. The yawning mouth of the railroad station, the rails slippery with wet, shunting of many cars, plumes of steam, the myriad of facts put before us synthetically abbreviated, and enveloped in an atmosphere that you could see, smell, taste, this canvas was a contribution to modern art as important in its intentions as in its omissions.

I have always envisaged Claude Monet as the only Impressionist, as I believe that Charles Baudelaire was the greatest French poet of the nineteenth century— Victor Hugo excepted, and only Hugo—and that the supreme realistic novel is L'Education Sentimentale by Flaubert. But the chief body of criticism rules otherwise. Baudelaire is "immoral"—what has morality to do with art? (don't ask this question of a literature "professor"). The public reads the vulgarisation of Flaubert and Manet in Zola. Oh! Manet is already old-fashioned. Zola himself speaks of "le bonapartisme sentimentale" which precipitated the downfall of the Second Empire, the Bonapartism which had proved the undoing of a generation patterned after his lurid writings. The daylight clearness of Flaubert, and the delicate

arabesques of the De Goncourts, was followed by the
sooty extravagances and violent melodrama of Zola and
his disciples. It is all dead and forgotten in Europe.
The Russians: Dostoievsky, Tolstoy, Turgenev, Tchekov,
Gorky, and Artzibachev intervened. The art of fiction
has become finer, and more spiritual, especially in England, where the influence of Henry James is more potent
than in his native land. But dear progressive America
is still in the throes of a naturalism which died at the birth
of Zola's vilest offspring, La Terre. Mr. Howells set the
fashion of realism, a tempered realism, though he stemmed
from Jane Austen and Turgenev. His is the art of the
miniature painter. Frank Norris followed him, and
Stephen Crane, both at a long distance, preceded by
Henry B. Fuller (in his With the Procession and The
Cliff-Dwellers). Zola was not a realist merely because he dealt with certain unpleasant facts. He was a
myopic romanticist writing in a style both violent and
tumefied, the history of his soul in the latrines of life. Life
as a whole he never saw steadily; it was for him more like
a succession of lurid lantern-slides. If, in the Court of
Realism, Flaubert is king, then Zola ranks only as an
excavator

But I must vault back to my early Paris; Paris which
is now, as it always was, the reservoir of spiritual and
artistic certitudes. I spoke of Degas, and Manet, Monet,
Pissarro, Sisley, and the other Impressionists. I must
not forget two names, each important in his own department, Renoir and Toulouse-Lautrec, the first a rare master, the second an incomplete genius but one whose im-
print on the art of the generation succeeding him has been
marked. Auguste Renoir still lives; old, semi-crippled,
an octogenarian, yet painting every day pictures that

are astonishingly strong. No need to pardon their
weaknesses, there are none. Vivacious, lyrical, happy,
his work never betrayed a hint of the bitter psychology
of his friend, Edgar Degas. His nudes are pagan, child-
women, full of life's joy, sinuous, animal, unreasoning.
His genre tableaux are personal enough, the luminous
envelope, the gorgeous riot of opposed tones, and delicious
dissonances literally transfigure commonplace themes.
In his second manner his affinities with Claude Monet, and
Impressionism generally, are easily noted; but his landscapes are more atmospheric, division of tones invariably
practised. Everything swims in an aerial bath. His
portraits are the personification of frankness. The touch
is broad, flowing. He was the first of the Impressionistic
portrait-painters to apply unflinchingly the methods of
Manet and Monet to the human face—Manet, while
painting in clear tones (what magic there is in his golden
brush) seldom employed the hatchings of colours, except
in his landscapes, and only after 1870, when he came
under the influence of Monet. In his third manner,
Renoir combines his two earlier techniques, painting with
the palette-knife and divided tones. Flowers, barbaric
designs for rugs, fantastic, vibrating waters, these appear
in the long and varied series of canvases in which we see
Paris enjoying itself at Bougival, on the Isle Puteaux,
dancing near the heights of Montmartre, strolling among
the trees at Armenonville; Paris quivering with holiday
joys, Paris in outdoor humour; and not a vicious or dis-
cordant note in all this lucid psychology of sport and love.
The lively chap who, in shirt-sleeves, dances with the
jolly plump sales girl, the sunlight dripping through the
vivid green of the leaves, dazzling the edges of profiles,
nose-tips, fingers, this human pair are not the sullen work-

people of Zola or Toulouse-Lautrec, nor are the girls akin to the "Sœurs Vatard" of Huysmans or the "human document" of Degas. Renoir is not abysmally profound; to him life is not a curse or a kiss, as we used to say in the days of Swinburne. He is a painter of joyous surfaces, and he is an incorrigible optimist. He is also a poet. The poet of air, sunshine, beautiful women—shall we ever forget his protrait of Jeanne Samary? A pantheist, withal a poet, and a direct descendant in the artistic line of Watteau, Boucher, Monticelli, with an individual touch of mundane grace superadded. In a private collection near Overbrook, Pa., there may be seen the finest group of Renoirs in this country.

To a gloomier tune goes the art of Count de Toulouse-Lautrec. In it is the perverse genius of an unhappy man, who owes allegiance to no one but Degas and the Japanese. At Paris I visited the first exhibition devoted to his work. His astonishing qualities of invention, draughtsmanship, and a diabolic ingenuity in sounding the sinister music of decayed souls, never before had been assembled under one roof. Power he has and a saturnine hatred of his wretched models. Toulouse-Lautrec had not the impersonal vision of Zola, nor the disenchanting irony of Degas. He loathed the crew of repulsive nightbirds which he pencilled and painted in old Montmartre before the foreign invasion diluted its native spontaneous wickedness. Now a resort for easily bamboozled English and Americans, the earlier Montmartre was a rich mine for the artistic explorers. Raffaelli went there, and Renoir, but Raffaelli was impartially Impressionistic, and Renoir was ever ravished by a stray shaft of sunshine flecking the faces of the dancers and recorded in charming tints. Not as these men was Toulouse-

Lautrec. Combined with chronic pessimism he possessed a divination of character that if he had lived longer and worked harder might have placed him near Degas. He is savant. His sensitive line proclaims the master. Unlike Aubrey Beardsley, his Japanese predilections never seduced him into the decoratively abnormal. We see the Moulin Rouge with its parasites, La Goulue and her vile retainers. The brutality is contemptuous, a blow struck full in the face. Vice is harshly arraigned. This Frenchman's art makes of Hogarth a pleasing preacher, so drastic is it, so deliberately searching in its insults. And never exaggeration or burlesque. These brigands and cutthroats, pimps and pickpurses are set before us without bravado, without the genteel glaze of the sentimental painter, without the attempt to call a prostitute a cocotte. His sitters with their cavernous glare, their emaciated figures and debauched expression are a commentary on the life of the region. Toulouse-Lautrec is like a page torn from Ecclesiastes.

With the years the arts have become too explicit, all except the art of music; even tonal dramas of Verdi and Wagner tell their story without the consoling veils of ambiguity. In literature, Browning was never obscure in intention; he tried to send a multiple message over a single wire, he packed too many ideas in a line; but Stéphane Mallarmé deliberately wrought a poetic art hermetic, like a flash seen in a mirror at midnight, charged with subtle premonitions of music unheard, the "silent thunder afloat in the leaves," faint adumbrations of a dream-prose or verse for those ten superior persons scattered throughout the universe, as Huysmans said. I have yet to meet any one of this sacred ten, this spiritual legion of Thebes. As Arthur Symons has shown us, even Mallarmé is not wholly cryptic. He has more than ten readers, scattered between two or three clubs in this city. Whistler was once an enigma. His evasive art when finally cornered proved to lack substantiality, robust vision, a vigorous brush. But a musically eloquent painter. In orchestral music alone do the secrets of the gods remain inviolate—almost, for we are become gods ourselves and we have learned to interpret their tone-language. Claude Debussy was the newest composer to take refuge in a lovely symbolism. What are the Cubists but searchers after an abstract that ordinary representation makes crudely obvious. Dancing in its highest estate is winged metaphysics. Sculpture and architecture are the most cruelly exposed of the arts; yet in an archaic symbolism such as Epstein's, or in the cold polished logical ferocity of Brancusi, sculpture evades the inexorable linear law. Rodin shivered the syntax of stone, only to replace it with his own sensuous rhetoric. Acting has its plasticity in attitude and gesture; occasionally we see a soul emerge from that prison house of the theatre, more ineluctable than the canons of the Medes and Persians. We seldom encounter a Duse, a Booth, a Salvini, a Modjeska, Sada-Yacco, or a Sarah Bernhardt who were supreme because they incarnated the poet's creations and not because of their professional technique. When we saw, heard them, the acceleration of our interior life became almost intolerable because of its poignancy. To comprehend and feel, as in a blinding simultaneous vision, a synthesis of the senses, what French psychologists call "multanimity" (as opposed to unanimity), is the dream of a few advanced artists. Nevertheless, mystery in art is its chief virtue. Is such

HELENA MODJESKA

an ideal to be compassed? How unhappy people would be if they were really happy. Supreme art, always about to be, but never is quite achieved. . . .

Later, when in Italy, I went to Bologna, to see a pianist, conductor, composer, Giuseppe Martucci, the director of the Conservatory there. For this Neapolitan musician I entertained much admiration after hearing him play the piano part of his own B flat minor concerto in true virtuoso style, and also old Italian music by Scarlatti. I determined to seek his advice. His concerto with his own changes and special fingering, I have preserved. It is very difficult. Runs of double-sixths abound. As a pianist he was the only one who could play double-sixths like Rosenthal. A brilliant, rather than an emotional artist, he was a conductor of high rank. I preferred Sgambati, of Rome, in chamber music, but I have pleasant souvenirs of Martucci. Returning to Paris by a roundabout route, I crossed the lovely Lake Constance on a cool, clear September morning. This lake is as green as fabled Erin, so green that the bellies of birds hovering about its bosom are tinged with emerald tints. The distant prospect of the Alps is enlivening, but it is the colour of the water, its soothing smoothness, and the pink mist garbing the base of the mountains that woo the eye. The transition to Geneva is easy. Three days in this city by the lake bred dreams of Italy. The weather was warm, the sky soft, and the River Rhône a celestial blue. I went to Ferney, saw the house of Voltaire; to the Salève, and wondered if Mount Blanc touched the tall stars; to the villas of Byron, Josephine, and Lola Montez; to Rousseau's birthplace, to the island with his statue; to the cathedral where Calvin preached, and finally to Montreux, passing Noyon, Morges, where Paderewski lived afterwards, Evian, Ouchy, Vevay, Clarens; then I found myself again in Paris.

I proceeded to Auteuil, dear, old, delightful, restful Auteuil. There, said I to my soul, I shall find the rest which passeth all understanding. "Vance," I wrote to the poet Thompson, "find me a poetic spot near the house of Goncourt, where I may sit on the balcony and hear the frogs parse the more irregular verbs in their sweet mother-tongue." He found it, did Vance Thompson. Never shall I forget my first night in historic Auteuil. From my window I heard and saw the trains of the Chemin de Fer of the Ceinture which girdles Paris. They run every five minutes and make more noise than may be heard at Thirty-fourth Street and Broadway. If I tried to sleep I was awakened by rude petulant voices which desperately wrangled choice phrases, "Cochon" "Cornichon" "Homard," and again Cornichon (as if one should say, pig, pickle, lobster), were wafted to my enraptured ears. I was in the "pickle" the other blind drunk. Then the climax most telling, an excerpt from municipal orchestration. A brutal machine, a steam-roller, marched to and fro for six hours, horridly crunching the stones and gravel prepared for its midnight luncheon. It settled my hash. I dressed, descended, went across the street to the police station on Boulevard Exelmans and talked cigarette French to the amiable officers on duty. The next day I told Vance that his frogs were railroad frogs, and he retorted by taking me over the district and filling me to the eyes with local anecdotes. He lived there in the Hameau Boileau, a retired hamlet, heavily wooded, containing a half-dozen villas. His own was the original Boileau house bought

by the poet for 8,000 livres in 1685. On the Rue Singer,
Benjamin Franklin lived; further down there is a street
named after him. Madame Helvétius lived there.
Franklin as well as Turgot wanted to marry her.

A perfect nest of artistic memories is Auteuil; Lamar-
tine, Victor Hugo, Proudhon, the philosopher-economist
—he only died in 1861 at No. 10, Rue de Passy,—Balzac,
Jules Janin, Spontini, and Rossini, who founded a home
for old musicians, Maison Rossini, lived in the neighbourhood; Sandeau and George Sand once kept house at
Passy. De Musset lived in Auteuil; Gavarni, Halévy,
the famous actress, Sophie Arnould, were there, and the
Goncourts lived at 67 Boulevard Montmorenci—in the
same park where Vance Thompson was. There, too,
is the Pool of Auteuil, a most poetic spot with willows
weeping over its green waters. Hugo, Turgenev, Flaubert, Maupassant, George Sand, Zola, and Goncourt sat
at its triste borders, and no doubt wondered when dinner
would be ready. Poets and artists are dreamers, but
not on empty stomachs. It was Mrs. Ralph Waldo
Emerson who said of Henry Thoreau that he loved and
led a lonely life, but he never went beyond hearing of the
dinner-bell.

Rossini's ashes are not in Père Lachaise or in Florence;
a joker to the last he had requested that they should not
bury him in a Jewish cemetery. Naturally I often went to
Père Lachaise. There lies my beloved Chopin—his heart
is in the Church of the Holy Cross, Warsaw, and his
statue and house that stood in his birthplace, Zelazowa-
Wola, Poland, were destroyed during the great war by
Russian Cossacks. The Paris cemetery is a most interesting place for one with a historic imagination. I was
never carried away by the graceless Clésinger memorial

to Chopin. The tombs of Abelard and Heloise do not mean much to the present generation, but the composer of "Carmen" is there, and the Countess D'Agoult, the mother of Liszt's three children, and Bellini, and Molière; but let us go to Montmartre, where Heine sleeps and the Goncourts, Henry Beyle—better known as Stendhal—Ernest Renan, Théophile Gautier, prince of marmoreal prose, Carlotta Patti, and Dumas fils. The grave of Ada Isaacs Menken, poet, actress, bareback rider, the greatest of Mazeppas, is there. Among her various marriages was a brief alliance with John C. Heenan, the prize-fighter. I think Ada hailed from New Orleans, and was not a Jewess despite her Jewish name. Her letters to the American writer, Hattie Tyng-Griswold, published after the death of the notorious and unhappy woman, revealed another side of her temperament. Extracts were printed in the newspapers. She was a Mazeppa doubled by a Sappho. Her slender volume of verse entitled "Infélice," was credited in part to Swinburne, but that is nonsense. The poet of Anactoria, while he sympathised with Lesbian ladies, never wrote bad poetry. But he knew her well enough to be photographed on the same plate. I have a copy. I have also a photograph of Ada sitting on the luxurious lap of the elder Dumas. She was as versatile in her affections as in her talents. A strikingly handsome woman according to the report of her day, her figure being the "envy of sculptors." I confess it is difficult to see the beauty in her photographs. A tormented, morbid soul, a virile soul in a feminine body, she led a stormy passionate life, and, like Lola Montez, died neglected by the world. On her tomb are the words "Thou Knowest!"

The real Paris is not the city of junketing visitors,

the Paris that clusters or once clustered about the grand boulevards, Maxim's, the hill of Montmartre—all memories, for Paris was spiritually reborn in 1914—and other absurd places. No, the real Paris is the Louvre, with its glorious marbles and canvases, the Luxembourg, its palaces and cemeteries, above all its noble churches. If ever I became religious to Paris I should flee. It is a city where they worship artistically. Religion is poetic in Europe.

VII

AT MAXIM'S

I spoke of Maxim's on the Rue Royale. It wasn't in existence when I first went to Paris. Much later I spent one of the jolliest nights of my life there, and notwithstanding Constable, the English landscapist, who declared that a good thing can never be done twice, I propose now to retell the story which is in The Pathos of Distance, but this time I shall give the true names of the dramatis personæ; some are reverend, grave, and bearded signors, perhaps married; and one at least is dead, and his death was a loss to American literature, for he had the voice and vision of an authentic poet. I mean George Cabot Lodge, the son of Henry Cabot Lodge, United States Senator. It would be hardly fitting to prelude a rake-helly anecdote by dwelling upon the virtues of this lamented young man's poetic art. That I shall attempt later on. His friend, Joseph Trumbull Stickney, another gifted youth, also at the Sorbonne, and a prize winner. He was with us. The affair came about in this fashion: in company with a friend from Boston, who was studying organ conducting and composition, Wallace Goodrich, by name, we heard a fair performance of "The Valkyre," at the opera where I had earlier "discovered" the barytone, Maurice Renaud, a vocally gorgeous Wolfram in "Tannhäuser"—and naturally we were thirsty. Behind the opera house at the junction of the streets called Gluck and Halévy was the Café Monferino. It was directed by an Italian and a Frenchman—who had been a head-

waiter at Delmonico's, New York. The cuisine was
Italian and French, and you could get Viennese pastry.
Pilsner beer of the purest made the Monferino a paradise
for artists and writers. The *Figaro's* office was around
the corner, and I often saw the editorial staff, for
the most part bearded and wearing silk hats during the
dog-days, sitting for hours, sipping the blond brew, ges-
ticulating and violently thinking aloud. Here it was I
interviewed an ex-King of Servia; more of him anon. I
asked Goodrich if he, too, was athirst. Yes, he was.
Soon the tempo became swifter. We drank from huge
mugs for several hours while discussing Wagnerian lead-
ing-motives. It was midnight long past when Goodrich
exclaimed: "Let's go to Maxim's!" "To any spot in
Paris," I answered, "where recollections of a French
opera can be drowned in amber, as is the fly of the
fable." We drove to Maxim's, which, as any church-
going American knows, is not far from the Place de la
Concorde. As we forced our powerful personalities
through a mob of men, women, waiters, and crashing
furious music I said: "Lo! art thou in Arcadia?"

Goodrich soon spied a table surrounded by a gang of
young fellows howling: "Constant! Constant!" I
wasn't foolish enough to interpret this combination of
imprecation and cajolement as an adjective; yet I couldn't
at first see Constant. I was speedily introduced to six
of my countrymen, mostly hailing from New York,
and after solemnly bowing and suspiciously staring at
their friend Goodrich, they quite as solemnly shook hands
one with the other, then yelled in unison: "Constant." I
rejoiced. My heart told me that I was with the right
crowd. Constant appeared, and as he bowed his round,
sleek head for the "commande," I tried to untangle the

fritilant delirium encompassing me. A red-haired woman, who looked like a big, salacious Chéret poster, furiously waltzed and sprawled and slid as the gypsy band vertiginously played. She had in tow a little chap whose eyes bulged with joy and realised ambition. He possessed the largest lady in the building; what more could he expect! The band was wonderful. It ripped and buzzed with rhythmic rubato rage, and tore Czardas passion to ragtime tatters. It leered, sang, swooned, sighed, snarled, sobbed, and leaped. Its leader, a dark gypsy, with a wide, bold glance, swayed as he smote the strings with his bow, and I was shocked when he collected coin, plate in hand. At the tables sat women and men. The moral weather was scarlet, the toilettes admirable. Occasionally there strayed in British tourists, but if they had their women folk with them they fled; if not, they remained. I saw nothing objectionable; the establishment simply overflowed with good-humoured deviltry. The tone was unmistakably scarlet, and as the night wore apace it became a rich carmilion—a colour said to be a compound of carmine and vermilion; also lobster, champagne, and rouge. Wallace suddenly cried: "Constant! Constant!" The singing ceased at our table. "Let's get a room with a piano." "Constant! Constant!" we screamed and soon the active Constant conducted us up-stairs into an apartment with a shabby upright piano. Beer had become a watery nuisance, champagne was ordered, and my voice trembled as I gave the order, for I knew the ways of young America when in Paris. We had already absorbed enough to float a three-masted schooner.

Constant left us after making a piteous appeal not to awaken Napoleon in his stony lodgment across the Seine.

Then Master Goodrich sat down before the shaky instrument, and without preluding began playing—what do you suppose? Old-time negro melodies, and those boys started to sing and dance with frantic and national emotion. It's a curious thing, but syncopation must be in our blood. Joe Hunt, the architect, and son of his famous father, Richard Hunt—he wore his hair and whiskers à la Victor Capoul—sang Irish songs with an enviable accent. He was a pupil of the Beaux-Arts, but it was his Saturday off, and he proposed to spend it in a reasonable fashion. Two young men studying at the Sorbonne "said" some cold, classic words from Racine, but broke into a wild jig when were sounded the stirring measures of that sweet old darky lyric: "My gal, My gal, I'm goin' for to see!" We fought double-handed. We improvised tugs of war with a richly brocaded table-cloth. We pranced, we galloped, we upset furniture, and every time a blue-eyed lad exclaimed in a fragile voice, "Oh! I want to dance with a nice girl!" we smothered him in the richly brocaded table-cloth. It was not the hour for girlish blandishments, but for stern masculine rioting. Accordingly, we rioted. Since, I have marvelled at the endurance of Wallace who braved the ivory teeth and cacophonous bark of a peculiarly vicious piano. When I asked him to resign his post and give my aching fingers a chance he refused, but he was pulled from the stool and a magnum poured down his neck. Then I sat down and started in with the Revolutionary study of Chopin. Darkness supervened, as I was lassoed by that revengeful table-cloth, and dragged over the floor by the strong arms of a half-dozen Yankee boys. I long nursed three violet-coloured bruises, a triple testimony to the Chopin-hating phalanx from the Beaux-Arts and the Sorbonne.

We relaxed not for a second our endeavours to chase merriment around the clock. After more big cold bottles a new psychical phase manifested itself; for raging and war's alarums was substituted a warm, tender sentimentalism. We cried to the very heavens that we were all jolly good fellows, and that no one dared deny. Constant came up to deny it, but corks, crackers, napkins and vocal enthusiasm drove him below stairs. Only when the two young men from the Sorbonne went out upon the balcony and in stentorian tones informed the budding dawn and a lot of sleepy coachmen that it was the Fourth of July, and that America was God's own country, did the counsels of the trusty Constant prevail, and order was temporarily restored. But the glimpse of awkward daylight began to tell on our nocturnal nerves. Our inspiration flagged as a beer thirst set in, and beer meant dissolution; among us were some who were no lovers of the barley fruit that grows in breweries; besides, the pace had been killing. Maestro Goodrich came to the rescue. Tossing off a celery glass of bubbles, he resumed his seat at the dog-house—meaning the piano— and began those mystically intense measures of the Prelude to "Tristan and Isolde." Another psychical tempest set in. The romping, justing hullabalooing ceased, and a melancholy madness prevailed. For some temperaments the music of Tristan is emotional catnip. We wriggled and we chanted and submitted to the spell of the opium-charged harmonies.

Wagner proved our Waterloo. Maxim's will stand anything but Wagner in the cruel early morn. Goodrich was a musical trance-medium, and as six o'clock sounded from adjacent belfries we tumbled down-stairs into the crude daylight. Six, or was it eight? American citizens blinked like owls as a small mob of coachmen hovered around them. A lovely Sunday morning. Huge blocks of sunlight, fanned by the soft breezes, slanted up the Rue Royale from the Place de la Concorde. A solitary woman stood in the modulated shadow of a doorway. The fantastic dream-flowers on her wide-brimmed hat clouded her features. Her costume was rich, her style Parisian. She waited in the cool shade. Her sullen, crimson mouth affrighted us. Her jaw was animal, and I detected in her countenance a blending of two races. Ah! how sinister she seemed. "It is the Morocco Woman," whispered one of the boys. "It is the Woman from Morocco," we shudderingly acquiesced as we moved across the way. I never discovered the identity of this mysterious Morocco Woman. Probably some nurse-girl going to early Mass. But we saw things melodramatically at that hour, and a vampire she surely was. After two of the crowd escaped arrest while trying to steal a sentry-box, we rented carriages and told the drivers to seek beer-land. The Madeleine looked grey and classically disdainful as we turned into the grand boule-vard, where, in the gleaming current of sunshine, we lifted up our voices and told Paris how happy we were. At Julian's we stopped. Up two heavily carpeted stairways we mounted only to find banality. There were a few belated nighthawks who preened as we entered, but we were Sons of Morning, and sought not the Avaries of the Night. No beer, but lots of coffee! We promptly scorned such chicory capitulation and once more touched the sidewalk. Our coachmen, who had been with us since we left the Café Monferino, began to show signs of wear and tear. They had celebrated our national holi-

day with a drink every fifteen minutes. Yet they did
not weaken, only swore that every place except the
churches was bolted. We had melted in number. Two
traitors fled. Cowards! we jeered, for we hated to give
in to sleep. After meditation the drivers uttered strange
calls to their rusty horses and then I lost my bearings.
We drove up side streets into back-alleys leading into
other alleys, through tortuous defiles, and into open
clattering squares. At last we reached a café, a rendezvous for coachmen.

Alas! it was too late to pick our company; our withers
were still unwrung, and the general sentiment was that
the devil could catch the hindmost. Oh! we were lucid
enough; it was our parched gullets that spurred us on to
new conquests. We pell-melled into the building and
found a choice gathering. Coachmen, cocottes, broken-
down foreigners, the rag-tag and bob-tail, the veriest
refuse of Parisian humanity. Our entrance was received
with a shout. They knew "a good thing." They were
disappointed. We were exclusive. Of course, we
"treated" every lost soul in the place, that was only
our chivalry. But the beer sobered us. One scion of
American industrial wealth casually remarked: "I never
knew Paris held so many thirsty people." It sounded
like an echo from the Tenderloin. We squared financial
matters, and, after fighting off the manœuvring of some
shady persons, we escaped. Our coachmen, who had
almost succumbed, managed to introduce to us an aged
bootblack from Corsica who had fought and bled with
the First Consul! We believed all he said for ten centimes, and with a last View Hallo! we drove down anonymous lanes cheered by the most awful crew of blackguards
outside a Balzac novel.

The hot sun set us to thinking of life and its responsibilities. One man spoke of his mother "way back" in Kansas, and as his voice broke the landscape was blurred by our unshed tears. Another blurted out that he had a déjeuner promised to an impossible cousin. Him we rallied. But we were all positive that we must appear midday at the American Embassy, there to hear the Declaration of Independence read by our Minister. Was it not the glorious Fourth? Were we not brethren and citizens? It was only eight o'clock, an easy engagement to keep! Wallace Goodrich left us, and his departure made a profound cavity in our united consciousness. The party was thinning. The Lord knows what might happen in an hour. Perhaps solitary confinement in my bed. I was foolish enough to confess that I had with me a letter of introduction to a young architect living in the Latin quarter. "Name, name!" was cried. "Aldrich. He is the brother of my friend, Richard Aldrich, the music-critic, of New York." A chorus of roars was the response. "Why didn't you say so before? He lives in our house. We'll drive you there." We were now four; the others had melted into the middle-distance. We forgot their names. But never shall I forget the introduction when we reached that house. On the fifth floor there lived sixteen architects, students all at the Beaux-Arts; that is, they seemed that number. I swear that two young men bearing the name of Aldrich arose from his bed to salute me. I laughed. "I didn't know Dick Aldrich had twin brothers in Paris," I expostulated. He was perfectly angelic, considering that he had been aroused from an enviable Sunday morning slumber. Perhaps my obliquity of vision was the result of atmospheric refraction, a liquid Parisian mirage. It never

happened to me but once before, and then, may the gods
give me joy! the victim of my optical illusion was a
girl. Can you conceive anything more delightful than
finding two girls you love where there was one before?
I say "that you love"; otherwise the experience must be
blood-curdling. But the young devils in whose company I found myself were not satisfied with this tame
climax. They went from room to room, bed to bed,
shouting: "Hello! old son, here is a man from New York
with a letter from your brother," and many pairs of
pyjamas, drugged with dreams, politely arose, bowed,
shook hands, and, cursing us heartily because not one
boasted a brother, they would fall into bed again.

All perfect things must end, and without remembering
the modulation to the street I found myself alone in
front of the Gare Montparnasse. I was cold sober. I
knew this because of the way the passing citizens gazed
at me. Presently I engaged in a discussion with a railroad employee about the comparative wage-earning of
Paris and Philadelphia. An hour later I enjoyed the
hallucination of sitting at a little table in the Café Monferino drinking white wine (said to be superior to the
hair of the dog that bit you), with a bearded and friendly
stranger who spoke fluently about the psychic life of
micro-organisms. The proprietor told me afterwards
that it was the illustrious scientist, Alfred Binet. How
I deplored my lost chance to ask him a lot of questions!
I was a member of the Academy of Natural Sciences on
Logan Square and had regularly attended the Tuesday-
night meetings, and heard lecture such giants as Leidy
and Cope, the paleontologist, not to mention the Reverend McCook, on bee-hives. At eleven o'clock I knew
the game was up and in a dignified though not chas-

tened mood, I rode over to the Impasse du Maine, where
I lived in a studio once occupied by Bastien Lepage
when he painted the portrait of Sarah Bernhardt, and
where he coughed in company with that brilliant consump-
tive Russian girl, Marie Bashkirtseff. I threw myself
on the bed for a brief snooze. I awoke feeling refreshed,
and as the blinds were down I scratched a match and
looked at my watch. Just twelve o'clock. I had no
time to lose. Brushing my hair, changing linen, I went
into the corridor. It was black as pitch. No wonder.
Midnight, and my "nap" had consumed a dozen hours.
I unfortunately missed the celebration at the American
Embassy, but I had dispensed much patriotism during
the night before. I learned that all of the boys were
at the Embassy. Other things equal, I didn't regret
our evening at Maxim's on the Rue Royale.

VIII

I INTERVIEW THE POPE

Perhaps Rome at a superficial glance affects the American visitor as a provincial city, sprawled to unnecessary lengths over its seven hills, as it did Taine more than a half century ago, and, despite the smartness of its new quarters, it is far from suggesting a World-City as do mundane Paris and London. But not for Rome and her superb and imperial indifference are the seductive spells of operatic Venice or the romantic glamour of Florence. She can proudly say "La Ville, c'est moi!" She is not only a city but the city of cities, and twenty-four hours' submergence in her atmosphere makes you a slave at her eternal chariot wheels. The New York cockney, devoted to his cult of the modern—hotels, baths, cafés, luxurious theatres—soon wearies of Rome. He prefers Paris or Naples. See Naples and die—of its odours! I know of no city where you formulate an expression of like or dislike so quickly as in Rome. You are its friend or foe within five minutes after you leave its dingy railway station. It is hardly necessary to add that the newer city, pretentious, hard, and showy, is quite negligible. One does not go to Rome to seek the glazed comforts of Brooklyn. I went there in 1905 to interview Pope Pius X. I am ahead of my story, but as we are in Europe we had better remain there till I tell it. Philadelphia is looming again with increasing distinctness on the skyline, and soon we shall be back again. The usual manner of approaching the Holy Father is to visit

the American Embassy and harry the good-tempered
secretary into promising an invitation card, if you are
not acquainted in clerical circles. I was not long in the
city before I discovered that both Monsignor Merry del
Val and Monsignor Kennedy were at Frascati enjoying
a hard-earned vacation. So I dismissed the ghost of
the idea and pursued my studies in pagan sculpture at
the Museo Vaticano. The pictures at Florence are more
varied, but at Rome there are only masterpieces. If I
admired the Raphael of the Stanze, how much more did
I admire his portraiture. Not in the Madonnas but in
the portraits of his contemporaries is to be found the
true artist of Urbino. Michelangelo is so massive in
his grandeur that at first he stuns. In the end I forget
the "Last Judgment" for his sculpture. I recalled what
Boucher said to Fragonard who was going to Rome: "If
you take those people over there seriously, you are done
for." Luckily for us, Fragonard did not take the Italian
school seriously and remained his own charming Gallic
self. Velasquez did not like Raphael. His opinion is
recorded. How could he and be Velasquezy, the greatest painter of them all, with the possible exception of
Jan Vermeer, of Delft? Michelangelo, Da Vinci, Rembrandt were great visionaries, yet the Spaniard was their
master in brushwork, and he, too, possessed supreme
vision, not nocturnal, but daylight vision; not a poet,
seer, philosopher, nevertheless he recreated every-day
life with the intensity born of veritable hallucination.
Go to the Museum on the Prado in Madrid and see
"Las Meninas," "Las Hilanderas," and the noblest battle picture in the world, "The Surrender at Breda," and
if the Dresden Madonna and "The Transfiguration" still
win your suffrage then your taste is to be commended

for its childlike piety, but not for artistic reasons. After
the electric vitality of Velasquez's line, after his tonal
magic, versatile characterisation, and atmospheric verisimilitude, few other painters there are who in comparison do not seem flabby, insipid, incomplete. Yet I love
Raphael's portraits of Pope Julius II, Pope Leo X, and
his two cardinals. These portraits are in the Pitti Palace, Florence.

The heavy hoofs of three hundred pilgrims invaded the
peace of the Hotel Fischer up the Via Sallustiana, where
I lived. They had come bearing Peter's Pence and
wearing queer clothes. The third day after their arrival
I got wind of a projected audience at the Vatican. Big-
boned Monsignor Pick daily visited the hotel, and when
I saw him in conference with Signor Fischer, I asked the
proprietor if it were possible. "Anything is possible in
Rome," responded the wily Fischer. Wear evening
dress? Nonsense! That was a custom in the more
exacting days of Leo XIII. Pope Pius X is a democrat.
He hates vain show. Possibly he has absorbed the
English antipathy to seeing evening dress on a male during daylight. But the ladies must wear lace veils in
lieu of hats. I was in high spirits. I was to see the
Pope.

The morning of October 5, 1905, the hotel was crowded
with Italians selling veils to the female pilgrims. Carriages blocked the streets and stretched around the Palazzo
Margherita (from my windows I often saw the Dowager-
Queen with her ladies of honour, slowly walking under the
palm and cypress trees on melancholy autumn evenings).
There was much noise. There were explosive sounds as
bargains were made. Then, after the vendors of saints'
pictures, crosses, rosaries—chiefly gentlemen of Jewish

persuasion, comical as it may appear—we drove away in
high feather, nearly four hundred strong. Through the
offices of my amiable host I had secured from Monsignor
Pick a parti-coloured badge with a cross and the motto,
"Cologne—Rome, 1905." It was as exciting as a first
night at the opera. The rendezvous was at the Campo
Santo dei Tedeschi, which, with its adjoining church of
Santa Maria della Pietà, had been donated by Pius VI
to German residents as a burying-ground. There I met
my companions of the hotel and, after an interrogation
regarding my religion by a priest, I was permitted to join
the procession. In Rome any road may lead to the
Pope. It was for me a matter of life or death. After
standing above the dust and buried bones of the forgotten dead, we went into the church and were chilled by a
worthy cleric, who, in a long address, told us that we
were to meet the Vicar of Christ, a human being like
ourselves. He emphasised the humanity of the mighty
Prelate before whom we were bidden that gloomy afternoon. We intoned the Te Deum and filed out in
pairs, first the women, then the men, over the naked
stones, till we reached the end of the Via della Fonda-
menta. The pilgrims wore their every-day clothes. Short
cloaks and Swiss hunters' hats prevailed. We left our
sticks and umbrellas in the garderobe, which did a thriving business. We mounted innumerable staircases. We
reached the Sala Regia. I had hoped it would be the
more spacious Sala Ducale.

Three o'clock was the hour set for the audience, but
His Holiness was closeted with a French Eminence and
there was delay. We spent it in staring at the sacred
and profane frescoes of Daniele da Volterra, Vasari, Sal-
viato, and Zucchero, and then in staring at one another.

The women, despite their Italian veils, looked hopelessly
plain, the men clumsy and ill at ease. They made uncouth and guttural noises. Pious folk, but without manners. Conversation proceeded amain. Some pilgrims
were heavily laden with crucifixes and rosaries for which
they desired the blessing of the Holy Father. One young
priest from America was bedecked with pious emblems.
It is against the rule to bring such things into the Pope's
presence, consequently every one breaks the rule. A
"pia fraus," as we said at the law school. The guilty
feeling which had assailed me as I passed the watchful
gaze of the Swiss Guard was dissipated. The Sala Regia
wore an unfamiliar aspect, though I had been haunting
it and the Sistine Chapel for a month past. At last a
murmur: His Holiness! The nervous tension was become unpleasant. We had been waiting over an hour.

We were ranged on either side of the Sala, the women
to the right, the men to the left of the throne, which was
an ordinary tribune. It must be confessed that the noisy
sex were vigorously elbowed to the rear. In America
these women would have been well to the front, but the
polite male pilgrims evidently indulge in no such ideas of
sex equality. They usurped the good places by sheer
strength. A tall man in evening clothes—solitary in this
respect, with the exception of the Pope's personal suite—
patrolled the floor followed by the Suisse (a murrain on
Michelangelo's taste if he designed such hideous uni-
forms!). I fancied this major-domo was no less than a
prince of the royal blood, so haughty his bearing.
When I heard that he was a Roman correspondent on
some foreign newspaper my respect for the power of the
press increases—He comes!

This time it was not a false alarm. From a gallery facing the Sistine Chapel entered the inevitable Swiss Guard, followed by the officers of the Papal household, a knot of ecclesiastics wearing purple; Monsignor Pick, the Papal prothonotary and a man of importance; then a few stragglers—anonymous persons, stout, bald officials— finally Pope Pius X. He was attired in purest white, even to the sash that encompassed his plump little person. A gold cross depended from his neck. He held out his hand to be kissed in the most matter-of-fact way. I noted the whiteness of the nervously energetic hand tendered me, which bore the ring of Peter, a large square emerald surrounded by diamonds. Though seventy, he looked ten years younger. He was slightly under medium height. His hair was white, his face dark, red, veined, and not healthy. He needed more air and exercise. The great gardens of the Vatican Palace were no compensation for this man, homesick for the sultry lagoons and stretches of gleaming waters in his old diocese at Venice. If the human in him could have called out, it would have voiced Venice, not the Vatican. The flesh of his face was what painters call "ecclesiastical," that is, coarse in grain; his nose broad, unaristocratic, his brows strong and harmonious. His eyes may have been brown, but they seemed black, brilliant, piercing. He moved with silent alertness. I saw with satisfaction the shapely ears, musical ears, their lobes freely detached. A certain resemblance to Pius IX there was, but not so amiable looking. I found another than the Pope I had expected. This, then, was the man of sorrows, the exile, though in his native land, a prisoner within sight of the city over which he was the spiritual ruler, a prince of all principalities and dominions. Withal a feeble old man whose life would have been imperilled if he had ventured into the streets of Rome.

The Pope finished the circle of pilgrims and stood at the other end of the Sala. With him were his chamberlains and ecclesiastics. Suddenly from a balcony came a voice which bade us come nearer. I was amazed. This was going back to the prose of life with a vengeance. However, we obeyed instructions. A narrow vista was made, with the Pope in the middle perspective. The voice, which issued from the mouth of a bearded parson behind a glittering camera, cried in peremptory and true photographer accents, "One, two, three! Thanks, Your Holiness!" And so we were photographed. In the Vatican and photographed on the same plate with the Pope of Rome. It seemed incredible. Old Rome sometimes has surprises for patronising visitors from the New World. Then His Holiness mounted the throne and received the director of the pilgrims. I had my turn, being introduced by Monsignor Pick, who informed him that I was an American music-critic in search of Plain-Chant. The Pope at once was interested, as he had recently inaugurated reforms in the church choirs of the world. He asked me how I liked the music in Rome, and then and there I expected excommunication, for I told the whole truth. The previous Sunday I heard a Mass which was sung with much satisfaction by the Sistine choir of male soprani and contralti in St. Peter's; I had been informed that the eunuch singer no longer existed, nevertheless, I heard a male soprano deliver with art and elegance the roulades, trills, scales, and flourishes generally, which no masculine throat could have achieved. The timbre of the artificial soprano is agreeable, boyish, yet with an ambiguous quality. In a word, sexless. His Holiness didn't relish my news. He said something in Italian to a secretary, who immediately jotted down the instruction on his tablets. We conversed in French. The accent of the Pope was Italian. I stood after the preliminary kneeling. But when I answered his question concerning the reception in the United States of the new law affecting church music I was poked in the ribs by Monsignor Pick, who didn't think my answer sufficiently diplomatic. Perhaps it wasn't, but again my naïveté compelled me to say that Gregorian chant was hardly popular in my native land. Feeling that I was lost, I fell on my knees and kissed the magic ring and the interview was at an end.

The Pope addressed his audience in a ringing barytone. He blessed us, and his singing voice proved rich, resonant, and pure for an old man. The pilgrims thundered the Te Deum a second time with such fervour that the historical walls of the Sala Regia shook with the vibrations of their lungs. Then the Papal suite trailed after the Pontiff and the buzzing began among the pilgrims. The women wished to know, and indignant were their inflections, why a certain lady dressed in scarlet, hats and gloves the same worldly colour, was permitted within the sacred precincts! No one knew. The men hurried to the garderobe and jostled the keepers for their umbrellas. Laden with their holy objects, unconsciously blessed by the Pope, the owners of rosary-beads, pictures, medals, and scapulars were envied. We broke ranks and outside we found sunlight. A happy omen. I waited for Monsignor Pick, a man and a brother. I took him in my carriage and on the wings of thirst we flew to the Piazza Santi Apostoli, which spot, notwithstanding its venerated name, has amber medicine for sore throats. The worthy Monsignor hailed from the land of the Czech, a giant in size, with the heart of a child. He related anecdotes of the Pope, who was a democrat and easy of access. He was musical, proud of his singing, and played the piano. I asked Monsignor if he had ever heard Pius IX, nicknamed Pia Nina, by Cardinal Antonelli, because of his love of music and friendship for Liszt. Pius X did not care for Liszt's religious music, always referring to the Hungarian composer as "il compositore Tedesco," which would have pained the Abbé, for he was proud of his nationality. The Graner Mass has never been sung at St. Peter's, although Liszt was so friendly with Pius IX. I made Monsignor laugh when I retailed that venerable tale about Liszt's repentance and withdrawal from the world to the Oratory of the Madonna del Rosario on Monte Mario, an hour from Rome. Pope Pio Nono conferred upon the Magyar pianist the singular honour of personally hearing his confession and receiving the celebrated sinner into the arms of Mother Church. (Perhaps the delightful old Pope was curious.) After the first day and night, Liszt was still on his knees, muttering into the exhausted ears of the unhappy Pontiff the awful history of his life and loves. Then, extenuated, Pio Nono begged his penitent: "Basta! Caro Liszt. Your memory is marvellous. Now go to the piano and play there the remainder of your sins." Liszt did so and for another day the sacred precincts of the Vatican echoed with the most extraordinary carnal and enchanting music. The wailing of damned souls, the blasts of hell, and the choral singing of cloistered cats were overheard. Liszt had never played so intimately, so epically. Not only was the spellbound Pope shaken by the thunder of the Apocalypse, by the great white throne and Lucifer in chains, but he had visions of the Mohammedan Paradise, with fountains, gazelles, and, quite worn-out, he fell asleep, and when he awoke the following week Franz Liszt was made an Abbé and a deacon in third orders. It is said, I told Monsignor Pick, that he never touched a keyboard after that in the Vatican. "Se non è vero è ben Trovatore," hummed the cleric. And it was my turn to laugh. I must not forget that next day the Syrian peddler descended upon our hotel with photographs for sale. I bought three copies; one I still possess. Why not? A man doesn't often get a chance to appear in the same picture with a Pope. And I still hear the summons: "Uno, due, tre!" of that too familiar Roman photographer.

ON THE TRAIL OF THE EARTHQUAKE

Several weeks previous to the interview with the Pope, I was living at Sorrento on the Bay of Naples. Marion Crawford, the novelist, in whose company I crossed from New York, lived not far away, at Cocuemella. There I visited the celebrated author of Mr. Isaacs and A Roman Singer, and saw the tower in which he wrote; it stood on a hill some distance from his villa which overlooked the Mediterranean. His yacht was usually anchored off the Hotel Vittoria and daily I swam out and around it. Not till later did I discover that it had served as a New York harbour pilot boat owned by Pilot Brown, the father of the young pastor, Father George Brown, of Morristown, N. Y. But the craft had an Italian crew, it was no wonder I didn't recognise its American origin. The summer of 1905 was a hot sultry one in Southern Italy. Mount Vesuvius in eruption through August and September was a magnificent spectacle from the esplanade of the Vittoria at Sorrento. In the daytime the crater lost its infernal lustre, yet it glistened; at night lava streamed down the mountainside. No one seemed nervous in Naples. Nor for that matter at Torre del Greco, in the direct path of the molten river. But the most enchanting spectacle was after sunset, when the black column of smoke, expanded at the top like the palm-tree, the classic shape described by Pliny, became a tremendous pillar of fire, showering sparks and huge incandescent masses over the landscape. The booming, as of distant artillery, was incessant, and it became so alarming that I asked the porter of the hotel if danger was to be expected. Being an expert liar he answered that every summer Mount Vesuvius shot its fireworks for the benefit of foreign visitors, and that the principal noise I heard was merely the gun practice of an Italian navy fleet anchored off Castellamare. Now, as several oldest inhabitants in Naples had informed me that such an eruption was a novelty—they carried open umbrellas in the streets when pulverised dust or ashes became too thick—I knew I was enjoying a rare and operatic performance conducted by impresario nature. Auber's "Masaniello" and its eruption scene was childish in comparison; but Bulwer's description in The Last Days of Pompeii struck the right keynote. The grand finale was to follow. I had been in Naples all day and a muggy day it was. I had taken luncheon at the "Gambrinus," a pleasant café on the water's edge kept by a fat Italian. He had smiled when I expressed my astonishment at the unconcern of the Neapolitans. They were used to the caprices of their beloved mountain. Even the inhabitants at its base returned to their devastated farms and calmly resumed work after an outburst. I took the afternoon boat to Capri which stops at Sorrento, and as I saw the gorgeous pyrotechnics from the upper deck, I congratulated myself on my luck. People have gone to Naples for years, yet missed a real Vesuvian blow-up.

The next morning I saw with some surprise that plaster had fallen from my ceiling. A storm during the night, no doubt. But when I went to the portier's lodge for my mail I found a mob surrounding the poor man, whose wits had deserted him. He could only ejaculate "very

bad, very bad," and it took me ten minutes to pluck out
the heart of his mystery, and then he pointed in the
direction of Naples. I eagerly looked. To my astonishment Vesuvius was normal. A hazy cloud of vapour
issued from its centre, the metallic booming had ceased.
I was mystified. I had seen Mount Ætna in Sicily, and
Mount Stromboli on the Lipari Islands, and it was thus
they had appeared, although the lighthouse of the Mediterranean was luminous after dark. "Very bad," repeated the portier. "Batuishka," I said, firmly grasping him by the neck—I forgot to tell you that he was a
Russian—"Beloved brother, speak, make yourself clear
or by the holy name of Rurik, I'll choke the beloved son
of your venerated mother." He spoke. It was very
bad indeed. At about three A. M., a shock had started
from the fiery mountain, traversed the country, and developed into a frightful earthquake in Calabria near
Reggio; the eruption stopped as the quake began.
Vesuvius had shot its bolt. In the cataclysm which occurred several years afterwards, Reggio was destroyed
and across the Strait, Messina, too. But the 1905
catastrophe was severe enough. It had lightly shaken
Sorrento and the household climbed down the steep in-
cline or went on the lift to the strand where they prayed
and screamed till daylight. My neighbour in the next
room had been thrown violently from his bed. I had
peacefully slept. The portier regarded me with suspicious
cynical eyes. What? A man could sleep through such
a shock! Oh! those Americans. Then he winked at
me with the sly wink of a little Russian. Ah! yes! the
foreign-born Barin had been over the gulf at Naples.
No wonder he slept soundly!

But I was too busy getting my kit ready and scouring

Sorrento for a conveyance to take me to Calabria. There was a fat newspaper story down there, and I didn't propose to miss it. The King and Queen of Italy had motored from Rome that morning; at last I hired a miserable old machine and a gay young chauffeur. To the Evvivas! of the hotel guests led by the portier—now quite overseas from excitement and a subtly dangerous liqueur called Strega—I went off on the job, though with an uncomfortable feeling that we should smash up before we reached Amalfi. We did. Worst of all was the behaviour of the driver. He was a thirsty soul and insisted on pointing out every trattoria on the route. He drank but kept sober. What I particularly disliked was his hospitable way of inviting a friend at each wine house to ride and keep him company. Those friends of his sat on the front of the car, and to have some dirty rascal blot out the view and let me enjoy his evil odour—no, it was too much! Halt! I finally cried, after we had dropped a woman with a dirty brat at a wayside inn, halt Antonio! I hired this motor, I continued, and you are renting the front seats to every newcomer. It must stop "subito!" I explained, and added "caramba!" and then remembered that it was not Italian. I'll get out if you take on another passenger. He smiled, showing ivory that an elephant might have envied. My threat didn't disturb this ingenuous youth. He knew. So did I. The road was hilly, dusty, and perhaps dangerous. But when I told him that he would not receive a tip he weakened and promised to be good. We proceeded on our winding way. Nevertheless, we reached our destination two days late, but I saw the desolated villages, saw the misery which those truly charitable souls, the royal pair, did so much to relieve, and saw the little girl

with her nanny-goat who was rescued after being penned
up in the ruins of her house. The continuous bleating
of the kid and her feeble wails led to their discovery.
When, covered with dirt, she came blinking into the
daylight, her arm about that blessed goat, she cooed
"Babbo! Babbo!" Her mother had died before she
was old enough to remember the loss, so there was no
one but "Babbo" left, and he was buried under the
débris in his cellar. The child was pacified with candy,
and the last I saw of her and the goat was as she stood
talking to the Queen, who was alternately weeping and
laughing. She is a stranger born, the Queen, but the
Italians adore her because of such pity for the afflicted.
I had seen the havoc wrought by the earthquake after
sleeping through its primal shock.

X

I TREAT A KING

I have mentioned the name of Milan of Servia. In 1896 he was an ex-King, simulacrum of royalty, and unworthy descendant of the Obrenovitches, originally O'Brians of Antrim, I could take an oath. Swineherds and Servian Kings. One torrid August afternoon I was writing at the Café Monferino, Paris, where I did much of my work (I tried to be very Parisian then). A furious gabbling at the table next to me caused me to curse the interruption. A dark, wiry chap was quarrelling with a fat, swarthy, whiskered personage in an unfamiliar speech. They became so noisy that I protested, using, I am sorry to say, violent language. But they paid no attention. It was evidently a dispute over money for they held up fingers, counted in the air, and took out wallets. I summoned the proprietor. He whispered: "Cher ami, it is the Milan King of Servia, and with him is his ex-Prime-Minister, Chancellor of the Exchequer Chamberlain, First Lord of the Bedchamber and Bottle holder." This fact altered matters. Ten minutes elapsed and I found myself sitting with the royal household and interviewing the King. He was a charming blackguard. His first question was: "Do you already know the families Vanderbilt, Astor, and Rockefeller? My son would like to make a rich alliance. He is King of Servia. His mother, Queen Natalie (Milan had the impudence to mention the name of that sainted and cruelly abused woman), will be happy if he marries an American."

305

I thanked him for the honour and confessed that while I was not precisely hand in glove with the people he mentioned—"But I will make it worth your while, young man," he importuned. I am not a business man, much less a Shatchen, a marriage-broker, as they say in Yiddish, yet I found something so comic about this diplomatic offer that I burst out laughing. The royal household took umbrage. I apologised. In the meantime the sun had vanished behind the opera-house and we went out on the terrace. The household could boast a thirst. They swallowed vast "doubles" of Pilsner, and soon the porcelain stands which also serve as tallies began to pile up. At midnight we were still discussing the tremendous question: Would a female member of the prominent American families aforesaid be induced to wed the scion of the Obrenovitches? If so—how much? By this time I could only see their faces, so high were piled the tallies. Parisian waiters easily forget, and this is a safe method for keeping the account before your eyes. I went indoors to select some cigars. When I came out no royal household was to be seen. I made inquiries in a sad voice. Arcades ambo! I said, and consoled myself with the thought that the story I had extracted from them would amply repay me for the outlay. I asked the garçon for his addition. At fourteen cents a "double" and with about one hundred "doubles" to be reckoned up (in less excited condition I voluntarily knocked off one-half of this number), I saw that there would be no excess profits left from the article. And so it came to pass. I paid the bill and when I met the same scamps a few evenings later, I told them what we do to such pikers in the land of the free. They shrugged indifferent shoulders, explaining that I had invited them—besides I was only a correspondent, an American, and because of the honour conferred by their company—I moved away. The poor son of a poor father married Draga and made her his queen, and with her was foully murdered in 1903. Peter Karageorgovich, the legitimate King, did not know of the conspiring that put him back on the throne, yet he was clairvoyant enough to reach Belgrade from Paris in surprisingly short time.

XI

HOME AGAIN

I returned to Philadelphia. I loved Paris but my parents loved me more. There was no fatted calf killed on my arrival. I came over on the Red Star line and my last bright memory was Antwerp and a September Kermesse. I was despondent when I went aboard the steamer and didn't dream that Bruges, Antwerp, Brussels would see me years afterwards as a regular summer inhabitant. My home city was shrunken. Paris is a dangerous criterion. It was the only criterion I had at the time. If I had come via Brooklyn the modulation would have been less painful. If I had landed at New York instead of on the Delaware I should never have gone further. Of that I am sure. Why the sudden distaste for Philadelphia? The only answer is Paris. That magic vocable filled my horizon. I was more hopelessly homesick for the city than before I saw it. But why explain? I came to consciousness as painfully as the moment when the balsam apple liniment burned into my flesh after my accident at the Baldwin locomotive shop. My family behaved beautifully. Not a reproach, but my friends were uncomfortable when they met me. I was like a man who is reported missing in an accident and is mentally disposed of by his acquaintances and then embarrasses them by appearing safe and sound. I should have stayed away longer. The prodigal son is always a bore. I went about my business as usual but teaching no longer appealed to me. A foreign correspondent and a piano teacher! I moped. I studied, in fact, for several years read enormously. A few cultured families opened their doors to me. I saw that one could live in Philadelphia and yet enjoy art and literature. With Franz Schubert I resumed the old-music-making. Max Heinrich and his brood had gone South. I met Theodore Presser and we persuaded ourselves that we must have the superciliary tendon of the ring-finger on the left hand liberated by cutting. Pianists are hampered by this tendon, one of those survivals in the human anatomy like the appendix, the pineal gland, and moral scruples. Bravely we went arm in arm to Dr. Forbes, a well-known surgeon, then on Locust Street west of Broad. We took our punishment without complaint or cocaine. The little snip of the steel hurt, but that night I played as usual at an exposition in West Philadelphia, where my old employer, William Dalliba Dutton, had an exhibition of pianos. I think I should have accepted an invitation to a lunar voyage so weary was I of my life. I suffered from the ordinary hyperæsthesia familiar to neurologists. Paris, I believed, was my "patrie physique," and I said so much to the disgust of sensible people. In my revolt against my environment I even went so far as to plan a society for the æsthetic and moral regeneration of society. It was to be called "The Children of Adam" after the chastest and most odouriferous section of Wicked Walt's Leaves of Grass. I drafted the formula of the scheme. It was comprehensive and pagan enough to have aroused even the interest of the police, if known. I found some disciples, intellectual, artistic girls, who saw the ideal through a hole in the millstone. There were plenty of windmills in the vicinity, but this particular group didn't wear bonnets, so nothing came of the enterprise. It languished and died of inanition. The chief trouble lay in the fact that I was to be grand Panjandrum, Pooh-Pah, and Brigham Young combined. No other males but I were admitted to membership. In such circumstances "The Children of Adam" could not have long endured. Nor I. It was the ideal of a happy chicken-coop. The consolation I had after a week of study was the long walk on Saturday afternoon in company with Professor Roth, Dr. E. J. Nolan, and Frank Cunningham. The professor, as my friend and only schoolmaster, felt called upon to exercise from time to time his classic prerogative of putting me through my paces. He knew of my passion for music, and at the beginning of the promenade he held me up on the river just where the boathouses stand. "James," he asked snapping his thumbs and forefingers, an ominous sign that made me shiver, emancipated as I was from the schoolroom, "James, man, what is rhythm?" The finger snapping increased, sure sign of repressed impatience. Bravely I stuck to my definition, "Professor Roth, the simplest formula is measured flow. Rhythm derives from the Greek—" He interrupted, "Greek or no Greek! Thunder and mud! For the last time, what is rhythm, James?" Dr. Nolan and Frank showed anxious interest. But I was not to be shaken. Measured flow, that's what rhythm is when we get to Strawberry Mansion. "Professor, I'll prove to you that rhythm can also become measured flow." I winked. The professor cordially shook my hand. The others laughed and I felt relieved. I knew his puzzling tactics. At the most inopportune moments he would pop out questions to rattle his old pupils not even the presence of a bishop could prevent from asking. "What is the origin of the mitre?" or, "If there are four synoptic gospels, how many rejected gospels were there?" Which was embarrassing. Edward Roth withal crochety had a very human disposition, and his old pupils are faithful to his memory. When they meet he is the first person they discuss.

Our walks seldom varied. We would meet at the Academy of Natural Sciences, proceed up Twentieth Street, occasionally cut into Pennsylvania Avenue, but usually followed Fairmount Avenue to the park entrance; thence along the west drive and sauntering, chatting, smoking, we enjoyed the loveliest natural park of them all. Strawberry Mansion achieved, we halted; Levy would play on his golden cornet—he had a French horn tone, this plump little Jew, born in Dublin—and we sat at table and didn't eat strawberries. I think that Robert Tagg, of Maennerchor Garden, was the manager of the café. The park then was not under dusty puritanical rule, and I can't for the life of me see any improvement in our civic virtues or human thought and activities. Roth was a well-read man, a linguist, and a classical scholar; Dr. Nolan, strong on the natural sciences with a bias towards modern literature, possessed the wittiest tongue in the town. He could scarify an opponent as quickly as a farmer's wife can wring the neck of a fowl. Battles royal were fought between Nolan and Roth; Frank Cunningham and I anticipated blood flowing, but the only thing that flowed was beer. At nightfall we returned tired and pleased with our outing. There weren't as many clubs as there are nowadays. The park was our summer club.

The old-fashioned hospitality of New Year's Day was

beginning to disappear. How well I remembered the
closed windows, lights burning at midday, the punch
bowl and the appearance of sundry young men more or
less speechless though fervently polite. It had its drawbacks, this immemorial custom, but the girls liked it.
The punch bowl has gone into the limbo of discarded
things and the world wags on. The same good old
Dr. Landis "lectured to men only." Don't be a clam!
was an advertising slogan. The Chestnut Street Opera
House was for me the wickedest place on the globe.
Startling posters revealing stoutly built "British Blondes,"
with grand-piano legs, stirred my curiosity, whatever
they were called, the Lydia Thompson or the Emily
Soldene burlesques. With the exception of Alice Dun-
ning Lingard, I thought Lisa Weber the most attractive
woman on the boards. Years after I had seen Lydia, I
went to Her Majesty's theatre in the Haymarket, London, then under the direction of Beerbohm Tree. Francis
Neilson was stage manager, and "Twelfth Night" was
truly a gorgeous revival. Tree played Malvolio, one of
his most convincing assumptions, for, despite his much
praised versatility, his range was extremely limited. I
sat in the front row, a guest of the management, and next
to a very old but active lady, who took the greatest interest in the performance. The Maria was Miss Tilbury—Zeffie, and she was so arch and charming that we
applauded her. Simply beaming with joy, my neighbour asked: "She is very good, is she not, sir?" I
praised the girl. "She is my daughter," she proudly
informed me. The entr' acte found me behind with
Neilson. He smiled. "Do you know the lady next to
you?" "Yes, Miss Tilbury's mother; she told me so."
"True," replied Frank, "but do you realise that she is

Lydia Thompson?" Good Lord! The years at once telescoped and I saw the handsome blonde Lydia of my boyhood, now a little old lady still interested in the stage and in her daughter's career.

At a little midnight supper I related to my host, Beerbohm, not then Sir Herbert, Tree, the story, and he told me a dozen better ones. To Neilson and myself he said: "They say the Beerbohms have Jewish blood. True, I was born in Berlin and my father, Julius Birnbaum, was a Russian, but if I had a few drops of what George du Maurier called the precious essence, I should be a richer man." Tree made money but spent it in costly production. He followed in the footsteps of Henry Irving. His "Darling of the Gods" was almost as elaborate as David Belasco's. I thought of a possible Jewish strain in the family when I was with George Moore on the esplanade of the Baireuth Opera House in 1901. We had been speaking of humour, and I spoke of Jewish humour. "What do you call Jewish humour?" said Mr. Moore in his most disinterested manner. I replied: "Heine, Saphir, Beaconsfield, Zangwill, Max Beerbohm." "I didn't know that Max was a Jew," exclaimed the novelist, Max is a half-brother of Herbert. "He may not be Jewish, but he has that delicate ironic touch which is Hebraic." It abounds in Hebraic literature. Then the trumpets from their balcony sounded the fate-motive, and we all trooped in to the last act of "The Valkyries."

You can't always tell from physiognomy. Sitting one afternoon on the beautiful Marina at Naples, after visiting the devil-fish and other extraordinary sea-monsters in the Aquarium, perhaps the choicest collection in existence, I was surrounded by a lot of little beggar boys.

Half dressed, dirty, impudent, and several of them as beautiful as the Infant Jesus, I saw that it was a hopeless hold-up. I shook my stick at them. Some ran away. I looked about me for the police; not one in view; it was the hour of the siesta. "Clear out, you scamps," I threatened. The leader of the gang must have been twelve years old. He never budged, though he kept beyond the reach of my stout cherrywood stick.

He remonstrated and did my ears play a trick? New York, East Side English: "What for you rich Yankee come to Napoli and no give money to poor Italian boy?" That settled it. "Here," I cried, giving him a handful of copper. "Where did you learn English?" "I came from New York; I was born there." "Born where?" "Mulberry Street," he answered, and with his band scooted towards the Santa Lucia quarter. He looked like the future chief of a black-hand blackmailing organisation. Then, Naples was in the temporary clutches of the notorious Camorra, who made themselves very unpopular with visitors. "Rich man," the boy had said, and at the very moment I was counting my wealth to see if I had enough to get as far as Genoa; if not, I should be compelled to ship at Naples on my return-trip ticket.

XII

ETERNITY AND THE TOWN PUMP

Let us rest now for a little gossip about Eternity and the Town Pump. I pause to recover my second wind. I've told you some things I remember about Old Philadelphia and the Paris of the seventies and eighties, therefore it might be a holy and wholesome thought to catch my breath and, incidentally, examine my conscience. I warned you at the beginning of these papers that I proposed to make a clean breast of everything (of course, I wouldn't dare all for fear the police would intervene), else how can you judge my estimates of music, painting, acting, literature? Out of the hodge-podge which I call my life I had to distill some sort of philosophy. I was never an agnostic. I always believed in something, somewhere, somewhen—as Emerson has it. In fact, I believe, and still believe, in everything. I am a "Yes-Sayer" to life. Any extravagance, but the denial of reality. The "vicar of hell" is he who teaches the negation of things. Man is a vertical animal. True. But he is also mobile, an animal that adapts. Because of his numerous aptitudes he is differentiated from his fellow-animals. His "fall" was when he went on all-fours and worshipped ignoble sticks and stones as gods. The gesture was well-meant, but the attitude undignified. It was a throwback to the anthropoids. It savoured of a return to animalism. Yet it is better to be a polytheist than an atheist. The gods are ever moving through the heavens to remoter constellations. Nothing endures but

315

mobility, changeless change. Nevertheless, we speak of stability, permanence, immortality, the absolute when nature abhors an absolute. The Eternal Return is now, it is the eternal recommencement. Hope of a future life is the aura thrown off by young healthy cellular tissue. The sap is mounting. Youth alone is immortal. With advancing decay the fires of the future pale and burn out. But we must believe, the very affirmation of belief —say in free-will—puts courage into actions. Wordsworth, in his famous sonnet, after deploring that the world is too much with us, late and soon—getting and spending we lay waste our powers—exclaims with noble indignation: "Great God! I'd rather be a pagan suckled in a creed outworn. . . ." Then he could believe in old Triton and all the gods of the waters.

Plato called Time "a moving image of eternity," believing that God was unable to make the earth eternal? To each man his mysticism. Everything that is to be has already happened; the tiny segment of the curve of events we call the Present is not the best vantage point from which to grasp the mighty wheel of life. Even the norm of our existence may not have been the norm of remotest ages past. As Ibsen said, perhaps two and two make five on the planet Jupiter. Our reason is the crystallisation of ancient experiences. The constancy of the human intellect proclaimed by Remy de Gourmont may be one more metaphysical illusion. Historical perspective is too limited to permit any but vague generalisations. As for fatalism, what else are those who write and speak of Free-Will, Immanence of the Deity, but fatalists? If the exterior world is a mirage of our inner-self then the lack of continuity, the fragmentary attempts,

the disjoined thinking without sequence or import, are
not all these things natural for the reason that they are?
The queer being that peers at us over the back wall of
our consciousness, our phantom twin, our true self, the
wanderer and his shadow, the old man of the sea, Sinbad's
unwelcome burden, our sublimal consciousness, as the
psychoanalysts call it—what is this mocking devil doing
there, sneering at our pretenses, and laughing when we
fall and skin our mean little souls?   Is he Brother Death?
We carry this companion from the cradle to the coffin.
We appease him with our heart's blood and with our
flimsy lies and sometimes succeed in stifling his importu-
nate and accusing voice.   What if the neighbours should
hear him scolding in the reaches of the night!   What
a scandal that would be!

Most men and women die disappointed with life,
which they think has played them a scurvy trick.   And
it has.   Its chief function is to illude and then dis-
appoint our false hopes.   The majority of humans die
of spiritual arterio-sclerosis, the result of a too high
blood pressure, caused by vain imaginings.   Your doctor
detects the danger with his sphygmograph, your spiritual
director also employs his sphygmograph; examination of
the conscience.   It is often efficacious.   The chief thing
it shows you is that life, at first a feast planned by the
almighty Barmecide host, proves to be a succession of
appearances; his guests never taste essences, only yearn
for them from afar.   Our five senses play the immortal
game to perfection.   The efferent nerves carry from our
centre a filament message to the exterior; our afferent
nerves return to us the message of the world without.
Literally we are imprisoned for life, with the privilege of

telephoning our cerebral central to ask it to phone us the news of outer existence. It's the greatest fairy-tale imaginable, our life. But it is not free—oh, no! In a physical sense we are the grandchildren of vegetables which live by solar heat; and of the so-called lower animals—query: why lower? Like them we, too, are automatons, ruled by the same rigid laws; we borrow vitality from the vegetable kingdom, and we are nourished by this triple-distilled solar energy. Nature is not always coherent, and De Vries, the Dutch scientist, showed me, when I visited his garden at Amsterdam in 1912, that nature can create by leaps, as well as by orderly progress. This philosopher-physicist actually produced new species of flowers overnight. Our nervous system is the whole animal. And these nerves may be so finely spun that they receive messages from the Fourth Dimension of Space. Life, asserts Bergson, is a division, a dissociation, not association, not an addition of elements. And at the end the philosopher knows as much as the peasant. But the philosopher doesn't believe this.

Personal liberty is another chimera. To be sure, man is born with a skin, not with a carapace like a tortoise, nor is he unwieldy like the elephant. He is the lord of the soil only for a certain period. Napoleon, the superman of modern times, remarked: "Liberty is the necessity of a small and privileged class, endowed by nature with faculties higher than those of the mass of mankind; it may, therefore, be abridged with impunity. Equality, on the contrary, pleases the multitude." He practised what he preached. Of fraternity he said nothing, probably because there is nothing to say, even if you call it by such a high-sounding name as altruism. It is like one of those ornamental banners that hang out in fine weather, but when it rains it is quickly folded and brought indoors. And it usually rains in the land of fraternity. I began my "dark saying on the harp" and I fear it is ending in obscurity. What am I trying to prove? Nothing. In life nothing can be proved, except disillusion, and that may be escaped by self-study, as does an entomologist a formidable bug; and by the same token anything may be proved, even the victory of Zeno's tortoise over the swifter-paced Achilles. The sea lives without the approval of man, collaborating only with the winds. But we live by a parallel of our sensations, so we worry if the tide and weather are not propitious. Hence the priest, hence the ruler in the scheme of civilisation. Voltaire was short-sighted when he said that mankind would not be free until the last king was strangled by the bowels of the last priest. Religion and government were not invented by priests and kings to enslave us. Our organic needs evolved them. What a cosmical joke it would be if, after the inhabitants of this planet had forsaken all gods, one really existed; a god of irony, smiling within the walls of some unknown dimension, the Nth of mystic mathematicians, a Moloch of the ether spying his hour to drop, as drops a boa-constrictor from a tree, upon deluded mankind. Perhaps, suspecting some such celestial denouement, Pascal made his wager with himself—the celebrated "pari de Pascal"—in which he demonstrated himself a more subtle Jesuit than the Order of Jesus he so denounced in his cruel, brilliant Provincial Letters. His bet was a bit of theological sophistication. If, he said, you make your peace with God before you die you are on the safe side whether there is a paradise or not. Pascal, a master of the iron certitudes of geometry and the higher spatial dimensions, has always been to me a giant intellect that could believe and disbelieve with equal ease. There are such anomalies in the fauna and flora of the human soul.